A GIRL FROM SCHINDLER'S LIST

A GIRL FROM SCHINDLER'S LIST

(original title: *Oczami dziecka*)

by

STELLA MÜLLER-MADEJ

translated from Polish by
WILLIAM R. BRAND

DjaF

Editor
DjaF
Kraków 2006

ISBN 83-86774-47-9

Cover design
Krzysztof Grzywna
Ris-Graf
ul. Krowoderska 61, 30-158 Kraków

Print
DjaF
ul. Kmietowicza 1/1, 30-092 Kraków
tel. 012 636 32 40, www.djaf.pl

Contents

Prologue

It was 1939. I was nine years old and, according to the grown-ups, a cute, smart, mischievous child. I had long black braids, big dark eyes, and regular features that were, as they say, "a rarity in the Semitic race". My whole family was made up of pretty or handsome people. Mummy was of German descent, and everyone on her side of the family had light blond hair. Like Greta Garbo, she was tall, slender and graceful, with lovely green eyes that were always smiling. Daddy was wonderful. He had beautiful coal-black hair, but above all he was sweet-tempered, patient and good. My brother Adam, four years older than me, was obedient and never got a spanking. Even though he lied like crazy, everyone believed him.

The saying around the house was: Adam is a perfect child, and Stella is a stubborn, nasty brat.

Mania, our maid, also lived with us. She knew how to deal with everything and everybody, and we would have been lost without her. Mania and I adored each other. To her, I was not a brat but a "doll" or her "darling little angel". I also had my very own dog, Puki, white with back spots, who slightly resembled an Irish terrier, but not very much. I loved animals, especially dogs, and I always dreamed of a big dog. But my parents used to say that I alone cause more trouble than a whole pack of mad dogs. Then one day when I had when I had a cold that they thought was pneumonia until the doctor came (I had never been sick before), they promised me a dog if I would only get better. So, they had to keep their word.

We had lived for tree years on Szymanowski Street in an attractive modern district of Kraków, where there weren't many other buildings yet. The apartment was spacious and furnished in a modern way thanks to the help of Uncle Zygmunt Grünberg, a well known local architect. Across the street from our building lay a vast splendid park, half-wild, ideal for playing in.

I was in the third year of primary school and not a very enthusiastic pupil, but I didn't have any trouble in school. My parents had decided, for the sake of our relatives and friends, that my brother and I should learn Hebrew. Until then I hadn't really understood that we were Jewish and, more generally, I hadn't realized that there was any difference between Jews and other people. A tutor was hired to come and teach us religion and Hebrew. However, these lessons did not go on for long because I gave him such a hard time that he quit.

I couldn't stand my brother's tutor either, but in that case my malice had no effect. He seemed to have a crush on Mummy.

During meals, Mania kept watch behind the kitchen door and as soon as she heard too much commotion, she entered under some pretext or other and took me out of the room so that I wouldn't get the spanking that would have been unavoidable if I had stayed there. Apparently I had a lot of bad instincts and Mania was supposed to be a positive influence on me. There were no misunderstandings between us. I would do anything for Mania. I accept every punishment or reprimand from her without talking back.

Towards my parents, on the other hand, I was so hostile that more than once, after what I regarded as an undeserved punishment, I wished them ill in my heart and imagined being freed of them in the cruelest way. For instance, I dreamed that they would be ran over by a tram car. I longed to be left alone with Mania and Puki.

I had no friends, because I didn't know how to play with other girls. They just whined all the time, and you could never tell why. I liked playing with boys, although the weren't always eager for my company. The only little girl I got along with was my cousin, Ziuta Grünberg, five years older than me. However, we lived in districts that were far apart and didn't see each other often, so I was lonely. This made me even more nasty and unbearable. All I ever heard at home was: What an insufferable, difficult child. How could anyone raise a child like that?

We came back several days early from the health resort of Rabka, where we had been on vacation. There was mad confusion at home and I didn't understand what was going on. Everybody was running around upset. Sacks full of sugar, kasha and all sorts of provisions appeared in incredible quantities. I kept hearing one word over and over: war! For me this was all great fun. I could do whatever I wanted and nobody paid any attention to me until, in the end, I broke a priceless vase (not on purpose, of course). Mummy got wound up and at the end of her scolding she stood in the doorway and said: "Just wait until this excitement is over, and then we'll settle accounts for these last few days".

My greatest wish from that moment on was that the war would finally start, because then Mummy wouldn't have time to settle accounts with me. I imagined war like this: the front doors of the buildings would be boarded up and the men would stand out front with sabres to defend the entrances, while the women cooked meals and bandaged the wounded. I could already see myself in the role of a heroic auxiliary, and I couldn't wait for hostilities to commence.

One morning, Daddy went out on the balcony and called excitedly, "Come here, Tusia dear, and see how the airplanes are diving. It's fascinating. They must be holding exercises".

Mummy took one look out of the balcony door, shouted, "Can't you see the war has broken out?" and dragged him back inside.

Of course, Daddy laughed at her. "Don't make a fuss, darling." "It's only exercises", he repeated stubbornly.

In the end, I had to open my mouth. "Will somebody please tell me what the war is really going to be like?"

I didn't get an answer.

***

And yet the war did start. Strange things were happening everywhere. We were fleeing. It was in constant despair over

9

Puki, whom I had not been allowed to take with me, and Mania, who hadn't wanted to flee from Kraków. She said she would take the dog and keep it at her brother's, somewhere near Rakowice. She was also supposed to keep an eye on our apartment.

We had been on the road a long time, and we often had to take cover in the ditches because airplanes kept strafing the road. I didn't have to wash, nobody combed my hair, and there were no scenes because once again I had lost a ribbon from my plaits. There were times when it seemed like great fun. But I didn't want a bullet hitting anyone in our group, and I tried to stay as close as possible to my parents. There were a lot of us; grandmother, aunts, uncles, and strangers who kept latching on. The names of the places we hiked through seemed nonsensical: Margola, Szczurowa, Terespol.

I think it was in Margola. At night, as we lay sleeping in a barn, we were awakened by a tremendous explosion that sounded as if it was right outside. Then the owner of the farm came in, stepping over our heads and generally trampling on everything. He stepped on my arm and it hurt so much that I started to cry. The peasant growled, "Quiet. If they hear you, they'll cut your nose off."

The next morning, the same farmer came into the barn again. Now he seemed different, holding himself erect and looking satisfied. He said: "Well, the Germans are here. The Germans are good, they're already giving people salt!"

We didn't want salt.

The grown-ups decided to go straight back to Kraków. It was a cheerless journey, with exhausted stranglers from the futile battles lining the roads and the corpses of people and horses everywhere. From the depths of the wood we often heard the wounded calling desperately, along with the whinnying of horses that hadn't been put out of their misery. We reached the city tired, hungry and tattered.

We continued to live in our beautiful apartment on Szymanowski St. until November, 1939. One morning, it might have been a Sunday, there was an alarming ring at the door. Mania went to open it. Three SS-men holding revolvers came in. One of them, who must have been higher-ranking, started walking around the apartment without saying a word. Then he stopped in front of Mummy, who looked glamorous again in a long, exquisite satin housecoat in yellow and black stripes.

"Ah, it's so delightful and European here," he said. "There must have been a mistake. This can't be a Jewish apartment."

"There's no mistake," Mummy replied in her impeccable German. "This is a Jewish apartment."

"But you, dear lady, are a German, if my ears don't deceive me."

"I am Jewish."

"Let's be serious, dear lady".

I was amazed that Mummy didn't invite the elegant German to sit down. Instead, she asked in a strange voice, "What do you gentlemen want?"

Now the German stiffened. "This apartment is to be vacated within half an hour. Understand? You are not to take anything with you. Please get dressed, and everything found here will be held by us on deposit. Nothing will be damaged. We will make a full inventory of everything, and you will receive a confirmation with an official seal."

Mania dressed me with trembling hands. I was soon perspiring heavily because she put several sweaters on me. Mummy managed to take some things from her jewel-box. Daddy ordered a cab. We drove to my Grandmother's on Bosacka Street. There, everyone was feeling sorry for us. Mummy, who really was of German origin, argued almost furiously that, after all, nobody knew better than she and grandmother that Germans keep their word. If they had given a receipt that they were holding the apartment and all its contents on deposit, then that was the way it was. And we were supposed to get a substitute apartment soon.

We got our substitute apartment a year later. It was on Czarniecki Street in the Kraków Ghetto.

1

The Ghetto

A lot of people were heading for the Ghetto, big groups and small. Some were carrying only bundles, and others had all their possessions loaded on horse carts. Daddy was pushing a nondescript wagon that he had borrowed from the janitor.

It was a beautiful sunny day, but no one was smiling about the splendid weather. The whole crowd around us was grey, gloomy and sad. I felt bad because we must have looked the same in such company. To cheer things up, I said to Daddy, who was pushing the cart with a vacant expression on his face, "Let's pretend it's our car, and we'll step on the gas and run from the bridge here down to Zgoda Square, OK?"

"Get up on the parcels and off we go!"

I must have jumped too fast. In any case, the parcels went spilling all over the street and I went with them. With a guilty look on his face, Daddy quickly started helping me to gather them up while Mummy looked at me accusingly and said, "That girl is no wiser than she ever was, and she's already ten years old."

That made me sad. After all, I had only wanted to cheer Daddy up, but nothing ever worked out right for me. If Adam had done it, I'm sure she would have said, "How inventive and sensitive he is!"

Daddy looked at Mummy. "But she's still a child," he said, and turned to me. "Hold on tight!"

We ran along, skipping and letting out Indian whoops. Mummy and my brother picked up the parcels that fell off along the way. Some people looked at us indignantly, while others laughed at the sight. I heard somebody say, "Quite right. We shouldn't let it get us down. It's not as though we were going to our deaths."

The apartment on Czarniecki Street in the Ghetto looked dreadful. Mummy was in shock, and shouted that she would rather not live at all than vegetate for even a week in such conditions.

Poor Daddy consoled her as well as he could: "Tusia dear, you won't recognize this place in a couple of days. It'll be beautiful."

I had an active imagination, but even I was incapable of envisioning how you could do anything with that apartment. It consisted of one gloomy room with a kitchen. The toilet was in the courtyard. Everything was terribly filthy and full of black bugs. Mummy was in such a state that Daddy asked her to go back to Grandmother's for a couple of days. We set to work, or rather Daddy did, and I helped a little. However, he was very pleased with me.

Grandmother, Aunt and Uncle remained free. I couldn't really figure out how it was that they weren't completely Jewish, unless it was connected with Grandmother's side of the family, but it was a mystery. I considered it fortunate that they didn't have to come to the Ghetto, because there were too many people there already. And if I were to be frank, I didn't like those people at all. I had not known that Jews, or more precisely, that many Jews look completely different, dress differently and speak differently from us. No, it didn't appeal to me at all and I felt no liking for those people.

Thanks to Daddy's efforts, the apartment changed greatly within a few days. The walls were whitewashed, the floors painted, and the insects seemed to have disappeared – well, perhaps not entirely, but they no longer crawled around during the day. Daddy brought in, from where – I don't know, a cot, mattresses, a dilapidated wardrobe and a few stools.

***

13

Our whole family is now living together and everybody leaves for work every day. Daddy works at Liban's stone quarry. He often has nosebleeds from exhaustion when he comes home, and he's lost a lot of weight. My brother is working at Bauminger's nail factory in the Grzegórzki district. Mummy has the best job. She works at the button factory on Agnieszka Street, where the commissar of the company is Frau Holzinger. Mummy first met her just after the outbreak of war when the Holzingers were quartered with Uncle and Aunt Grünberg.

>From the beginning, the Holzingers were said to be decent Germans, from Austria. Mummy runs the office, Frau Holzinger doesn't interfere and she even likes Mummy; they are somewhat alike and Frau Holzinger is also very pretty. Thanks to Mummy's job, things are not so bad. Frau Holzinger brings incredible packages of goodies to the office, and since Mummy leaves the Ghetto on an individual pass it seems to be easier for her to smuggle those delicacies back in. They obviously treat her as "somebody" at the gate.

No German who came to the office ever imagined Mummy was a Jew. Laughing, she told us more than once in the evenings how she would pick quarrels with them, and afterwards they occasionally sent her flowers. Daddy wasn't happy about this. He thought it could end badly.

Mummy came home from work upset one day. Frau Holzinger had given a reception at her home and insisted on Mummy's coming. She promised to drive Mummy back in the evening, right to the gate of the Ghetto. The reception was supposedly charming, but Mummy came home very depressed. It turned out that the armband with the star on it had fallen out of her purse by accident. There was a lot of confusion and Frau Holzinger explained to her guests that it was a sort of joke, but it might be the end of Mummy's wonderful job because there were too many SS-men at the reception.

***

I feel terribly abandoned. When the grown-ups go out to work, I am left alone. I kick around the Ghetto streets as if I were in a bewitched world. Everything here is alien, bustling, loud. People are speaking a language that I cannot understand at all. I find the children especially irritating and call them "little rabbis". Daddy tries to explain to me that we are the same and that is why we have ended up here. I don't argue with him, but I cannot accept it. Everyday, before my parents go to work, I have to listen to a full set of do's and don'ts – don't go out anywhere, don't go near Krzemionki where the boundary of the Ghetto is, don't talk to strangers or, God forbid, pick any quarrels with children. I generally sit in the window and observe what is happening in the street. It is a big plus that we live on the ground floor and the window looks out on a busy street – Rękawka. I try to be as helpful as I can by cleaning a little, and from time to time I manage to cook some kind of soup. In this way, the days pass.

It was beautiful and sunny and I couldn't hold out any more, so I found myself heading for Krzemionki. I wanted to watch them building the wall that was supposed to separate the Ghetto from the normal world. I went a little bit further. A lovely little shrine stood there, and several children were running around it. I stopped to watch them playing hide and seek, and really wanted to join in the game. One of them came up to me and asked, "Where are you from?"

I pointed down, there, below.

"From the Ghetto?"

"Yes, from the the Ghetto."

They started pulling my ponytails then, and ran around me shouting: "Jewish girl! Jewish girl!"

There were several of them, and in the end their pushing and jostling made me fall down. I was not hurt, but I started howling terribly. Suddenly, someone was bending over me. It was a labourer who had been at work on the wall. He shouted at my persecutors: "Get out of here! She's a child just like you!"

I got up. Then another worker called, "Leave her alone, let the kids have fun with the little Jew. Hey, Sarah, here's an apple for you," and with an unnatural motion he flung out his hand and hit me hard right in the nose with the apple.

Blood gushed out of my nose and I started to roar as if my throat was being cut, or maybe in fury. My rescuer also became furious. He jumped at the other one, smacked him in the face and shouted, "You son of a bitch, I'll show you! Aren't they putting them through enough hell without us...?"

He didn't finish his sentence, but came over to me, wiped my face, and said, "You'd better not come back here any more, little one, because something really bad might happen."

I stood there feeling miserable.

Perhaps only to say something, he asked, "And what's your name, little one?"

"Stella."

"Ah, Stella. Well, that's a strange name, but pretty."

For a moment I recalled my old complaints to my parents about my uncommon name. Why could my brother be a regular Adam, while I had to struggle with such a strange name? I always wanted to have any other name, Zosia or Frania, as long as it wasn't Stella. In school I was the only Stella; I was the only Stella anywhere.

"You know what?" my rescuer asked. "If there's good weather, you come on back here. This work'll go on a while yet, and I'll bring you something nice and you can sit out in the air. I've got children just like you, and maybe they'll give me a toy for you."

"But Sir, I..."

"Call me Antoni..."

"But Antoni, please, I'm big and I don't play with toys."

"You, big? How old are you?"

"I'm eleven."

"What? My girl's thirteen, and she plays with dolls all the time."

"Well, perhaps," I held my head up proudly, "but I already have a household to run." He looked at me, put his hands to his sides, and burst out laughing. This made me sad, and I thought I must have sounded really stupid.

When I got home I looked in the mirror. I was a dreadful sight, with my face scratched and my nose like a potato. I washed, but nothing helped. The worst came in the evening. My brother was the first to remark upon it.

"Oh, I see little sister made a friend today!"

Mummy inspected me. "Oh, look, Musiek, your daughter's been in combat. The way she looks! Now just wait for people to start coming round because she's been beating up their children," she went on, without stopping for breath.

"But don't you see. Tusia darling, that this time she's the one who got it?"

Daddy took me by the hand and led me into the room.

"So tell me what happened," he said gently. "You were supposed to stay at home, and if you went out, why did you have to start fighting immediately? You must learn to get along with people."

I guessed that he was speaking more to himself than to me, and I was trying to figure out how to cover up the fact of my having made the acquaintance of Antoni. I didn't notice Adam coming into the room.

"Why bother, Daddy?" asked my brother in a superior tone. "All it takes is one look at that face of hers and you feel like giving her one." We started fighting. We jumped on each other, Adam laughed at me and I punched him.

"Children, settle down!" Mummy said. "You should be ashamed of yourselves. You pretend to be grown up, and you behave worse than babies."

Adam never let me have the last word, so I cried and went to the darkest corner.

"You shouldn't be so hard on her, son," I heard. In my thoughts I repeated, "Son, son, monstrous son." Then I heard: "She's really lost, all alone. You're her older brother. You ought to help her somehow."

After Daddy's "speech" I felt unhappy, ugly and abandoned. Of course, I thought, nobody could like such a wretch.

"Calm down, dear," said Mummy. "I'm going to try to get some books so you can write and read. The war will be over soon, and you ought to learn something. Now go and wash, because you don't exactly look pretty."

"How am I supposed to look," I mumbled, "when I'm the ugliest thing in the world?"

"You're not ugly, dear. It's just that you don't have to be so rebellious all the time."

Nothing came of the reading and writing because no one had the time or presence of mind to think about it. I started my reading with so-called forbidden books. My education thus made rapid progress, but not in the direction my parents would have wished.

At this time I felt that I was "growing up." At first I was terrified and didn't know how to cope. My stomach cramps were a torment, but I was still happy. "They" didn't know anything about me, and I was already a woman!

A couple of days later I went back to Krzemionki. I met Antoni.

"So, little one, all healed?"

"Sure. It was nothing."

"You're a brave one," he praised me. "I brought you something to play with," he said taking out a package, "that I got before the war when my little one was sick, and this was given to my wife by an engineer where she worked then. They were also Hebrews."

"Why don't you just say 'Jews,' Antoni?"

"Well, because that might be offensive."

"No, it isn't. It's what one says, and it's not offensive. Jews are just Jews. What's wrong with that?"

"Oh, aren't you a little philosopher?" he said, impressed.

This made me feel better, because I had been afraid that my remark had hurt his feelings.

"I wonder what could have happened to that engineer," Antoni pondered. "He was a decent man, he gave me a job, he paid well, and I always got clothes for my family from his wife. I wonder if he's here now. Maybe they went to England. They sent their son there to study. I think they had a pretty little daughter, and she had a strange name too." We started to play at guessing the name, but neither of us could come up with it. Antoni stroked my head and told me to go.

"You understand," he said "This is piecework." I didn't know what "piecework" meant, but I made a knowing face.

He added, "They're after us to finish this cage for you as fast as we can, as if they didn't have anything else to worry about, those Huns, except to wall people off, God knows why. You'd think there was a plague."

"Well I'm going."

"Come again."

My days passed one by one. The visits to Antoni were my secret. Mummy chuckled over the way I had lost my enthusiasm for cleaning and cooking. I started worrying because the wall was almost finished, and Antoni had talked with me in such an adult way.

Once, when I went to Krzemionki, Antoni said that he was going to Lwowska Street where his engineer lived. "Maybe now I can help him somehow," he said. "People have to help each other, whatever you call them, Jews or Turks, right, little one?"

I told him that I could go with him to Lwowska, because I had relatives there called Grünberg. "You don't say! That's my engineer's name, and so they must be the same people."

In the end, I didn't go to Lwowska with Antoni. Aunt Tusia (Daddy's sister had the same name as Mummy) came to see us that evening. She told us that one of Uncle's old employees had visited them and informed her about our acquaintance. I was ready for a big scene, but nothing happened. I had to recount how I had met Antoni, and, of course, how he had defended me. My parents renewed the ban on my wandering away from home, and that was all.

I went back to Krzemionki a couple of days later. Antoni spotted me from a distance and came up with a mysterious look on his face, holding a little bundle.

"Sit down," he said, "and close your eyes. I've got a surprise for you."

I closed my eyes and it took my breath away when I felt some-thing wonderful in my hands. A warm, miraculous, tiny

19

puppy! I was speechless, I wanted to cry, laugh, jump. I sat down and cuddled the beautiful, little, living, black ball. "There, you see what fun he'll be," Antoni pronounced.

"But how did you know, Antoni, that I love dogs best in all the world?"

"Well, you told me once about yours, and mine had puppies. So, I brought you one and that's all there is to it."

"He' so nice, black as coal. I'll call him Blackie."

"You take him now and give him some milk. He's whimpering because he's been hungry since morning."

I ran home happily. But the closer evening came, the more worried I grew. I realized that it wouldn't be pleasant when my parents saw the "new tenant".

Daddy came home first. "What's this?" He hadn't finished when Mummy walked in.

I stood there with a stupid look on my face and Blackie went wild, running up to everyone, catching their trouser turn-ups, rolling over. Mummy recovered her voice first, and she let off a tirade.

"Where did you steal him? You return that dog immediately to wherever you took him from! These are no conditions for keeping a dog. You can't be so foolish!" She was plainly upset.

I realized that things were bad when Daddy said nothing.

"Get going," Mummy insisted. "Take him and go!"

I picked up the dog and took a deep breath. Without batting an eyelid, I calmly decided to lie, which I never did. "But Mummy, I don't have anywhere to take him. I found the poor thing in the street."

"So leave him in the street."

I turned around and said decisively, "In that case I'll go on the street with my dog."

As usual, Daddy took my side. "You know, dear," he said, "It'll soon be the curfew. Perhaps we can keep him for today, and tomorrow we'll think about where to leave him."

The tension subsided. Everybody picked up the puppy and agreed that he was indeed lovely, and home seemed more cheerful. I sat quietly, happy that the storm had passed. I knew that I wouldn't give him up, and that my parents would have nothing more to say to me on the subject.

The Ghetto is finished, which means that we are now separated from the city by the wall. There are watch-towers and three gates, two on Limanowski Street and one at Zgoda Square. A real town has arisen among these dozen or so streets. It is strange to see how much energy appears among these people who have been ejected from society. A multitude of shops has sprung up. There is a hairdresser's, a baker's and, supposedly, even a cafe. Young people arrange dances, and I hear my brother coming home in the evening and telling my amused parents where the party was this time and how much fun it was.

It's not fair that I do everything at home and am not allowed to have any fun of my own; that they talk about everything in front of me but, when I speak up, it turns out that I am still too young and silly to have my own opinion. Why? I ask myself. I know who is being unfaithful to whom and with whom, and I already know that children are not born through the belly button. I think I know everything, and so again the feeling of rebellion and hostility towards everybody rises in me.

Today, Daddy came back from the quarry in a state of utter exhaustion. He said that he would go to the doctor to get a couple of days' sick leave because he was ready to drop. It is evening. I hear a heated discussion: Daddy's recounting how, on the way back from the doctor's, he met Symcha Spira.

"You know, Mummy, he was a messenger boy or something in my father's firm. And so I look: Symcha Spira in an OD uniform, and let me tell you, decorated like a marionette, like a general, but one in a circus. I didn't know that he's the commandant of the Ghetto," he goes on, excitedly, "because after all he's practically illiterate. How on earth did they choose him as commandant?"

As Daddy tells it, Spira looked at him, stopped, and asked, "You're Müller?"

"Yes," Daddy answered.

"Zygmunt Müller? The son of Bernard Müller? Why have you got such a silly look on your face? You know me. Aren't you aware, you idiot, that I'm the commandant here?"

21

"So I see," Daddy said.

"War is war and a man makes a career, that's the way it is in life. You have to push to the top."

Daddy stood there like a fool and just nodded.

"And what are you doing, Müller? You've become poor, oh, you've gone down in the world."

Daddy said that he worked in the quarry and had just got sick leave from the doctor.

"You come and see me some time. I'll give you better work."

There was a discussion at home about whether he should go or not. Daddy decided to try in the *Arbeitsamt* instead. Maybe they would give him something better. Unfortunately, he wasn't offered any better job and he went to ask Symcha Spira for help.

The OD, or *Ordnungsdienst,* is the Ghetto's law enforcement service, Jewish of course. After waiting for a long time, Daddy was called in to see the commandant. He said later that it would have been easier to get to see Hitler himself than Commandant Symcha Spira. The worst thing is that he can't speak any language, Polish, German, Yiddish or Hebrew, properly. He's supposed to be learning German urgently. After many propositions that didn't interest Daddy, Spira accepted him for service in the OD as a regular private. Daddy absolutely refused any higher function.

Spira was never happy with Daddy's work, and supposedly threatened to send him back to the quarry whenever they met. "You, Müller," he said, "are no OD-man, you're just an ordinary *shmo.*"

People liked Daddy very much and he tried to help whenever and however he could. There were two camps in the OD, the bad OD and the good OD, and Daddy was among the latter.

***

People are saying that a car full of soldiers has been driving around the Ghetto. They are shooting people on the streets, like birds on a roof. I am under strict orders not to go outside, especially on the main street. My only joy is Blackie. My parents seem to be happy that they gave in. The dog keeps me occupied. I go to Krzemionki in the morning so that he can run, and have met a couple of little girls there who visit me sometimes. We are even trying to organize something like education. Some of them are older and can read and write better, so they give me lessons. This makes my parents happy.

Lately, when I was out walking, I noticed a very good-looking boy with an Alsation dog, which he called "Juhas". The boy noticed that I was watching, so he showed off what his dog could do, while looking at my little mongrel with contempt. I didn't know who to pay more attention to. The dog was beautiful, but the boy was different, too. He spoke to the dog loudly and not in Polish, perhaps in German. He was certainly three or even four years older than me, yes, he must have been fifteen. Everything on him, his shoes, socks and shirt, looked as though they came straight from the shop. I became aware of how poor I looked in comparison with this boy. My pony-tails had long since stopped being pony-tails, they were mouse tails tied with pieces of tape. Since there was no one to comb my hair, I had been snipping them off a bit at a time. Then there were my arms that were too long, my misshapen shoes, my too short old dress that wasn't very clean. I called my dog and ran home as fast as I could, in despair over the way I looked. Something in me sobbed: "God, I am so ugly!"

Over the next few days I behaved horribly and kept picking fights with Adam for no reason, and I got spanked for pulling his tie. I pouted: Why was he, a boy, beautiful and well-dressed, while I wasn't? I'll go up to the wall at Krzemionki, so that they shoot me. What good is somebody so ugly? My parents said that I must be sick and should stay in bed. I lay down. Nothing mattered. I felt so unhappy that, despite beautiful weather, I slept half the day. It was September already.

As I said, the window looked out on Rękawka Street and was very close to the pavement. I didn't even notice when someone hopped up on the window sill. I heard him calling: "Anyone in there?"

"Yes, I'm here. What do you want?" My heart stopped. It was the elegant boy from Krzemionki.

"I need water for my bicycle. Flat tyre." Heavens, he murders the Polish language with that accent of his.

"Please come in through the window. There's water and a bowl in the kitchen".

I was ashamed to get up because the shirt I had on was hardly suitable for receiving guests, and unfortunately I had no robe. It was a good thing that he took no interest whatsoever in who had allowed him in. He only went on explaining something, not exactly in Polish. When he left the same way I relaxed, but only for a moment. After all, he would have to come back to return the bowl. I jumped out of bed, got dressed, and sat on the edge of the bed without knowing what I should do. Run out of the apartment or sit there? After all, he might recognize me.

I didn't even see him come back with the bowl in his hand. Blackie started barking joyously at him, the way he greeted any old fool. "Blackie," I called. "Come here. None of that".

"Let him be. I like all dogs." The way he talked – that strange accent surprised me again.

He looked at the dog. "I've seen him somewhere." Yes, of course, the worst possible thing happened: he recognized me. "Maybe you walk that dog not far from here?"

"Yes, that's me, and you," – I didn't know how to address him – "you've got a beautiful Alsation."

"That's right." He perked up. "Juhas is beautiful and trained. He came from Germany with us two years ago now. I understand Polish but I don't speak so well."

"Do you like it in Kraków?"

"Oh, yes, it's beautiful, but once this is over I'd prefer to be in Leipzig."

"What's that?" I was sure that this was an intelligent question.

"What's that?" He stared at me. "That's the city I come from."

"Oh, yes." I tried to look wise. "I didn't catch what you said."

Like an idiot, I picked at the ribbon on my pony-tail while the boy went on.

"I've learned to talk, but my Mutti and sister not at all. My Father also speaks a little Polish, but we Germans don't like living here."

"So why don't you go back where you came from?" Now I was angry.

"Well, we can't. Don't you know they drove all the Jews out? But this will end soon."

I don't know why I wanted to slight him, but I picked up a book and started flipping the pages.

"What are you reading?" he asked.

"A book, as you can see."

"Yes, but what book?" I had no idea.

"Ehh, you're not reading, you're just turning the pages," he laughed.

"What else do you want here?" I don't know why I took an arrogant tone. "To bother me? So please go!"

"I don't want to bother you."

"Bother, bother." I mocked his accent. "First you'd better learn to speak Polish properly, and then you can be a wise-guy."

I could see that I had hurt his feelings. He went to the window, and I said that he was free to leave by the door. On the way to the door he bent over and smacked Blackie.

"How dare you beat someone else's dog!" I roared wildly.

"I'm not beating him," he explained. "But is he supposed to do this?" He held one of Mummy's shoes, with the heel chewed off, in front of my nose.

I didn't know what to say. Mummy had got those shoes a few days ago, brand new, from Frau Holzinger. He stood there holding that shoe without a heel, and I started to cry.

"Please don't cry like that." Now he was unhappy." Your mother will forgive you, or maybe I could come and say that Juhas did it?"

"Please give it to me. I'll hide it for now and think of something later."

"Well, I'm going then. I'll come again tomorrow."

The shoe was completely unimportant, but I couldn't stop thinking about the boy. He might not have been very big, but he had lovely curly hair, dark brown eyes, even white teeth, a funny turned-up nose, and, well, he was terribly clean and beautifully dressed. After he left I again realized how I looked, with my long arms hanging down and those silly-looking legs sticking out from under a very old threadbare dress that was far too short on me. I tried to figure out how to force Mummy to get me some clothes, and I knew that it would be hopeless and she would say: "Who has the time or presence of mind for such things?" So I decided to feign sickness. I would put on one of Mummy's night-dresses and I wouldn't look so wretched.

In the evening, when everybody was home from work, I moaned, "I don't think I'll go out tomorrow, Mummy. I ache all over."

She gave me a thermometer and soon told Daddy, "She hasn't got a fever."

"You know, Tusia darling, maybe she should stay in bed anyway. She might have caught a cold when she was out with the dog."

I started cleaning as soon as they left in the morning. Then I washed, brushed my hair and plaited it as well as I could, and dug through the wardrobe trying to find a night-shirt of Mummy's that I could wear. It didn't matter if I tripped over the hem, as long as it looked good at the top. Finally, I got into bed, pulled the covers up to my chin, and waited. I was sure that the boy would come as soon as I lay down. At each rustling outside the window I closed my eyes and pretended to be asleep. In the meantime, hours passed. He did not come. My bitterness rose because I had thought he would feel sorry for me and come. And he had probably forgotten all about that unfortunate shoe, because after all, he was a grown-up boy and no companion for someone like me. Anyway, maybe it would be better if he didn't come. He was a German, after all!

He hopped soundlessly onto the window sill. "Hello. Still sick?"

"No, and you didn't have to come, because I wasn't waiting for you." I was angry. At what, I didn't know, but I was.

"What's your name?"

"Stella."

"And I'm Bubik. My real name is Siegmar Schleifer, but at home everybody calls me Bubik."

My anger suddenly left me.

"How old are you?" he asked.

"Well, in the winter I'll be twelve."

"What?"

"What 'what'?"

"Because I thought you were fourteen. You're just a kid."

"No I'm not. I might not be very old, but I'm quite mature." I was terrified that my age could stand in the way of a promising friendship. "And how old are you?"

"I'll be fifteen on January fifth."

"Oh! I took you for seventeen," I lied. I had thought no such thing.

He started laughing, until my eyes hurt from the whiteness of his teeth. "It won't be any problem that we both thought something different, will it, Stella?"

"No," I answered. "Why should that be a problem?" I thought.

"Good, so we'll be – what do you call it?"

"Friends, you mean?"

"That's right. Do you like the accordion, Stella?"

"I like it very much."

"Then I'll bring mine. I live two houses from here at number fourteen."

"Really? And we never met?"

"I saw you many times, but you always had such a scowl on your face that I thought it was better not to start. And now you're fine. I'll be right back with my accordion."

Before I could get over my amazement about Bubik and the accordion and my being 'fine'... he was back. He put something huge on the table and sat down. I praised the accordion, which made him happy. He asked what he should play. I do not know how long he played, but he played so beautifully that, from that day on, the accordion would always be my favourite musical instrument. Then he offered to try to fix Mummy's shoe. He was in a hurry and had to get home for dinner.

"You're the first girl I've known," he said. "We'll be friends."

"Well, of course," I said eagerly.

Everybody noticed that I was much more polite and less rowdy. I didn't say anything about my new friend, because what business was it of theirs?

More and more people were arriving in the Ghetto, apparently brought in from smaller ghettos that were being liquidated in nearby towns. The things these people said were hard to believe. They told us that the Germans were murdering, beating, and shooting children and old people. We couldn't believe it, but they just kept nodding. These people were being quartered in apartments. Several families often lived in one apartment. We were not in danger of this, because our apartment was small and Daddy's half-brother was also living with us.

Sundays were the most pleasant time, as long as the weather was nice. The only green place was Krzemionki, where the grass had been trampled flat but was still green. People swarmed there. Women sat together mending, darning, and of course gossiping. The men argued about politics and the young people flirted. I often saw young people hugging each other or even kissing when I was taking a walk and found it very embarrassing. The more pious adults only quickened their steps and mumbled about licentiousness. I didn't know what "licentiousness" meant. I resolved to ask.

Some kind of confusion jolted me out of my reverie: people were running towards the place where Krzemionki ends at a high cliff. Down below, outside the Ghetto, the Baudinists, whom we called "the Blacks," were stationed. I stopped a woman and asked what had happened.

"A horrible thing, child. One of the Blacks came over to our side and pushed a boy who was lying at the edge of the cliff, and the boy fell. They say he's dead."

I didn't listen to the rest of what she said, but started to run in that direction while horrible thoughts raged in my head. After all it might be Adam, or perhaps Bubik. Adam loved showing how brave he was. As I ran I bumped into people and was not even aware that I was crying.

Someone grabbed my arm. "Stella, what's wrong?" It was Bubik. Good. I sat down where I was and started howling.

"What's wrong?"

"You're here," I sobbed, "and you know that they killed somebody, murdered them ... over there," I stammered.

"I know, but what's wrong with you?"

"You're stupid. It could be Adam!"

"Hey, girl," he shouted. "Calm down. I was there. It was a little boy not more than eleven years old. I know your brother!"

What he was saying finally got through to me. I hugged him. "I don't know myself who I was more afraid for, Adam or you."

"You were afraid for me?" He stood there in surprise. "You know, Stella," he said after a moment, "when this is all over and you're bigger, I'm going to marry you and take you away, only not to Germany. You're right not to like Germans. I'll take you to America."

On the way home I thought that when they gave me a hard time and said, "Don't interrupt, you're just a child," I would answer that I'm no child because I have a husband and I'm going to America with him. But what was America? It was certainly a country, but I had no idea if it was far from Kraków or near. I would ask Bubik one day. He knew everything.

In the evening I heard Daddy telling Mummy that they were preparing a transport that would take people away. Limousines carrying various important SS dignitaries had driven through several times during the day. There was supposedly a camp in Auschwitz where they killed people in gas chambers and there was also a labour camp there, and they were going to build a camp not far from here, at the old Jewish cemetery in Płaszów. I heard Daddy saying nervously that they were supposed to take the old, the sick and children away first. The regulations had been tightened up recently. No one was allowed on the streets after curfew on pain of death, and those who returned after eight needed special passes. Shots could be heard more and more often in the Ghetto.

Bubik found a passageway between the houses into our courtyard, so that if there was something urgent he could get through even after curfew and call me with our agreed whistle signal. Everyone here had an agreed signal and no one ever mixed them up.

He whistled. All upset, he said that his father had been talking about the transport at home. His father also worked in the OD, but Bubik never wanted to tell what he did there or what position he held. I have to sniff out what's behind this.

The first thing in the morning, after everyone had left for work, a lot of trucks drove in with armed German soldiers. They looked as threatening as if they had come to confront wild beasts, yet there were only unarmed people here. A limousine drove slowly through the streets and the German in it announced through a loudspeaker: "All Jews are immediately to go to their dwellings. Do not leave your homes until further orders. Do not approach the windows under penalty of death."

They staked out the whole Ghetto and its perimeter so that not even a mouse could have moved unseen.

I was alone in the apartment with Blackie. The building was quiet as if there wasn't a living soul around. None of the Weisses next door had a work assignment, and I had heard them creeping down into the cellar earlier. I was terrified because I clearly heard it said that the children were going to be taken away. I could hear more and more shots, and horrible screams and wailing. The noises in the street were drawing closer.

I sat on the floor in the darkest corner holding Blackie who was also terrified and shaking all over. Oh God, why didn't Daddy come? After all, he was here in the Ghetto. I was so scared. I pressed my hands to my ears so that I wouldn't hear anything. Just so I didn't hear! I felt sick to my stomach and I got hiccups which I couldn't control. I wanted so badly to stop hiccupping because if it was quiet they might not come in, or they might not see me, it was so dark in the room.

Suddenly I heard dreadful screaming in our building. I recognized voices. They were starting in the cellar. *"Rrrraus – rrraus!"* There were moans and crying, and then a shot and horrible howling. "My child! My little Ernestine!" I pressed my hands tight over my ears. Nothing helped. In a moment they would come for me and it was bound to be the same. I was so terribly frightened! I heard the clomp of boots. Those characteristic hobnailed boots were right outside. I covered my face with my hands. This must have been how every animal feels when cornered by evil people. I vowed to myself that I would never again so much as step on a bug. I couldn't finish the thought. Footsteps, a blow from a rifle butt, the door slammed open against the wall and the pane of glass in it shattered. There was a horrible buzzing in my head.

"Raus!"

I can't, I'm unable to get up, they'll drag me out... or else right here on the spot...

"Noo, was ist den los!"

Suddenly, it must be a miracle, I hear an agitated voice in the hallway, yes, it's Daddy's voice! If only he gets here before they shoot. I see the barrels of two revolvers right in front of my nose. When I stand, my legs seem to be made of cotton. Daddy comes in, holding a piece of paper in his hand. They look around and talk with him, but I can't understand anything. Then Daddy takes out his identity card.

"Ja, das ist meine Wohnung" I hear him say as he stands at attention.

And where is Blackie? Under the couch, maybe. They point at me, they show each other the paper, they talk to Daddy. He tells me, "Walk in front of me and don't look around."

I summon up all my strength to be able to walk out.

The streets are empty. Every ten metres stands an SS-man with his rifle ready to fire. Not moving my head, just by letting my eyes range around, I see people lying every few feet. They must be corpses. We are stopped several times on the way. Each time, Daddy pulls out the paper and explains something.

"Where are we going?" I whisper.
"Don't say anything. To the OD."

Suddenly an old woman comes out of a door, and several more people behind her. Two SS-men are herding them with their rifle butts. The woman grips the door-knob and cries, *"No! No! Ich bitte, Ich will nicht!"*

The Germans lay into her with the rifle butts and blood flows from her nose, from her head, she is covered in blood. An SS-man raises his rifle. There is a scream, and a shot.

"Faster, don't look there!" I hear a whisper from behind me.

The journey seemed unending. When the gate of the OD closed behind us, Daddy leaned heavily against the door and took his cap off. Then I could see the sweat running down his forehead. He took out a cigarette, but his hands were trembling so badly that he had to ask someone else to light it for him.

"You stay here until I come for you, sit in the corner there. No one will take you away. I've got to go back, I'm on duty collecting corpses."

I did not answer, and my hiccups started again. I didn't know how long I sat there. Then I became aware that someone was calling someone else "Schleifer". I started looking at the men in the room. This was the OD duty room. I did not know Bubik's father and I could not imagine which one he could be. Finally I couldn't help asking the nearest one. "Excuse me, Sir. Which one is Schleifer?"

"What's it to you?"

"I have to tell him something."

"That's him there," he said, pointing to a short, fat man.

I went up to him. "Excuse me, Sir." He looked at me warily. "I only wanted to ask where Bubik is." I couldn't control my hiccups and felt embarrassed.

"What does it matter to you?"

"I just... I only wanted to know where he is."

"At home," he barked, and walked away.

I thought that Bubik must be safe if his father was so calm. A moment later, I heard laughter. I looked in astonishment to see who could laugh at such a time. It was Bubik's father, imitating my hiccups.

It was all over. We sat around Daddy, who was telling us how he had gathered corpses and that among them he had found three members of his own family, two uncles and an aunt. He looked broken. "Mummy, would there be any vodka in the house?" he asked hesitantly, since he never drank.

Mummy came back a moment later with a bottle.

"You know, Tusia," he said, "Maybe she should drink a little, too. I'm worried about those hiccups. She might be suffering from shock. She's been through a lot today."

Mummy thought for a moment and then decided that I wouldn't get any alcohol because I had to get used to it first. Besides it was only the beginning of such horrors.

The bottle was already empty. Daddy stood up, tottering slightly, and put his arms around me. "Come on, dear, get into bed. That's enough for today."

He sat beside me and began humming a lullaby that he often used to sing to me at home. Something in me ached at the sad intonation in his voice.

The door opened and my brother came in. His group was always among the last to return from work. His hair was ruffled and his eyes looked jumpy. "Is everyone here? Where's Stella? I heard terrible things along the way, that children..." He saw me. "She's so pale. Is she hurt?"

"Adam, calm down," said Mummy. "She's only exhausted."

He came up and started showering me with kisses. "My poor little sister. My darling."

We both cried. I think that was the moment when a true bond was formed between us.

The doors opened again and a man with a beard and side curls came in. "Müller, come pray, we have to say kaddish for the dead and every decent Jew is going to pray. You're a *gites mensch* and a man has to pray."

"No, I'm not going to pray," Daddy said sadly. "Today I have already prayed over each one that I picked up. The time is coming when there won't be anyone to pray for us," he said more to himself than to other men.

"Oh, *nicht git* with you, I'll have to pray for you too," he muttered under his nose as he went out.

Bubik came a moment later. He knew nothing about my day's adventures, so Mummy started telling him in German (I didn't like it when they spoke German to each other) about what Daddy had been through with me. During her account he looked at me with more and more concern. I felt good lying there surrounded by my dearest ones. It had been a long time since I had felt so loved and so secure.

"So, Bubik, you'd better go now," Mummy finally said. "They'll be worried about you at home."

"Oh, I almost forgot, Stella, here's some chocolate for you," he said with a smirk. "Chocolate is the best thing for sick children."

He gave me a piece of milk chocolate, which I loved, and I was too tired to be offended by that "children".

Everything in the Ghetto went back to normal. Nothing was heard of those who had been transported, and of the numerous reports that were circulating, the most common was that they had gone straight to the gas. The Ghetto was empty, but there were already rumours that a new transport would arrive from Bochnia. If they bring new ones in, I thought, there will be a new transport out. So is that how it will go, down to the last Jew? Friends and relatives visited us in the evening bearing various predictions, according to all of which the war should end soon. My brother had different comforting sayings, such as "A comet will sweep us with its tail and that will be the end," and whenever there was an air raid siren he laughed and shouted, "Presents flying overhead from Tommy to Adolf." Our parents often told him not to jest. Then he would ask maliciously if they would rather he speeded things up and just hanged himself. He felt that you had to make light of the situation. Such discussions were frequent occurrences when everyone was at home.

***

Bubik is a darling. He has traded his boy's bicycle for a girl's so that I can learn to ride. At first he ran along behind and held the saddle as I pedaled, and then one day I looked

34

around and saw that he wasn't holding on. So of course, I fell immediately. I became angry with him and he told me that I was being hysterical, because he had only been pretending to hold on for several days now. After that, I got on the bicycle by myself and rode. I was as proud as if I were piloting a plane.

Bubik became my protector. He announced one day that I should start learning things. He brought me a lot of books, maps and so on, which did not suit me at all because I preferred riding the bicycle and playing with my dog. But Bubik explained with irrefutable logic that the war would end, and what would I do then if I couldn't find America on the map and didn't know my multiplication tables? I could not really understand why he was so strict with me – he set times for lessons and was unyielding. During the first lessons even I noticed that I knew absolutely nothing and asked idiotic questions. Bubik tried bravely to fulfill his pedagogical mission.

Boys and girls made a big thing of us and when we walked down the street we often heard them calling, "Oooo! There goes the engaged couple!" I didn't mind and held my head up high, but Bubik must not have been very happy about it.

He would say then, "They're fools. You're still a child. Maybe you'll be my fiancée someday, but they're acting stupid."

It made me angry to be treated constantly as a child, when I was already starting to hunch my shoulders because I didn't know how to hide the breasts that were visible under my dress. I was dissatisfied with myself again and had gone back to feeling low.

We had our favourite place at Krzemionki. We often sat there and Bubik would review our lessons. One day, when he had deflected my troublesome questions by saying that I was still little and stupid, I grabbed his hand in rage and laid it on my breasts. "Feel them," I said. "I'm hardly a child anymore."

He got up and walked away without saying a word.

I waited in vain the next day and the day after that. He did not appear. I lacked the courage to ask Mummy if what I had done was terrible. But if he reacted that way, I must have been in the wrong. In the end I couldn't stop myself from heading towards "our" place at Krzemionki. I spotted Bubik from a long way off. I wanted to apologize to him, even though I didn't know for what. When I was almost there, I saw that he was not alone, and that knocked the breath out of me! My theoretical education had been brutally completed. I went home sobbing, feeling a terrible revulsion, hatred, and I could not really say what else, towards everyone, towards my parents – but Bubik had become the most disgusting of all.

In the evening, Daddy asked if anything was wrong because I was crying in the corner. I replied haughtily that he should leave me alone.

Daddy got angry: "Do you think, snotnose, that nobody has anything more important to worry about than your tantrums? Go to bed!"

Later I heard my parents talking in the kitchen about how it was better not to pay any attention to my behaviour, that perhaps I was going through puberty and in such conditions, where they had no time for me, I would encounter things that shocked me. Then they talked for a long time about how they could help me.

Mummy invited Ziuta, my dear cousin, to visit. I hadn't seen her for a long time because she was working. I looked at her with envy. She was such a lovely, grown-up girl, nicely dressed and not sloppy like me. She asked, a little awkwardly, what was new. How was I supposed to answer? So I didn't. Finally, as if it were an offhand remark, she said, "I hear you've got a wonderful boyfriend, Stella."

"He's no boyfriend," I prickled. "We're not speaking. He likes older girls and only wanted to show off how clever he was in front of me..." I broke off, thinking I had already said too much.

"Don't worry, kid," Ziuta said with a superior expression. "Emil and I" – she also had a boyfriend – "are always quarrelling about something, but we make up quickly."

Sure, I thought. If I looked the way you do, Bubik would be here now.

I had developed an ugly habit of eavesdropping when my parents talked in the evening.

"Have you noticed, Zygmunt," my mother whispered, "how distracted she is over that fight with Bubik? I admit he's a nice boy, but I'm happy he's stopped sitting here all day because he's older, and these children are growing up too fast."

"Oh, Tusia, come off it," Daddy said, and started whispering something that I couldn't catch.

I only heard that I should have a new coat because it was nearly winter and I was going around like a ragamuffin and had grown out of everything. I was already imagining how I would parade in a new coat. Then I heard Daddy say that they were going to suspend passes to the city and reduce the area of the Ghetto, from which nothing good could come. I went to sleep with all rancour eased, hoping for that new coat.

Everybody was running rather than walking these days and looking anxious. I had no idea what was happening. The worst thing was that it was getting cold and I was still waiting for my coat. I put on a black jacket of Mummy's with a fur collar, pulled a belt around it and, feeling exceptionally elegant, took Blackie out for a walk. I had not gone far when children were dancing in a ring around me: "Hey, Miss High Fashion, go back home," they shouted, "and give your mother her jacket, because she won't have anything to wear!"

I was dying of shame because at that moment Bubik came walking past with Dodek Reich, who used to tease him about having taken a job as a baby-sitter. In horrible anger I began striking out blindly at the children, and when I broke free I ran home. Along the way I could hear them singing "Stupid Stella's all upset, Bubik dumped her and she can't forget." I wished a car with a gun on it would come along right then and shoot me.

I have one piece of bad luck after another. Blackie is dead! I let him out into the courtyard, and he ran into the street right in front of a German car. Daddy saw it on his way home from work. He was explaining that the dog hadn't suffered a bit.

I cut him off and wanted to run outside.

"Where are you going?"

"To look for Blackie. It's not true that he's dead!"

"Wait! I carried him over and he's lying at the door. Be reasonable. Think how many people have been killed!"

"I don't care about people," I sobbed. "It's my fault, your fault!"

"How is it our fault?" Daddy asked, dumbfounded.

"Because I don't have a coat. It's all because of that coat!" But Daddy still couldn't understand.

I had stopped crying and sat in the corner all puffed up, but nobody spoke to me. Mummy had also cried in the evening, and then said, almost in a rage, "I told you that this was no place to keep a dog. I was right when I asked you to get rid of him, as if we didn't have enough troubles, and now this."

"All right, stop," Daddy said, not letting her finish. "She's suffering enough."

"We'll go together in the morning and bury him, dear."

Bubik arrived early in the morning with a box he had nailed together from little boards. I was so depressed that I didn't even wonder where he had come from or how he had found out.

"Where's the dog, Stella? We'll bury him at Krzemionki. I could bury him myself and show you where afterwards if you want."

"Fine, go by yourself," I moaned, "I don't care where you bury him."

"It's good that you're being reasonable."

I even forgot that we weren't speaking. He put the dog's body into the box and left. When he returned he hung around, not knowing what to do with himself. "You know, Stella," he said suddenly, "I've got an idea. I love my Juhas, but I can bring him here if you want."

Then I remembered my anger at him and my decision that it was over between us. "You're stupid," I shouted. "Stupid! Go, go to Krzemionki to your other girls!"

He stood with his head hanging down like a convicted man. He would have been wise to have left.

"What are you standing there for, you, you... Hun!" The anger rose in me.

"Stella, that wasn't nice. I didn't kill your dog. When you are older you'll understand that you shouldn't get angry at me, and that you are the most important."

I felt better knowing that I still meant something to him, although I went on pretending to be angry.

***

It was 1942. The winter was snowy and frosty and I had got my coat and shoes. Girls came to see them and they must have been envious because they had nothing nice to wear. I was so proud of my coat. Whether it was necessary or not, I ran out in the frost so that everyone could see it.

German trucks turned up quite often, catching people and taking them into town to shovel snow. They often stopped groups on the way home from work, and tired people sometimes had to spend the whole night clearing snow in the city.

Daddy was pacing around the apartment and we were not saying anything, although we were both very upset because Mummy should have been home long before. She still went out on a pass, not in a group, although of course she wore the armband.

Daddy worried out loud: "She's so unpredictable sometimes, she might have been insulted by a German. I've asked her so many times not to carry those big bags full of food. They might have stopped her at the gate. Or she might not have put her armband on, and some informer might have pointed her out..."

"Daddy, I'm going down by the gate a little," I cut him off.

"Just you be careful, because I've got enough to worry about."

"Only for a minute." Before he could answer, I ran outside.

I whistled for Bubik. He was downstairs a moment later and I told him that Mummy hadn't come home yet and I was going to walk towards the gate on Podgórski Market Square where she always returned. Bubik went with me, of course. Along the way he delivered a long, involved explanation of what had happened at Krzemionki but he spoke in such a way that I stopped understanding what he wanted to say and what it was

39

I had been offended about. I caught something about "men's matters" and how young I was. Little got through to me. Only one thought kept going around in my mind – I wanted to see Mummy. That was all that mattered.

Both sides of the gate were deserted. Our people preferred not to get too close and those on the other side were forbidden to approach. At the gate stood a German and a "blue policeman."

"What are you children looking for here?" asked the "blue". "Maybe you want to slip out? Not a good idea, all the groups have returned. You'd better go away, children."

"But, Sir, my Mummy doesn't go with a group and she hasn't returned."

The German went over to the "blue" and was obviously asking him what was going on. Before the "blue" could think of something, Bubik started talking to the German. They spoke like old friends. The German patted Bubik on the shoulder, looking around to see if anyone was coming. I strained my eyes until they ached, looking at the figures moving about in the distance. Later I learned that the German came from the same town as Bubik and had said that Bubik should come to him at the gate if he needed anything.

I was getting more upset. The curfew was approaching and we were getting ready to leave, when I thought I saw a small group of people in the distance.

"Look. They might be coming!" I shouted, excited. Now I was sure: there were a dozen or so people under escort, with my Mummy among them.

When they got through the gate, we ran up to her. "What happened, Mummy?"

Bubik took her bag and I bombarded her with questions. "Why with a group? Why so late? You're terribly tired, Mummy." It all came out in one breath.

"Yes, I'm terribly tired. Imagine, children, I was coming home as usual at four and near the bridge, not far from here, stood a truck and they were catching people with armbands walking alone. They came up to me. It did no good to say that I was on an urgent errand for Frau Holzinger. They took us to the Market Square, gave us shovels, and made us clear snow.

It was very unpleasant. Many people stopped to watch. Some shook their heads sympathetically, but there were others who were amused. Later I stopped paying attention. Stella, do you remember engineer Górecki who used to come with his wife to play bridge?"

"I remember."

"They stopped, and Górecki practically screamed, 'Mrs. Müller! My God! You, here?' 'Well, after all, I'm in no way better than the rest of our people behind barbed wire.' His wife started to cry. She took off her gloves and gave them to me. 'Please put on a second pair, it'll be warmer.' I said that it was very nice of them not to be ashamed to know me. 'Ashamed?' they both stammered. 'Please come with your family and we'll hide you and get you out.' Then they had to go because a German came and shooed them away. I felt like smashing his horrible face with my shovel."

So we got home, where Daddy and Adam were sitting motionless. When they saw how tired and wet Mummy was, they raced to bring her a bowl of hot water and her slippers. The sheets were already on the bed.

However, Mummy caught a cold and had to take several days off work. This was a wonderful time, because it was homely again. In the mornings, Mummy combed my hair.

"You know, dear," she sighed over my unkempt hair, "you've grown, you've grown up, and I've hardly noticed because we're together so little."

I could see that Mummy had changed a great deal. She used to smile all the time, but no more. She didn't lose her temper with me. We talked a lot and made plans. She asked what I would like to be when the war ended and said I had vast gaps in my schooling. I answered that I would like to be a vet. Mummy said that was no job for a woman.

"So, a musician," I mumbled without conviction.

"What? Not even the threat of spanking could induce you to practice the piano with Ziuta. You acted as if there was a drawing pin on the seat."

"Well, then maybe a dancer? I was always good at exercise class in school."

"You've grown a lot," Mummy closed our discussion, "but you're still childish. Maybe that's good."

In the evenings while she was ill, Mummy was adorable. Friends came, like Uncle and Aunt Grünberg and Ziuta with her faithful beau Emil, who worked with Adam and the two were inseparable. As in the old days, Uncle took me on his knee and made fun of my lisping. It used to amuse me, but now it made me angry. Ziuta cooed over my long eyelashes. This cheered me up a little bit but also embarrassed me. I didn't like myself and always wanted to be similar to "somebody", as long as it wasn't me.

During these evenings there was also vodka on the table. Emil organized drinks, Bubik played the accordion, the young people danced and the older ones played bridge. You could hear Mummy's and Uncle's voices as they argued heatedly over the cards, although in general they liked each other very much.

It is New Year, 1942. But this is not the normal New Year, this is the Jewish New Year, and I simply cannot get used to these Jewish holidays. For me there remained "our holidays", as I call them to the despair of my parents. We got into heated discussions, because when there was that holiday during which you are not allowed to eat bread, I went ostentatiously onto the street with a slice of bread, pretending to eat it. The more devout ones who passed me spat and shouted, "Shabbes goy". Daddy met me with some bread in my hands. He got angry and shouted at me. This was not a minor matter; he had never shouted at me before.

"Won't you ever behave properly? Do you have to be such a perverse goose?" The discussion went on long into the evening. "You must understand, we don't insist that you observe all that. It's our fault you were brought up the way you were, but just think, they'll treat us as outcasts!"

"But we're Poles," I stuck to my guns.

"Of course you're Polish, but you're also Jewish and here, in the Ghetto, you have to go along. You can do what you like at home and eat bread while the others fast."

"Daddy, what's a *shabbes goy?*"

"Exactly. It means a renegade, an outcast."

"I'll try never to do it again, but just tell me, who puts out the candles for those religious ones on Friday?"

"Who's been telling you such things?"

"Isn't it true?" I wouldn't leave him in peace.

"It's true!" I could see that Daddy was losing patience. "If you want, you can go and put them out."

Today is New Year, but the real one, as I call it. The table is set for a holiday and the curtains drawn tight. Everybody is already home from work. There's no hiding the fact that Adam and Emil, giggling, have already started. They both make strange gestures as if they intended to drop their trousers. I can't believe my eyes when each of them pulls two bottles out of his trousers on strings, and sets the bottles on the table to shouts and laughter.

"And now let's sing a carol, Adam," Emil cries.

"Only quiet!" everybody warns. "There are extra patrols today."

"Adam, you sing beautifully. One, two," calls Emil.

"Today in Kraków there's merry tidings, a thousand bombers are bound for Berlin. Berlin's in flames and Hitler messes his pants..." he sang to the tune of a Polish carol.

"Well, calm down now," the adults say. "That was beautiful, but enough." Then the stories begin.

"Germans came to the factory today. They received vodka, and when they were drunk we taught them to sing that song in Polish. It was great fun, we were rolling with laughter, and the Germans were so happy they could sing that they fell to their knees." Emil and Adam made such fun of them that we all laughed until we cried.

Suddenly, what was that? The dumping of boots. "Halt! Halt!"

Somebody said, "Put out the lights!" There was darkness, silence, then a shot and moaning.

"Everybody stand against the wall," said Uncle.

"Why are we so quiet? There's a couple of men here, damn it. Let's go out and show them that we won't take this," said Emil in a blustering tone.

They didn't let him finish. "Sit down and shut up, idiot. You can show them how you wet your pants, drunken baby," I recognized my aunt's voice.

There were a couple of more shots and a window broke. My parents decided that we would make room and no one would have to go home that night, except for Bubik who had an easy passage through the courtyard fence. It was an anxious, uncomfortable night. We learned the next morning that there were several corpses and a few wounded. Everybody took it as a bad sign for the New Year – that nothing better should be expected.

***

Nothing interesting has been happening lately except that I occasionally hear someone being shot or beaten. It no longer makes any impression on me.

The snow falls in large flakes but its whiteness doesn't show here; it is grey, too many feet walk over it. At home it is cold because they give us too little coal. Many girls and boys come to visit. Dosia Wasserlauf has brought the card game called "Flirt", which bores me. Dosia is a lot older than me and very pretty, even though she has freckles. Dziunia Buchbinder is stunning, with lovely dimples in her cheeks when she smiles. I would give anything for such dimples. When no one is watching, I sit in front of the mirror and press my fingers into my cheeks until it hurts, but the dimples still don't form. When we play "Flirt" the boys usually send their cards to Dosia or Dziunia. This game is absolutely not for me, and even Bubik barely sends me any cards, so I behave sharply.

Today, February 5, is my birthday. I am twelve at last, and perhaps they will stop calling me "little" and "kid". Mummy returned from work early bringing many splendid things, but the most important is a navy blue dress from Grandmother which has a white collar and a belt. Mummy says it is too long, but I am thrilled because it makes me look grown-up.

Everything is ready. I am dressed, Mummy has combed my hair and then stepped back and stated with satisfaction that I look the way I should always look. My palms start to sweat from nerves as I wait for the guests. Maybe that stupid Bubik will come, although he has been angry at me again for some reason. Daddy has just come home.

"How beautiful my daughter looks! Just like before the war, but so big already!" he says with a smile.

The guests start arriving. I get a lot of presents. Aunt Grünberg has brought me lovely things that Ziuta has grown out of, and Uncle picks me up, kisses me, and pinches me. Uncle and I love each other very much, and he always says that I am like a second daughter to him. I feel wonderful. Today, I am the most important.

"Stella dear," Uncle calls, "Let me raise a toast – to your health! May you live happily until the end of the war and grow up into a lovely young lady."[1]

Adam butts in. "What, are you wishing that my sister becomes an old maid? No danger of that!"

"Just look," says my Aunt. "They used to fight like cats and dogs, and now he's so proud of his sister."

"Well, she's already got an admirer," Adam laughs maliciously. "Except that today he seems to have forgotten about her birthday."

I don't know what to say. That was such a mean blow, and if it had not been for my new dress I would have given him one in the face. "Adam," says Daddy, "no caustic remarks today, please."

We youngsters get some ersatz wine and Emil has brought a gramophone, so it promises to be great fun.

I forgot to mention Sula Frankel. She came to me in secret, because her father, one of those devout ones who wore a *chalat* and side curls, has forbidden Sula to spend time with apostates such as us. Sula is very tall and I like her, although

---

[1] Note: The word used here in Polish – 'panna' – refers to an unmarried woman. Hence the following remark from Adam

I am put off by her ugly drawling way of talking and the way she mixes up her sentences. She is also pigeon-toed, dresses sloppily and is always pulling at her nose. But in general, she's fine. So Sula is also there. I stay close to her because everyone else seems to be avoiding her, which makes me feel bad.

Dziunia looks, well, I don't know how to put it, like Snow White in a film that I saw before the war. She's lovely. She comes up to me and asks casually about Bubik. What's wrong with you, asking about Bubik when it's supposed to be my birthday? I put on an indifferent expression because I really thought that he probably wouldn't come. "Oh, he'll be coming, it's just that, you know, he's such a dandy and he'll want to look especially good on my birthday."

It worked. I looked proudly at Dziunia's uneasiness. If he really doesn't show up, I'll think of something else later.

There was so much laughter and noise that no one noticed Bubik come in. He stood in the doorway with the accordion he always carried, holding a package in his other hand. He was dressed beautifully indeed. Where did his mother get such splendid things? I felt a gentle poke. It was Mummy indicating that I should greet my guest. I went up to him all embarrassed because everyone was watching.

Bubik was also embarrassed and said quickly, "This is for you, Stella," handing me the large package. "I wish you all the best," and he kissed me on both cheeks.

"Bubik! On the hand! You kiss a lady on the hand!" Emil is insufferable, but I like him.

Bubik kept his wits and shot back at Emil: "You kiss her hand if you're not allowed to kiss her on the face."

"Bravo!" cried Uncle. "That's a man for you, he doesn't let himself be embarrassed."

Perhaps out of anger I sat Bubik next to Dziunia. Emil picked me up, put me on the couch and announced that to satisfy tradition, I should be showered with delicacies. He's such a trouble-maker that he spilled a whole bag of beans over me. Bubik played *Sto lat* and said that he would play for me all the time. I felt very well.

I unpacked his present. It was a lovely case with a key, and inside were wonders: a headband, a hairbrush, cologne. "But Bubik," Mummy said, "that's too expensive a present. You shouldn't have."

"It came as a set." He spoke better Polish all the time. "And here's something else," he took a whole package of bobby pins out of his pocket, "so you don't have to go around with your hair in your eyes."

Adam already looked quite drunk. He recalled something suddenly. "Do you remember, sister, how when we were little we were in the park once and I was fighting with a bunch of boys and couldn't handle all of them? Suddenly they all started running away. I look, and there she stands, and I ask, 'Stella, what did you do to them?' 'Nothing, Adam, just my head in their stomachs and a kick in the ankles.' Afterwards, when I took her to the park, they shouted, 'Here comes the one that butts.'"

***

And so it is true that the size of the Ghetto is to be reduced. They are already building new gates and entrances. There will be Ghetto A and Ghetto B. I have no idea what is going on. Why are they supposed to divide one from the other? They say that it is for working and non-working. Now the Ghetto will be very small. Only one side of Limanowski Street will be left, with Józefińska, Targowa, Zgoda Square, one side of Lwowska and a few side streets. We won't all fit in such a small space, so again they must be up to something, but what? People have been going around asking these questions for several days.

Mummy has a very bad headache. She sends me to the pharmacy. We have one pharmacy, on Zgoda Square. There is a very elegant man there, completely unlike our people. "Mummy," I ask when I come back, "who is that man in the pharmacy?"

"Why do you ask?"

"Because he's different."

47

"He is a very nice, good man, Mister Pankiewicz. He is engaged in a continuing campaign to be allowed to stay in that pharmacy."

"Why does he bother? After all, we have a lot of pharmacists."

"You're right, but this way he can help us. He helps a lot of people stay in touch with their families who are in hiding."

"And he brings medicines that we could never get otherwise," Daddy puts in.

It has happened. We are moving to 29 Józefińska Street. Daddy says that this is a house for OD-men and their families, and that some of them are so unbearable that he would rather live elsewhere. I have also been hearing about these good and bad OD-men. Many of them are informers. I did not know for a long time why Bubik preferred not to speak about his father. His father is supposedly an informer who always goes in plain clothes and has a mistress, so Bubik's mother cries all the time. That is why he said he hates his father and is ashamed of him.

We live in a shared three-room apartment, in the smallest room. In the first room are Igo Braw and his wife. Then there is Rottersmann with his wife and four-year-old daughter whom they call Malinka or Little Raspberry, and she does look like a raspberry, pretty with a curly black head and a merry red face. In the middle room are the Neigers with two children, not nice at all with their noses always running, always getting a whipping and screaming. Bubik lives in the room above ours. His sister Rutti has married Dudi Goldstein. She is not yet eighteen, but Goldstein supposedly has Hungarian citizenship and Bubik says his parents have plans in connection with this, although he doesn't know what.

It is bearable in the room during the day, but in the evenings there is no room to move once we start unfolding the cots. I have asked Daddy to set up a hot plate, because the housewives will not let me put even a pot of potatoes on the kitchen stove.

The new apartment started having a bad effect on me. First, I got a bladder infection. I suffered for a long time because

I was ashamed to tell my parents. In the mornings, everybody was always looking for things and arguing. Everybody pushed their cots against the walls, and when they were gone I struggled to fold them up. This morning the fighting started early because everybody kept asking me things and I did not even answer because it felt like my eyes were full of sand.

"Stella, what's going on?" Mummy asked. "Get up. We've got to move the beds because there's no room too move."

"I feel ill," I said, almost crying. "My eyes hurt so much I can't see."

"Look, Zygmunt," Mummy said. Look at her! Her whole face is swollen and covered with spots. Give me a thermometer. Just as I thought," Mummy lamented. "She's got a temperature. What can I do? I can't go to work, and we'll have to find a doctor we know so that she won't be sent to the hospital. Remember how they shot everyone in the hospital courtyard during the last action? Oh, God, what am I going to do? She was always so healthy."

I had never heard my mother so upset.

"Calm down, Tusia. Maybe it's nothing, maybe it's just indigestion," Daddy said.

In the end, Mummy went to work saying that she would decide what to do with me in the evening, and in the meantime she would tell Frau Holzinger that she was taking a few days off.

I was left alone with my grandfather. He hovered helplessly over me and I asked him to lower the blinds because the light bothered me so. Bubik came; I had forgotten that I had asked him to start teaching me again. "What's going on here? Why is it dark? Why are you still in bed?" he asked.

Grandfather stood beside him waiting to get a word in. "Leave her be. She is ill. Her mother will be home from work soon and will bring a doctor."

"How can she be ill? She was all right last night." Bubik stood there helplessly.

Mummy came with the doctor. He was what I had always imagined a real doctor to be. He was fairly old, perhaps fifty, with splendid white hair and beautiful gentle blue eyes. His name was Otto Schwarz and he came from Bielsko, where he had his own clinic. He examined me and said that I had a bad case of measles. There was a measles epidemic and the hospital was overflowing, so I should stay at home. Mummy would have to be very careful since there were several children in the apartment.

I was really ill. I made it through the days, but when everyone came home from work in the evenings it was terrible. The light hurt my eyes and my head ached.

Mummy was angry at Bubik from the start because he sat around our place and could catch the measles. He said that he had already had it, but was he telling the truth? He promised her not to get close to me. Since Mummy hardly ever left the room he turned out to be very helpful.

Doctor Schwarz came back a couple of days later. He was not happy with what he saw and said that I could use some lemons. Mummy sighed that if she went to work for one day, Frau Holzinger would be sure to help. The next day Bubik did not come until evening. I could see that Mummy was upset by his absence, which to me was a matter of indifference. He came in with a mysterious look on his face, handed Mummy a bag, and said, "These are for Stella. I heard the doctor talking about lemons yesterday..."

Mummy cut him off. "Bubik! What are you doing? You can't do this," she stammered. "It's very nice of you. How much did they cost?"

"I have my own money. I get an allowance every month from my father," It was the first time he had mentioned his father. "Please don't refuse them!"

"Heavens, so many lemons. There must be half a kilo, where did you get them?" She was no longer angry. "I was worried about you."

"It's a long story," he replied. "I went to find 'my' German at the gate, but he was on duty only after two o'clock, and I told him that my mother was ill, so he changed with somebody else and went with me to the shop. It was simple, we even talked with each other. The swine, he said it was a shame I was a Jew because I was a fine boy. We came back together, he let me through the gate, and here I am."

"What will your mother say with you gone all day?"

"Sorry to admit it, but I lied and told her I was going to practice music with a friend."

"Bubik, Bubik," Mummy threatened him.

I got delicious lemonade and now I appreciated what true friendship meant.

My strength returned slowly. I couldn't manage to do anything right. I was weak and Bubik helped me. He stopped bothering me about lessons. Once, when he was sad, I managed to draw from him the news that he had had a fight with his father. The latter had said that he didn't want his son hanging around with "Polish swine" and Bubik replied that he, the father, didn't mind hanging around with Polish women, or words to that effect, and his father slapped him in the face. Bubik swore that he would never speak to him again.

Daddy has an uncle who was transported from Vienna. There he was a very wealthy and respected man. He always gets upset when he comes to visit, especially if Emil is here. Uncle wears a bowler hat and a worn-out black suit, but the bottoms of his trousers are always immaculately pressed. He is in a white shirt as well, frayed, and a bow-tie. Upon entering he greets everyone elegantly and waits until he is asked to sit down. Mummy sighs that he lives in his old world and perhaps he is lucky. When Daddy offered Uncle a pair of his shoes because Uncle's were falling apart, he said, "Zygmunt, don't you know that a gentleman doesn't wear such shoes?" and added a few words in verse.

"Mummy, what's he saying?" I asked.

"That's from Schiller. But what could it mean to you, dear?" And in fact, I didn't know where or who that was.

***

We didn't have Krzemionki any more, so I often walked with other girls through the few streets of the crowded Ghetto. We

51

were not surrounded by a wall any more, but only by barbed wire. I watched the tramcars running along Limanowski Street. "Normal" people, not wired-off like us, rode them.

Rózia Faeber and I went for a walk along Józefińska. There was a bath-house there. A group of prisoners had just been brought in from the *julag,* a sort of camp. Suddenly, there was an awful commotion – somebody was running away. *"Halt! Halt!"* People were falling over each other, stumbling, not watching who they were chasing or where.

"Let's get out of here, Stella!" Rózia pulled me by the hand.

We had almost reached a doorway when somebody stumbled and I tripped over them and fell. Rózia jumped over me, kicking me in the head. They were shooting at us! My head was underneath somebody and I had my legs on top of somebody else. I heard a groan.

"My leg, oh, it hurts!" I recognized Rózia's voice.

Untangling myself and standing up, I could feel that my face was wet. I touched it – blood, but I wasn't hurt anywhere. I could see them leading the poor fugitive back and hitting him with their rifle butts. "Stella," Rózia moaned, "I've been shot in the leg."

The hospital was across the road and I ran there crying that my friend was lying in the street. They came immediately and I followed the stretcher and waited in the packed corridor. The hospital was terrible, with people lying everywhere on stretchers or on the concrete floor. It stank awfully. They finally carried Rózia out of the emergency room. She was pale but conscious. "Go to my Mum, but don't frighten her. Say it's nothing serious."

I met Mrs. Faeber on the way. She was running and shouting, "My Różele, *mein kindele!"* Someone must have already told her. I wanted to tell her that she shouldn't worry, but I couldn't stop her.

The Ghetto was now so crowded that whenever you went out on the street, you met even the people you did not want to meet. So, of course, I ran straight into Bubik. "What are you doing wandering around?" he shouted. "There's been shooting."

"I don't need a baby-sitter," I said, although I wasn't so sure.

"You should be sitting with a book and reading."

"Shut up about those books, you, you scholar, you." I don't know why, but at times I adopted a very haughty attitude towards him.

"This time I'm going to tell your mother," he threatened, "and we will be not speaking for the rest of our lives."

"You see?" I smirked at the funny construction he used, "you bore me with those lessons and you yourself can't speak properly."

They set up a *kinderheim,* a children's home, in the building next to ours. There were children there of between two and ten years of age, mostly those with working mothers. I often saw them and many of them were lovely. I also liked Raspberry a lot. I forgot about my lessons and spent every free moment playing with dolls and bricks with her. I would probably have played by myself, but I pretended to be amusing her.

***

Summer has started with sweltering weather. There is a growing sense of overcrowding and of the lack of any quiet place to sit down and cool off. A sickly, dirty-sweet kitchen smell hangs everywhere. I crawl around the cellar looking for a place to shelter from the heat and people, but even here every corner is taken. Longingly, I recall Mania. How wonderful it was when she would suddenly appear before me, take me by the hand, and say, "Come on, little doll, let's go for a long walk into the unknown." She always talked that way and walks with her were always wonderful. During heat waves we would sit in the shade and I would put my head on her knees while Mania told me all sorts of fantastic stories. We often went into churches, partly for the coolness and partly because I liked walking around churches, especially when the organ was playing.

One day, when we were coming out of St. Mary's Church, a woman came up to Mania and started screaming at her:

"I know you! And that Jewish brat too. You should be ashamed to sin like that and take a Jew into the House of the Lord! Don't you know that they are an accursed people?"

She went on and on, and I had no idea what she meant. Only today can I understand the reason for her fury.

Mania told her, "One more word and you get it in the face. God's House is for everyone." She took me by the hand and we marched away. Yes, Mania was superb.

I remember that Mania once went to Sucha, where she had relatives, for a vacation. Mummy walked around the house with her hands on her head, screaming that she would go crazy with a terrible child like me. Mania saved our lives by showing up four days later. I don't know who was happier, Mummy or me. "What are you doing here?" Mummy asked, without concealing her joy.

"I couldn't sit there any longer. I missed my child so, and I was afraid," she said shyly, "that you might not know what to do with her. My little angel is so good when she's with me."

Mummy listened with an expression of amazement. "It's good you're here, because I'm going crazy. I'll buy you a nice present, Mania."

I snapped out of my reverie and looked around, returning to grim reality. I had to cook supper because they would soon be home from work. The heat, the noise everywhere, the people like ants made me terribly shiftless. It was exhausting.

I woke up frightened, but why? The street was already humming and everybody was getting up. For the first time I said to Mummy, "Please don't go to work today."

"Do you feel ill?" she was surprised.

"No. It's just that I'm afraid. Please."

"Don't be silly. After all, Daddy is around."

Grandfather stated that I must have been walking around in the sun too much and caught heatstroke. Adam was especially nice to me: "She must be exhausted. You know what? From now on I'll wash my own socks."

I repeated stubbornly that I was afraid.

"But of what?" Daddy interrupted.

"I don't know. All day yesterday there were cars coming to the *kinderheim*. I saw them. There was SS-man Pilarzik, and later von Malotchki."

Daddy looked at me with concern. "That's true. They were at the OD yesterday. A lot of them went in to see Commandant Spira" – he always said "Commandant Spira" ironically – "but I don't know anything because they sat the whole time behind closed doors."

"I'm frightened. I won't stay alone," I whined.

Morning activity was already in full swing. The Neiger children had had their spanking and were howling. Daddy went to the window every so often; there was a view of part of Limanowski Street through the barbed wire.

"Why do you keep going to the window?" Mummy asked irritably.

My crying was getting on everybody's nerves but I couldn't stop. Grandfather repeated over and over, "Heat-stroke," until Daddy shouted at him, as he had never done before, "Keep quiet, Father!"

Adam went to the window. "I wonder what the weather will be like today. If only this heat would let up ... Hey!" he shouted, "We're..."

"We're what?" Daddy cut him off sharply.

Adam looked at Daddy and then at me, and started running his fingers through his splendid dark hair. "Nothing. I don't remember what I wanted to say."

Mrs. Rottersmann burst into the room.

"My husband was on duty last night," she gasped in one breath, "and we're surrounded, just look through the window, they're standing every few metres and they've got dogs. They're supposedly going to let only some of the people out to work, only the ones employed in the most important factories. My husband wanted to know what's going on and he even summoned up the nerve to ask Spira. There's supposed to be a new registration."

When she left, we all stood there in silence, looking towards the window. Adam was the first to speak. He said to me, with forced jollity, "Remember how, when you were little, I called you a witch? I take it back. You heard them surrounding the Ghetto in your sleep and that's why you're afraid."

I loved that brother of mine for the way he could always cheer me up. "Now, little one, don't be afraid of anything. They're only going to write down names and they'll leave. My group will go to work for sure. I'll see you in the evening," Adam said in an unnatural tone. He kissed me and left with an embarrassed look on his face.

I sat watching Mummy dress. What was going on with me? I couldn't stop crying.

"Listen, Stella," she said energetically, too energetically, "they might let me out. I have to go to work because I've got all the keys to the safe with the important documents."

"Mummy dear, my only one, don't go. They won't let you out for sure."

She got angry. Daddy called her aside and they whispered in German for a long time, the way they always did when they didn't want me to overhear. In the end Mummy told me to stop carrying on and act like a grown-up, because now I was behaving worse than Malinka. No, she wasn't going to work.

Then a car drove up again and you could hear distinctly how they shouted through a megaphone: "Everyone is to go immediately to their apartments! Any civilians appearing on the street will be punished by death! Prepare all available documents so that the action and inspection can be carried out quickly! Approaching the windows will be punished by death. All employees of the OD are to report immediately to the station!"

We were left alone with Grandfather.

"Mummy, isn't there any other punishment besides death?"

"It's easier for them that way. Stop asking stupid questions and find something to do."

"Why do they hate us so much? You can hate one person, but why all of us?"

"There's a war on, and we're the enemy."

"But we're not fighting against them. We don't have any weapons. And Bubik told me the Germans are regarded as the most civilized nation."

"Well, that's what I thought, too," Mummy said and got angry. "But now give me a little peace and stop asking all these questions, because there are lots of things that I can't even explain to myself."

I heard shots. The action was beginning in Ghetto A, towards Węgierska Street. Germans were yelling everywhere. Why do they always have to yell so horribly? For me, the yelling was worse than the shooting.

"Maybe I'll close the window," I suggested.

"Don't you dare go near it."

"I can use a broom handle."

"Out of the question. We'll suffocate. Everybody is smoking and the room is overcrowded."

There were a lot of strange people there and I did not know where they had come from. The OD building offered a sort of security. Every so often, one of the OD-men looked in. He was showered with questions. Did they only want papers? He answered yes, without conviction. Would this building be passed over? There were a lot of strangers sheltering here, and nobody knew from what. Rottersmann said that a delegation had submitted a request that this building be omitted. They had agreed to exclude it from the registration and had stationed guards, who supposedly had a paper with a swastika seal on it, at the front entrance. I thought that was good, they wouldn't come bellowing at us in here.

Daddy showed up covered in perspiration, pushing two more women into the room. I heard him telling Mummy that there had been a massacre at the hospitals and the patients had been shot in the courtyards, or in the wards if they were unable to get out of bed.

"I managed to get Doctor Löw out the back by a miracle. She didn't want to leave her patients and I don't even remember which building I pushed her into."

"But what's going on?" Mummy asked. "They were only supposed to register people again."

"That was just talk to prevent panic. They're loading people, the ones who don't have work assignments and ones who have assignments, too, on to trucks at Zgoda Square. One 'blue' told me that they're taking them to the railway station at Płaszów and pushing 120 people at a time into cattle trucks. Terrible things are happening, people are suffocating."

I had lost track of time. The whole building was terribly quiet, even the children were silent. An old lady, who was with a woman who looked like her and must have been her daughter, quietly hummed a few bars of a song and then started sobbing. She started humming again. Her daughter held her hand and stroked her because she could plainly see that people were looking at her mother impatiently. She explained that her mother had been acting that way since she saw the Germans kill her father, that something had gone wrong in her head and the doctors were no help. I peered at that woman and saw that she wasn't looking anywhere and her eyes completely lacked expression. I felt cold in spite of the heat.

Daddy was back. He took a drink of water and told Mummy that they had killed his uncle from Vienna. He ran out. Mummy lowered her head and discreetly dabbed at her eyes. Daddy was on duty leading people out. He had asked Spira to let him collect the dead. He said later that he would rather gather corpses than listen with an aching heart to people pleading for help.

Trucks pulled up in front of the *kinderheim*. I stood watching from the side of the window. They were leading children out in pairs and loading them onto two trucks with their canvas tops down. Many of the children held their most treasured possessions, dolls or puppets, in their arms. Then a passenger car drove up and two SS-men got out. They must have been drunk because they were laughing and staggering. They spoke to the ones who were bringing out the children.

I did not realize that I had been hiccupping. Somebody told Mummy to give me a little sugar because the hiccups were maddening.

"Nothing will help," Mummy explained. "It's nerves." Somebody else said to leave me alone, because there wasn't anything that could be done about the woman who was humming all the time, either.

"That woman has lived through a tragedy," a woman gobbled, "but what has that little brat been through?"

"She's going through the same thing we're going through, but she's less resistant."

"What's she going through? The little shit!"

Mummy got angry. "If you don't shut up, I'll throw you out!"

The whole argument was in whispers.

"Just try it, OD wife! You think you can get away with anything!"

"How dare you, when she gives us shelter here," said another, taking Mummy's side. "You sit here in safety and attack her! Mr. Müller and his wife are such decent people."

"Did I say they weren't?" the woman began crying.

A deadly quiet fell over the room. From outside, we could hear the terrible cries of the children, cries for help, and the hideous chortling of the merry Germans. They were throwing children out of the windows onto the trucks, and at times they missed. One of them stood across the street shooting at the children as they fell.

A little girl ran out of the front door and down the middle of the street, holding her doll to her breast. I could not take my eyes off her. She could not have been more than five. A soldier crouched. There was a shot. The girl lay motionless, still holding her doll while a red spot spread around her.

Everyone in the room was nearly demented. In order not to scream, women scratched their faces until the blood ran and held their children so tight that they whimpered.

The louder the children in the trucks cried, the louder the Germans laughed. A man in the room was praying. How is he able to pray? I wondered dully.

The lorries full of children had driven away. There was a little square containing a statue of the Virgin Mary across the street from our building. They were driving people into this square, which was already so crowded that the people were piling up into a pyramid. The heat was terrible. There was no shade in that square and I could see people fainting and stepping on each other, while from below came appeals for water and the growling of the Germans: *"Ruhe, ruhe! Verfluchten Juden!"*

Every so often one of the OD-men came in to report on what was happening in the streets. Braw had come in a moment earlier. He claimed to have gone with a Red Cross group to the railroad siding in Płaszów, where the cars loaded with our people were standing. They wanted to spray water on the cars, because those inside kept tossing dead bodies out. They were chased away and allowed neither to spray the cars nor to pass out any water. Then someone came in and told us that a *sturmmann* had shot himself when our children reached the siding.

I sat senseless in the corner with my persistent hiccups. Thoughts and dreams ran through my head. If people all over the world got together they could help us. Bubik had taught me and shown me on the map how big the world is. Perhaps they, those other people, had no idea what was being done to us.

Rottersmann came in and said that it was safe to go out, they were just gathering up the corpses. One of the attendants at the *kinderheim* had hung herself in the attic.

Oh, Bubik is here. At the beginning I had not even been surprised at his absence, thinking his mother must have wanted him to stay with her. We went out into the street, not out of curiosity but because it seemed to me that it would be cooler there. Groups of people were on their way home from work. Mothers and fathers were running towards the *kinderheim* like mad people. Some of them were in loud, heart-rending despair. They ran into the building and ran out again, unable to believe that their children were gone. The worst sight, however, was the people who just sat on the ground across the street clutching children's toys. Their faces lacked all expression and they seemed like mannequins. You could not speak to them, because what could you say?

I looked around instinctively and saw something falling – no, it was someone. There was a smacking sound against the sidewalk, not very loud, and a big, a huge woman lay there. Or perhaps she seemed that way to me. People were already gathering around. Somebody said she was dead and somebody else said that it was Mrs. Grynszpan, who had three children in the *kinderheim,* worked in Optima, and whose husband had been taken away during the previous roundup. A man in a *chalat* said, indignantly, that it was impossible to condone what she had done. He even shook his fist as if he were threatening someone. "The Lord gave life, and the Lord takes it away!"

"Get out, you fanatical idiot!" someone shouted from the crowd. "Is each murdering soldier our Lord?"

There was a huge commotion. Two groups formed immediately, waving their arms and shouting as if the dead woman at their feet did not exist.

Bubik and I went off to see if anyone we knew had been taken. Dosia Wasserlauf lived closest. We entered her apartment through the open door. It was dark inside and dreadfully quiet.

"Bubik," I whispered, "all of them?"

We went into the room, where it was a little lighter, and there was a shadow near the bed which I thought might be a blanket. I was already making for the door, and Bubik was pulling me by the hand.

"Wait!" I shouted. "It's Dosia! Maybe she's alive. Call for help!"

Bubik wouldn't let go of me. He went over, knelt down, and then stood back up immediately. "Come on, she's almost cold."

Outside, we both cried like real children. Sobbing, I said, "I saw that she was holding on to one of the legs of the bed. She must not have wanted to leave, or perhaps she was hiding under the bed."

"Don't think about it. Try to keep calm."

I started crying even harder. "I used to tease her about her freckles, and she was so good, she always laughed and said that if I wanted any she would give me hers."

Bubik had stopped crying, and he tried to calm me down.

"I'm going to be afraid, I'm going to be afraid for the rest of my life." I don't know if my eyes or my nose were running worse. Bubik kept wiping me with his handkerchief.

"What are you going to be afraid of? You know there are no ghosts."

"Stupid! I'm not talking about ghosts. I know they don't exist. I'm just afraid. I want to live!"

"You'll live. Of course you will."

We went home. There were tears and wailing all around. I felt sick. Bubik kept explaining that I have to be reasonable, that I have to be brave, that I have to learn to control myself. Yes, there are so many things "I have to" do and so little I can do. One thing was sure – I was lucky to have such a wise friend, who could explain so much and understand so much.

Everybody had returned home except Adam.

"Where the devil have you been, and why? As if there hasn't been enough today, without worrying about where you are," Mummy screamed at me.

"I was looking for my friends."

"What an idea!"

"Dosia is dead..."

"Why do you jump to the conclusion that she's dead? She went with the transport, but that doesn't mean she's dead!"

"She's dead, she's dead! I saw her lying by the bed!"

"Why, for the love of God, did you go there?"

"It's nothing, Mummy," I said in a stifled voice. "You have to be brave. Please give me something to eat."

Mummy took her hands away from her face and she and Daddy both looked at me. Whether they were surprised or frightened, I do not know. She gave me food, but I couldn't swallow a bite. There was more and more in my mouth. I couldn't manage this bravery and started to cry. Mummy hugged me. "Yes, dear, you have to be brave. Now go to bed and sleep. That'll help."

Adam returned. Mummy was angry with him today and hollered at him for coming home late. I looked at my brother and saw that his eyes were red. "Have you been crying, Adam?"

"Olek Mett, my friend from work..."

"I remember. Did they take him in the transport?"

"No, they shot him here. He was always so pale and weak when he worked with us that they laid him off."

"Maybe it's an ugly thing to say," Mummy stated emphatically, "Let's cry for our friends, but I don't want to live to see the day we cry for our dearest." The tears rolled down her face. This was new. She never cried.

62

They are saying officially that a camp is being built for us at the old Jewish cemetery in Płaszów. The world has forgotten about us and renounced us. Not the least help comes from anywhere and no one cares. Those brought in from living on "Aryan papers" report that many Catholics say, "The Jews have no God and are doomed to destruction." I cannot understand this at all because I have always been told that there is one God, for everybody. I do not believe in Him. Many old Jews pray all day and all night, without eating, drinking or sleeping, and they dry out like husks and die first. For me, something doesn't fit in these stories of a "good" God. The worst thing is that everybody shoos me away impatiently when I ask about it.

"Daddy!" I caught him in a free moment, "Daddy – what is it with this God?" Why does He permit us to suffer like this? And those little children in the *kinderheim?*"

Daddy looked at me in surprise. "You know, dear, it's plain that He has many more important problems now."

I said no more because I knew that Daddy didn't think so at all.

Symcha Spira often threatened to teach Daddy some real discipline. Daddy always said that he wanted to get out of sight whenever he saw that "illiterate commandant". This time, however, he did not manage. Daddy came home very much changed in the evening. "Tusia dear, go immediately and fetch that doctor that treated Stella. I must get sick leave."

"What's going on? He's a pediatrician, remember? The way you're talking, Zygmunt, I don't understand anything."

Daddy calmed down and started explaining. We listened, holding our breath. So, Spira had assigned Daddy to a hanging detail. The next morning, six OD-men were supposed to march under escort by a *sturmmann,* they didn't know where, somewhere near Płaszów. Prisoners were to be brought from the Montelupich Prison. Poles.

"Poles! I am to hang a man! A Pole!" He was shattered and reeled around the room. I had never seen him like this in my life. He was talking to himself. "He knows, the bastard, the illiterate, that people like and respect me. He has threatened so many times to teach me a lesson."

"Zygmunt! Get a grip on yourself!" Mummy shouted. "You have to think. We must come up with an idea. You can't do it, but you have to be smart because he can finish you off. Who else did he assign?"

"Rottersmann, Braw. I can't remember."

"Yes, well, the most decent ones. I can't think of anything. My mind is a blank, a complete blank. Stella, run to Uncle Grünberg. He might be able to help."

I couldn't explain it to Uncle and mixed everything up. The way I told it, it came out that Daddy was to be hanged. This was enough for Aunt to come running with us and for Uncle to stop to take his pills on the way. I had always heard that he had heart trouble.

They conferred a long time and decided that there was no way Daddy should take part in that detail. Aunt advised him to pretend to faint at the last moment. Mummy and Uncle said that was idiotic because he could be shot on the spot. Uncle went out and came back soon with Dr. Löw and some man. I couldn't follow much of what was said. Daddy dressed quickly and went with them. Then Dr. Löw came back for a moment and gave Mummy a piece of paper.

Mummy left early in the morning. She was very upset when she came home and kept saying, "Bastards! Swine!" In the end I managed to find out that Daddy would be in the hospital for several days because he was slightly ill and she, Mummy, was upset because when she had taken the certificate from the hospital to the "commandant", he flew into a rage and stormed around the station saying that he, Commandant Symcha Spira, would send that idiot, that screw-up, meaning Daddy, off on the first transport. He apparently shouted many other terrible things in reference to Daddy. But the most important thing at this moment was that Daddy did not have to murder "his brothers", as he defined them.

Uncle Grünberg is the chief engineer for the construction of the camp in Płaszów. He visited us in the evening and said that they have set a completely unrealistic deadline for bringing the camp to a habitable state and inspection commissions are continually snooping around. The barracks are already near completion. The camp is to be made up of several sections divided by barbed wire. People in the Ghetto are talking more and more openly about how we will all be transferred there. Panic is spreading. Many people are trying to go over to the Aryan side. A few of them make it, but many come back. They say that they have nowhere to go because people are afraid to shelter them even in exchange for valuables. The Germans catch others, bring them terribly beaten to the OD, and hold them in the jail there.

Something bad, worse than anything that has happened so far, is hanging in the air. Mummy doesn't go to work any more. They have taken away her pass even though Frau Holzinger tried very hard to keep employing her. Nothing helped. Grandfather fell ill, had to be taken to the hospital, and died after two weeks. I know how much Daddy loved him. When he learned he had died, all he said was, "How fortunate that he died naturally and I won't have to collect his body from the street."

I was shocked because I had thought that Daddy would cry and break down because he is so good and sensitive. I could not understand it. We must really be in trouble if Daddy has so little to say after the death of his own father. I was tormented for several days over this indifference and harshness. Yet I did not know how to put it, and was afraid to ask any questions because I knew that my questions would only upset and trouble everyone.

Mummy wasn't home when Daddy came in. "Where is she?" he asked.

"I don't know. She went out somewhere."

"Put together a food parcel for me. Give me the best things we have."

"Why?"

"Don't ask, just do what I say." Daddy was upset
"But what's going on?" I persisted.
"I told you not to ask!" he shouted.
"But you can tell me, Daddy," I pleaded.

When I handed him the bag, Daddy paused. "Don't tell Mummy that I've taken anything," he said from the doorway. "They've brought in her brother, Uncle Ignac. They brought him in on a transport and he's in the jail at the OD."

"Why?"

"Well, a man he knew from school recognized him on the street. He had illegal leaflets in his bag. His old schoolmate went right up to a couple of sentries patrolling nearby and they grabbed Ignac as he was trying to throw the bag over a fence. Things look very bad because of those leaflets. And that rat of a 'classmate' also asked where he lived, alone or with his family. Fortunately, Ignac said that his family had stayed in Bielsko."

"Does that mean that Aunt and Grandmother are safe?"

"Maybe so, Stella, but I don't want Mummy to know about this for now."

"Daddy, I won't say anything," I promised. Mummy came home soon and asked if Daddy had been there. I lied and said that he hadn't.

"What do you mean? I met Mrs. Rottersmann and she said Daddy had been here."

"Maybe he was," I squirmed, "but I didn't see him. I must have been in the kitchen."

Daddy came back in the early evening and sat there listlessly.

"Zygmunt, why aren't you eating your supper?" Mummy asked.

"I don't feel like it. I'm not hungry, and anyway I have to take something to the OD because they've brought in an acquaintance of mine. You know. Tusia, when a man's fed he looks at the world more optimistically."

Mummy gave him a bag full of food.

"That's not very much, darling."

"Not much? But you know that since I've stopped going to work the food situation has deteriorated." She shot a look at Daddy. "Who is this acquaintance?"

"You wouldn't know him. We were in school together."

"What's his name?" Mummy insisted.

Daddy never lied, so a change came over his face and he stammered hesitantly, "Stop quizzing me, Mummy. His name has slipped my mind."

"Zygmunt, you are keeping something from me."

"What's got into you? What would I keep from you? Come on, give me the food. I've got to go. Aha, one more thing, Tusia dear. I've got night duty."

"What? You had night duty yesterday."

"But today I've got an extra duty."

Mummy watched him go with a thoughtful look on her face. As usual, Bubik was sitting there and already knew the whole story from me. He started playing softly on his accordion. Mummy turned around suddenly. "Don't be angry, Bubik. I like your playing, but I'm upset today. Please stop. Stella, did Daddy say who that acquaintance was?"

"Why would he tell me? No, he didn't say anything."

Mummy went to the cupboard. "Why is there so little bread? There was more lard, too." My heart was in my throat. Mummy was sniffing around like a retriever.

"There isn't much left," I mumbled, "because Bubik and I got hungry."

"Strange," she said. "Such wolfish appetites." She sat down, lit a cigarette, and thought for a long time. Then she asked again: "Was Daddy wearing a sweater?"

"Yes. The nights are cold, after all."

She went to the wardrobe and started rooting around. "Where's his other one? And his vest?"

"I don't know. Maybe he wore two."

"Impossible. He's always warm."

"So maybe Adam..." I felt as though I would start crying and tell everything.

Just then Adam came home, and of course Mummy saw that he wasn't wearing any sweater. "Adam," she said, "ask Rottersmann to come here."

When he came in, Mummy bombarded him with questions about why Daddy was on duty tonight when he and Rottersmann had both been on duty last night: why he wasn't at home, and what had happened? Rottersmann did not know what to tell her. Mummy finally asked him to take her to the OD station. When they had left, I told Adam what had happened. We sat there numbly, waiting for Mummy. She returned with Daddy and her eyes were red with crying, but she was composed.

Daddy did all he could to get Uncle out of the OD jail, at least so that he could stay with us in the Ghetto. He received a promise of release every day. Daddy used intermediaries, because a direct approached to Spira would have backfired – Spira couldn't stand Daddy. Being held in the OD jail was dangerous because whenever something happened, they always struck at the jail and the hospital first. Every day Daddy told Mummy that Uncle was sure to be released the next day. The next day came, and Uncle was not released.

Daddy took me once to see Uncle Ignac. He was cheerful, trying to pick me up as he used to do and declaring, "It's unbelievable how she's grown."

He looked like a young German with blonde hair, blue eyes, a straight nose and a merry expression on his face. "Stella, don't look so gloomy. Aren't you happy to see me? I'm going to stay with you. If you can live here, so can I."

Mummy got a work assignment in the *schreibstube,* the bookkeeping department of the Płaszów camp. Once again, she went out early to work and came home tired, because apparently it was a considerable distance just the one direction. She kept us up to date on the construction of our "new health resort." Each evening, she asked if Uncle Ignac had been released. Then she would cook something and run straight to the jail. The jailer was Wiluś Kranz, whom the prisoners liked, as did everyone, because he was always cheerful and had a good word for everybody.

The car with a loudspeaker is driving around again. We are all waiting anxiously to see what will come of it. Nothing dangerous this time. All residents of the Ghetto are to turn in their furs, even fur trim. Under penalty of death, of course, as if it could be otherwise. If they find so much as a bit of fur piping in anyone's apartment after the deadline, it will mean the death sentence. A truck stops in front of each house and people throw on everything that resembles fur. Many look downcast, because even an old fur often represents their only warm coat. Others bitterly cut fur up into little pieces and throw it into their coal stoves. The staircases stink. Then the Germans rush in, following the smoke, and beat people with their rifle butts until they drop.

Mummy sits in the corner angrily cutting everything made of fur into tiny pieces with a razor blade. Then she makes a bundle and throws it on the truck.

All the next day passenger cars pull up in front of the storehouse, the former *kinderheim*. Laughing German women go in and come out wearing furs, even fur rags, torn from the "Jewish swine".

One day Bubik said mournfully: "Stella dear, I've found out what my father intends to do. He's arranging papers for us to go to Budapest. I told you that Rutti's husband is Hungarian."

"Yes, you told me." I had not supposed that the news would hit me so hard. I could not imagine that my "teacher," protector, friend and defender would simply go away, leaving me. I wouldn't know whether he died or survived.

"I told him to forget about it," I heard Bubik saying. "I won't go anywhere without you! There was terrible fight. He hit me, and *Mutti* cried. Hey, don't look at me that way. Don't you believe I'll stay? Speak to me! Don't you believe me?"

I suddenly felt very old. "Bubik, don't you understand, there's no way out. Your father certainly wants the best, he wants you all to be safe, and you can't change his mind. We're the children, and they're the parents."

I think it was the first time I had said anything reasonable the whole time we'd been friends. Now he was the one who couldn't understand. "So you don't believe me!" he said with his eyes full of tears. "I'll hide. They'll never find me."

"But I believe you." What I believed in fact was that every day brought our parting closer. I repeated over and over the words he had taught me: "Stella, you have to be brave, very brave." Bubik had changed, lost weight, become quieter, and I too had the feeling that something in me was crying.

***

The autumn cold has set in. Transports to the camp in Płaszów have been under way for two days. One more massacre, directed this time by the Płaszów commandant, Amon Goeth. People say that we have a terrible new god, because "Amon" means "god' in Greek. Our Amon is cruel. He is never seen without a pistol in his hand, and he stands beside the trucks that people, constantly beaten and wailing, are being loaded onto. If he doesn't like somebody's looks, he grabs them by the hair and shoots them on the spot. He is a huge man and cuts a superb, dignified figure, with gentle, handsome facial features and a gaze that is even more gentle. Yet he is a ghastly, murderous monster. How can it be?

Right next to the wall on Krakus Street there is a manhole to a sewer that comes out on the bank of the Vistula. Doctor Rozalia Blau tried to lead a group of people through that sewer. A couple made it, but only a couple. At the outlet, somebody informed the Gestapo. The rest of the people being escorted by the Doctor walked right into the arms of the Germans. Doctor Blau came last carrying a woman with a broken leg and they were both shot on the spot. The others were brought back to the Ghetto and shot against the wall on Krakus Street.

Adam and Uncle Adolf, Mummy's other brother, are at the camp all the time now, and Mummy is going crazy worrying about Uncle Ignac, who has still not been released. There are rumours that all those in the jail are to be moved to some unknown destination, in any case not to Płaszów.

Our turn came. Bubik stopped being "brave and manlike" and paced in the corner, crying like a little child. I was the stronger one and consoled him, saying we would certainly meet again.

"Yes, Stella," he replied, "I have decided that I am going with you to the camp and we will be together." I thought with pity that he could decide nothing and would have to go with his family, but I nodded.

The next day he turned up full of enthusiasm. "You know, Stella, I heard that after the liquidation of the Ghetto they are going to leave several families behind. They will form a cleaning detail to liquidate the apartments and people will be brought from the camp to help." I had no idea what he was talking about, but I listened as he went on breathlessly. "The Rottersmanns are staying, and my family, and Symcha Spira and his family, too."

"So Symcha Spira won't be our OD commandant in Płaszów? That's interesting. Does that mean that the Germans themselves will guard us?"

"No. Apparently there's already a new OD commandant there." I wondered about that new commandant, whether he would be as bad an idiot or perhaps even worse.

"You know," I heard Bubik saying, "you can come out with that cleaning detail."

"Yes, of course," I said without thinking.

Mummy was feverishly packing our most essential possessions. We were allowed to take only two small suitcases. "Stella," she said, "put on all the clothes you can. You might need them."

A couple of days earlier, Daddy had managed to get me a pair of ugly lace-up boots, several sizes too big. He ordered me to put on as many socks as would fit. This made me anxious. I knew that we were going to much worse conditions, but how much worse? I was silent and frightened. "Mummy, when do we go?"

"Late in the evening. Daddy has arranged for us to go as late as possible, and he will be escorting our group – with the SS-men in charge, of course. You know," she addressed me like an adult "there are quite a few people who have to be smuggled into the camp, because anyone left here, aside from the ones legally assigned to the cleaning detail, may be shot tomorrow."

"How does Daddy intend to smuggle them?"

"I don't know exactly, but he said we will come under the control of the SS-men at the exit from the Ghetto. He's put people near the gate on Józefińska Street, and when our group goes past they are supposed to join us."

By now I understood a little, and so I kept worrying. "Good enough, but what about the list? Everyone taken to the camp should be written down there." Mummy paced the room in a mad dance of nerves, but I was afraid too, and could not stop asking questions. "It's a terrible risk! They'll put the whole group in danger!"

"Be quiet!" she shouted. "I know, I know all about it, but somebody" – she stressed the word "somebody" heavily – "has to save those people. If people only thought of themselves, we would all be dead." Then she added, softly, "that's what Daddy said, and he's right."

"How big will our group be?"

"Around two hundred people, I think."

"Don't worry, Mummy. We might make it."

I was ready to go. I must have looked like an overstuffed clown doll, I had so much on. And such big boots. My appearance was the last thing I cared about, but I was suffocating under all those clothes. What time was it? Almost seven. It was completely dark, and drizzling. "Can I go to the kitchen for a minute, Mummy? Bubik wants to play me a tune for going away."

"Have you lost your mind?" she jumped to her feet. "At a moment like this? At a moment like this she feels like hearing a little music? Maybe you have lost your mind?"

"Mummy," I pleaded with tears in my eyes, "he'll only play for a minute, as a farewell."

72

"It could cause trouble."

"No. We'll be very quiet."

We went to the kitchen and Bubik played the tune of our whistled signal. We both cried. We didn't say good-bye when he finished.

Daddy came in. "Go down to the front door," he said. "I'm going to lead the whole group to the OD. We'll assemble there and set out. Well, Bubik," his voice also wavered, "take care." He kissed him and left quickly.

At the front door, Daddy ordered us to line up by four and then led us to the OD courtyard. There were a lot of people there. Mummy ran around crying. Her crying always upset me, perhaps because I had seen it so seldom. She had been promised that Uncle Ignac would go with us to the camp, and he was still sitting locked up a few steps away, with no means of getting out. It was cold and wet, and I was shaking all over – but perhaps not from the cold, since I had so many clothes on.

Symcha Spira appeared, decked out in all the "commandantorial" insignia he could support. He strutted between the ranks like a dwarf turkey, and pulled several children out of line. I peered at those children in the darkness, trying to see if they were older or younger than me. Daddy was one step behind him. Spira shined a flashlight around. He noticed me, stopped, and started. I could feel myself shrinking. He grabbed me by the sleeve of my coat and pulled me out of line. "All right, Müller," he said to Daddy in an authoritative voice. "March the group out."

Daddy stiffened and enunciated distinctly, "No, Commandant."

"What is this?" Spira's mouth hung open in amazement. "Who gives the orders around here, you idiot? March them away," he shrieked in rage.

"No, Commandant," Daddy answered calmly. "I was assigned to escort a group and unless the group is complete, I will not march them out."

"These are children," Spira replied, shaking with fury. "They will go tomorrow, by truck."

"I know they will go, Commandant, but to their graves," Daddy answered.

Spira went crazy. "I will order you shot immediately. Long ago, I should have..." He did not finish the sentence.

Daddy replied very quietly and calmly, "You are worse than the Nazis."

"I will have you shot, you animal. You are putting all these people at risk!"

"My wife and daughter are here. Please keep us here."

Spira turned and ran into the building, with Daddy following. I might be wrong, but it seemed to me that people had started to look at me in a hostile way. I heard someone whisper, "Are we supposed to die because of one brat? You can't hold up the entire group because of one child." Suddenly everyone wanted to be in the camp as soon as possible.

All thoughts and feelings left me. I started backing away like an insect, not knowing what to do. The only thing I was sure of was that I could not endanger those people. Bushes grew near the fence and I squatted beside them. I must have stopped breathing; all I wanted was to disappear completely and for the others to march away. I felt my legs starting to go to sleep. I would run out into the street where the Germans were, and they would see me and shoot at once. Then poor Daddy and these people could go. But I remained there motionless even though I was sure I wanted to be shot. When I heard a quiet voice, I did not move. Then there was the glare of a flashlight shining in my face.

"What the hell are you doing here? You little piece of shit, did you have a pee?" An OD-man was dragging me by the arm towards the group. "We've been looking for you for half an hour, stupid brat!" He towed me along in fury.

Mummy slapped me in the face, and then hugged me with all her might. "Did you think for a moment that we would leave you behind?" she asked in tears. "Always remember, dear, that whatever happens to you, happens to me, too."

They were lining us up again and I asked Mummy what would happen next.

"Daddy has taken full responsibility. Either we make it or ..." She left the sentence unfinished. We started out. Mummy took one last sorrowful look back at the jail where her brother was being left behind. The Ghetto was empty and lifeless now, and made a ghostly impression. From time to time we heard the desperate howling of a dog abandoned in an apartment.

We went along the pavement and not, as we should have, through the street. Dark figures slipped out of doorways and joined the ranks. Daddy instantly put them in the proper places. He led us slowly along the short part of the way, looking around all the time like a thief. At one point he shoved a child, a little smaller than I was, between Mummy and me. "Cover him with your coat, Tusia, and walk close together," he whispered.

We reached the gate at Węgierska Street. "Why is Daddy staying behind?" I whispered.

"He must be changing the list of how many people there are," Mummy whispered back.

"How does he know?"

"Don't worry, he'll know. Daddy is wise enough to manage."

I could feel the trembling figure under Mummy's coat. I was carrying one suitcase and Mummy the second. "Keep the suitcase as low as possible," she whispered, "to hide his legs."

Daddy was standing by the gate now, and as we walked past in fives, the SS-men counted us. They stood with their rifles levelled at us. Up front, a German was yammering. What was he saying? Mummy explained that he was warning us that if anyone tried to escape, they would open fire. Daddy was moving freely among the ranks, and as he walked past he signalled that he had succeeded and they had signed the list without noticing anything. On the streets it was quiet and there was not a soul to be seen. Rain was falling and mud squished under our feet. Our footsteps were the only sound.

I tried to keep in step as my terror at the situation awaiting us grew. Perhaps it would be no worse than in the Ghetto. Why were they marching us like bandits? I would never understand it. After all, we had done nothing wrong. Shouts and the sound of feet stamping tore me away from my reflections. Someone was running toward the gate, close enough to be seen clearly. There was a shot and then a whole series of shots. Two SS-men went to check their accuracy, ordering us not to move. Escorted by an SS-man, Daddy walked to the gate and returned a moment later.

We start moving. Daddy is beside us. "Naïve," he said. "She thought she could make it. Be careful, Tusia love, when we even up. Get the boy behind you."

"And what if they figure out at the gate that there are too many of us?"

"Don't worry. I only pretended to cross out the one that made a run for it. And they might not check so painstakingly this late at night.

We watched carefully to see whether Daddy came near. Mummy cautioned the poor boy under her coat. He kept tripping, and she grew weary because it wasn't comfortable for her, either. Every so often, Daddy came near and whispered, "One from the middle to the rear, one from the middle to the rear." Everyone caught on immediately and knew just what to do. I did not even notice until the boy was already behind us, marching in place in a row of five. A German screamed at Daddy, who calmly explained that he was telling "those idiots," meaning us, to march calmly.

I was already tired and it was hard to keep lifting my feet out of the mud, but perhaps it wouldn't be so bad since, aside from shooting the woman who tried to escape, they hadn't been beating us or hurrying us along. Mummy whispered that we were nearly there. I could not see anything and had no idea where we were. A tiny light glimmered ahead: the gate of the camp. They ordered us to stop and counted us again. Daddy stayed behind and handed the German the list, and then as he passed he whispered that everything was all right.

2

Płaszów

The gate closes behind us – the heavy gate of the old Jewish cemetery. Will it be our cemetery? We march on. The road leads slightly uphill, and we have to pull our feet out of the sticky mud. Gloomy silhouettes of barracks loom around us.

"Men to the right, women to the left," Daddy says. "Wake-up is at five o'clock. For now just settle in wherever you can find room. Permanent places will be assigned tomorrow."

I am reeling from fatigue and have absolutely no strength left. Daddy leads us to a barrack. I look around appalled, the way Mummy did when she first saw the Ghetto. A light bulb, or perhaps it is an oil lamp, shines in the middle and there are three-tiered double bunks against the walls. Then there is the stench, a stench of dampness, of filth, and of something hard to pin down. This must be how destitution smells. My eyes adjust to the semidarkness. There are grey blankets, grey faces, everything is grey and dismal. I sit down on my little suitcase.

"It would be good to give her something warm to eat or drink," I hear my mother's voice from what seems like a great distance.

Daddy replies quietly that it is impossible. "Let me see if your shoes are wet." He leans over me. "They're soaked. They'll never dry by morning."

I sit indifferent to everything. How good we had it in the Ghetto. Daddy leads me to a bunk.

"Stella dear, when you're putting your shoes on in the morning, wrap your feet in paper first. Remember, you're not allowed to get sick here." Perhaps he said more, but I was already asleep.

I didn't manage to wrap my feet in the morning. The people in the barracks were jostling and bumping into each other in a mad rush while I staggered around, asleep on my feet. Mummy couldn't wake me up. Everything I had on was damp and probably already stank like that barrack.

The sound of a trumpet suddenly brought me to my senses. "What was that, Mummy?"

"That was Wiluś Rosner. Now our whole lives will be determined by his trumpet at wake-up, dinner break, lights out and special occasions."

I don't know if I was already awake but I was shaking all over and dreaming of clean sheets and dry, warm pyjamas. Mummy grabbed me vigorously by the arm. It was still completely dark but everybody was running in the same direction in panic and confusion, running into and tripping over each other. Mummy clutched my arm tight as I stumbled and my feet stuck in the mud.

We found ourselves in a huge square among a crowd of people milling around in disarray. It began to get light. Everybody looked wretched with the men unshaven and the women, like me, bundled in a hotchpotch of garments. "This is the *apelplatz*" Mummy said. It was the place where we had roll-call.

It seemed vast. In the very middle of it stood a writing desk surrounded by several SS-men. Others were bustling about with whips in their hands, followed by gaggles of OD-men. I did not know if being in that mad crowd was a dream or reality. Every so often a woman pushed me and I staggered in one direction or another. Mummy shook me again. "Four God's sake, pay attention! Remember! You're not a child any more," she practically screamed in my face.

Her desperate tone really did sober me up. "Where's Daddy?'

78

"He's got a job in camp bookkeeping. He'll report to that table there with information from all the groups about the camp population, living and dead, ill and healthy."

"But there are so many people here. Will he manage? It doesn't sound safe. What if he makes a mistake?"

"He's not allowed to make any mistakes. Stop annoying me, child. Nothing's allowed here." I started trembling and my teeth were chattering. Mummy must have noticed. "Look around and see if you can spot Adam or anyone we know. And pull yourself together. You pretend to be so brave, and look at you. Remember one more thing, dear, our tormenters don't like frightened people. You have to control yourself!"

I could see that Mummy was in despair. She wanted so much to help me while she herself was terrified and was losing control. I wanted, oh how I wanted to stop shaking, but I couldn't. Maybe it's only today, I consoled myself, and afterwards it'll stop for certain.

We were kept standing there until seven o'clock. The decent OD-men were having trouble getting people in place, but order was established more quickly where the whips and canes flew. We were finally formed up into a square facing the desk in rows of five with a block supervisor in front of each group. Their duty was to report on the number of people in their barracks, how many were ill and how many were going outside the camp in the work details called *aussenkommando*. Next, a German walked between the rows again counting the groups, helping himself out with his whip and making notes on a piece of paper that he then carried to the desk where Daddy stood writing things down in a big notebook, or there might have been several notebooks there. Finally, Amon Goeth drove up. A big, powerful man, he got out of his car. Daddy stood straight as a ramrod, picking up one notebook after another and reporting to him, apparently, on the population of the camp. Another car drove up and a German alighted from it with great dignity. He wore white gloves, which struck me as funny. He walked slowly towards the desk. "And who's that one?" I asked in a whisper.

"That's Obersturmführer Neuschel, and stop asking questions! There are too many of them for me to know who's who or who's most important."

"Is he such a bad one?" She didn't reply and I wondered how it was that they all looked so dignified and well-groomed and moved so delicately. We kept standing there endlessly and I felt that my legs were going numb and sinking right down into the sticky, clay-like mud. I wasn't aware that I was quaking all the time, but Mummy kept squeezing my arm every so often to calm me down.

"Mummy, I have to go to the toilet! I really do! What should I do?"

"How should I know? Go in your pants." Then she added more gently, "Just hold out a little longer."

We must have stood there for four or five hours. Amon Goeth finally went up to the desk where Daddy was waiting. Daddy reported, standing rigid at attention. He's a tall man but next to the Commandant he looked like a runty little boy – everybody seemed small beside Goeth. Then the Commandant walked around inspecting the groups, and at his approach each supervisor cried out, *"Aaaachtung!"* All the people in the ranks drew themselves up and stood absolutely motionless. No one dared look at him as he walked slowly past; everyone kept their eyes fixed dully, straight ahead. When our master finished his inspection, the command *"Antreten!"* was given. The prisoners walked towards their work assignments or dispersed among the barracks.

I ached from "holding out". Mummy and I trudged towards the barracks. "Now what?"

"We get coffee, if you can call it coffee, but first I'll take you to the latrine."

"What's that?"

"What's that? A long barrack containing a plank with round holes, which you might call a toilet or water-closet, as you wish," she said with painful irony, "and in the middle are sinks and a couple of taps where a little water dribbles out now and then."

80

"And everybody's there at the same time? With no partitions?" I asked, even though I knew it was stupid. I just couldn't help it.

"You'll see for yourself."

There was no way that Mummy could have had the patience to keep answering my obviously idiotic questions. I knew we had entered the latrine when the unbearable odour hit me. I stood there dumbfounded. Women were sitting along the whole length of the board with their knickers down, and the fatter ones rubbed thighs. Others stood waiting for a free place, jiggling up and down and urging the seated ones to hurry. "Oh God," I blurted out, "I'll never manage, it's worse than animals."

"You'll manage, you'll have to, and also you've got to go along with everything without discussion and stop making stupid faces at me" – I knew that Mummy had had enough and it was better to keep my mouth shut.

There was a terrible crowd around the sink with women pushing, elbowing each other and even coming to blows as they tried to catch a couple of drops of water. "But we'll rot here! This is supposed to be washing?" I gasped.

"So we'll rot." Mummy pulled me by the sleeve and we left.

Daddy was waiting in the barracks. "How was it, dear? How was your first roll-call?"

"My legs ached dreadfully." I though he would understand.

"That's nothing. You've got to get used to it. You know, Tusia dear, they're going to set up a *kinderheim* here for all the children in the camp. They'll have better food, they won't have to stand during the roll-call and they'll be taken care of by a very decent OD-man, Koch, who's good and kind."

I was sitting on the bunk hungrily devouring a piece of dry bread Daddy had given me. The expression on Mummy's face seemed odd. She was listening to what he had to say without replying; she just kept looking at poor Daddy in a way I could not exactly define, but it might have been contemptuously.

"Well, so what do you say to that, dear?" Daddy asked with none of his initial enthusiasm. "She wouldn't have to stand in the roll-call at dawn", he continued, without taking his eyes off Mummy's face.

"Have you lost your mind?" she snarled in fury. "You, her father, want to sentence her to death? There will be no talk of any *kinderheim.* Understand? Don't even think about it! I refuse!" Mummy almost choked and could not go on.

"But, Tusia dear, they swear those children won"t be touched, and besides she can't go to work. She's too young, they won't permit it, they won't give her a work assignment," he said, all conviction gone. I was taking in every word and thought it would have been better if I had been shot in the Ghetto; I was a problem for them again.

Mummy wiped her brow. "How old do children have to be to work?" she asked.

"Sixteen."

"In that case we have to alter her file."

"But Tusia, nobody will believe she's sixteen. Look at her!"

"The discussion is closed. I will not send her to the *kinderheim.* You can do what you want, but I won't part with her. That's final," she concluded sharply.

Mummy was working in the *schreibstube;* before she and Daddy left I heard a multitude of prohibitions and repeated warnings not to leave the barrack. What I wanted most was to lie down because I was tired, but it was against all the rules to lie during the day on the grey blanket drawn precisely over the bunk, so I sat. My head kept drooping. It was quiet in the barracks. I thought about Bubik and, perhaps for the first time, about how good it had been to have a friend like him back in the Ghetto. I felt terribly alone.

I started talking with the woman who occupied the bunk next to ours. Her name was Hanka Kleiner and she had a lovely little boy, Marek, about five. There was also Mrs. Rosenblum with her two daughters, four and six, and her baby son, Szymon. I asked Hanka how such small children had been brought here, and she said that most of them had been brought in knapsacks. The toddlers had had it so strongly drummed into them not to make noise or talk out loud that they sat like mannequins, with grave faces. I studied the children for a long time and was appalled.

I started wandering around the barrack and looking at other people who obviously hadn't been given work assignments yet. They all sat with blank expressions on their faces. I walked to the door without thinking.

"What do you want?" I heard.

It was the block supervisor, whose duty was to stand at the door. I didn't want anything, in fact, but I exclaimed, "Can I go to the latrine?"

"Right now you can. There isn't a *blokszper.*" I did not yet know what this meant, but I decided to act as if I understood. I heard shots, a whole burst of firing, so I stepped back and asked again if it was all right to leave.

"Go ahead. They're finishing off the people who were hiding in the Ghetto. They're shooting them on Chuj Hill.

"What's Chuj Hill?"

"There's a ditch there, on that ridge," he pointed, "and that's where they shoot people, but where the name comes from I can't say."

People were working in front of the barracks. Our camp stood on the grounds of the old Jewish cemetery, as Daddy had said, and so they were making pavements out of the gravestones. Others were dragging wooden beams to build barracks. They stood shoulder to shoulder pulling, but made no headway with the enormous beams in the mud. It was drizzling all the time.

I could hear my parents' voices over and over, saying, "You are not allowed to go outside under any circumstances." Yet I could feel that I was going to disobey their orders. I did not want to be disobedient. It just happened. Out I went. On the hill above the latrine ran three rows of barbed wire and a sentry carrying a rifle and accompanied by a dog, a beautiful Alsation, was walking between them. Further on, I could see a guard-tower with a sentry who seemed to be watching the camp through binoculars. There were searchlights at the top of the hill. I stood there amazed: the place was a fortress.

I felt a tug at my sleeve. Two women were warning me, "Don't stand there like that, you idiot! They could shoot you at any moment from the tower. Which barrack are you from?"

"She must be new," said the other one. "Or maybe she's retarded. Come on, we'll walk you back." I was speechless. The dreadful nightmare of the camp had been invisible at night.

I snapped out of it. "No, don't worry, I'm going." I went to the latrine. It was less crowded but the stench was worse and I stood in the corner watching. The majority of the women sitting there were chatting as if they were having coffee in their living rooms, although others "did their business" with miserable, humiliated expressions, avoiding looking anyone in the eye. I went back to the barracks. Time was dragging and there was no way to hurry it along; time was finished for the people killed by the gunshots, but they had surely wanted time to stop passing entirely.

I was hungry and felt around the bunk to see if Mummy had left me a piece of bread. I found nothing. Then the trumpet sounded with a different melody, quick and lively, the dinner trumpet. They brought in a cooking pot. I received a tin bowl and a spoon and lined up for my portion like everyone else. When I carried the bowl back to the bunk I was struck by the unpleasant odour that the food gave off. I was famished so I raised a spoonful of soup to my lips. No, this was impossible. It was awful brown garbage that stank of the cooking pot and stuck in my throat. I fished around with my spoon for a piece of potato, but there was nothing, only a few groats. I held my breath as if I were swallowing cod-liver oil. I felt unhappy and hungry, but I also felt like throwing up. I looked to see how the others were doing. A few were eating while others stirred their spoons around like me. I managed to force a couple of gulps down.

Uncle Adolf, who worked in the kitchen peeling potatoes, found me. "I got out for a minute. Here, eat this, this soup is better."

"No, thanks." I wanted to cry.

"Hurry up and eat." He pushed a mess tin towards me. "I can see you haven't eaten. Remember, you have to eat in this place."

Why was everybody constantly ordering me to "remember" that everything here had to be the way it was?

I felt silly because I had always assumed that this Uncle did not love me one bit, he was always so stiff, and now he was sitting there urging me to eat and stroking my head.

"You have to get used to it. Bye, little one, I've got to run." He took the tin – by now almost empty – from my hands.

"How long is the break?"

"Half an hour."

The trumpet sounded again. "That's it. I've really got to run."

I had already become acquainted with all the women in the barracks. I tried to play with the little children but it didn't always work out. Hanka Kleiner's little Marek was an outgoing, cheerful boy. But little Samuel Wiener, only three, was tragic: he sat on the bunk like a mouse with his eyes darting back and forth. "Hide Samuel," he lisped. "They're coming for Samuel. Bang, bang," he kept repeating and tried to crawl under the bunk.

Each time, his mother replied with a catch in her voice, "Don't worry, dear, Mummy will hide you when the time comes."

Nothing helped. He broke out every so often in muffled sobbing and repeated his "Bang, bang."

Then there were shots next to our block. Just in case, I retreated into a gap between the bunks. Samuel was out of sight; he had crawled under a bunk like a dog. An OD-man came in; it was Marek's father, Ignac Kleiner. "No need to panic. They're only hunting a Jewish dog."

"What does that mean?" I came out of hiding. "Hunting a dog?"

"Well," he said, "it must have followed its owner to the camp. They spotted it and they're hunting it down. Everybody stay indoors; they've already shot two people."

"But what have they got against the dog, Mr. Kleiner?"

"Are you stupid, or what? It's a Jewish dog. That's enough."

Now the shots were very close and I could hear the sentries shouting. I edged towards the window. The barracks were built on pilings, without foundations, and there was a space underneath. A little white dog, trying desperately to get away, was scrambling between the pilings. A bullet must have grazed him because he tumbled over, let out a miserable whine, and then went back to trying to escape. He was howling for help when a whole series of shots hit him. He rolled into a ball and his white fur turned pink first, and then all red. The Germans walked away laughing. I stood by the window with tears streaming down my face, thinking how good it was that Blackie was dead. I couldn't understand why even a dog wasn't allowed to have a Jewish owner.

"Hey you! Müller! Don't stand so close to the window!" somebody behind me shouted. I turned around. "What are you crying about? Aren't you ashamed of yourself, bawling over a dog. Our little society lady, supposed to be all grown up, wailing over a dog, while so many people are being killed and the shooting on the Hill never stops. You should be ashamed."

I burst out, "Why should I be ashamed?" I was sobbing as loud as I could. "You're like them! Heartless and bad! He came full of trust looking for his beloved master and you're the ones who ought to be ashamed, because he didn't know his master was Jewish. We knew, but he didn't. A dog doesn't know!"

"Look at that! She seems so quiet, but she's got a mouth on her!"

"What's going on here?" I heard Daddy's voice.

"That's quite a daughter you've got, Mr. Müller. She already knows how to talk back to her elders. She'll be a joy to you when she grows up, for sure," one of the women said.

"What's that supposed to mean?" Daddy spoke to me more sharply than he ever had. "Have you been impolite?"

I sat on the bunk and said nothing.

"Come on, tell me," he continued more quietly. "I believe you, but I asked you to be nice to people. Why are you causing trouble for me?"

"I didn't do anything," I stammered, still crying.

"Try to calm down. I don't understand you at all. Try to control yourself. You can't be a child here. You've got to remember that you're a grown-up like Mummy, me and the others."

His speech at least stopped me from howling.

"So what was that all about?" enquired Daddy.

"I was standing by the window and I saw them hunting that dog. Don't you know about that?"

"Yes, I know. And then what?"

"Somebody noticed I was crying over the dog. At first I didn't say anything but when they all started shouting at me I couldn't hold back and I told them what I think. I didn't insult anybody."

"Listen, Stella dear, I don't think you should judge your elders. It might have been unpleasant for you, but you should have sat there without saying anything."

This made me furious. "So what the hell do you want? You order me to be a grown-up, and then I'm supposed to keep my mouth shut because I'm a child. Which is it to be?"

Daddy looked at me in amazement, then he waved his hand in despair, jumped off the bunk and left.

The trumpet sounded for evening roll-call, a different tune, of course. Now things went better, without so much running back and forth. There were signs on the *apelplatz* with the block numbers and I stood by our number. Mummy came soon. "So, how was your first day? I hope you didn't go out."

"I went to the latrine once."

"And how did it go?" she smiled.

"It didn't" I said with the face of a person condemned. "I walked right back out. I'm hungry." I hadn't wanted to say that. I knew it would hurt Mummy, but the words just slipped out.

"There's nothing I can do, dear," she frowned. "After roll-call everybody will get a piece of bread and some coffee."

The groups that had been working outside the camp all day came back and each reported where they were returning from and how many there were. The *kapos* and SS-men at the gates counted the people and frisked some to see if they were carrying anything. The *kapo* who led the group shouted: *"Aaachtung! Mützen ab! Augen links!"* or *"Augen rechts"*, depending on which side the gate supervisor was standing.

This time the roll-call might have lasted more than an hour, but not as long as in the morning. Upon returning to the barracks we got our ration of bread, which was supper. There was one loaf, perhaps two kilograms, carefully divided into eight pieces and with it went a tiny piece of margarine, not more than twenty grams, and then that cold stuff that was supposed to be coffee. I wolfed everything down and Mummy watched me; I think she wanted to give me hers but I managed to say in time that I was full, even though I could have eaten the whole loaf of bread.

For the next hour we were allowed to move freely around the camp. Adam, Ziuta, Emil, Aunt and Uncle and many friends visited us. A man came in and asked if I was Stella Müller. He handed me a sheet of paper and I recognized Bubik's handwriting. My heart leapt with joy. "Do you work in the Ghetto?" I asked.

"Yes. We go there every day. That boy wanted to give me a parcel but I couldn't take it because they search us at the gate. But you can always get a piece of paper through."

After a lot of trouble I found some paper and a pencil, but then I realized that I didn't know what to write. Finally I put down a couple of lame sentences, that everything was fine in the camp, that I didn't need anything but I missed him. In that way we kept in touch and I knew that Bubik was still there.

Dziunia came to see me and we went out in front of the barracks. It was already dark but we could see couples with their arms around each other. Some were even kissing. "What are you looking at?" Dziunia asked.

"At those people, who are still in love even here," I said in a whisper. "Perhaps it will be easier for them to survive."

"Oh, keep quiet, you're an awful philosopher, always nosing into things."

"It's important," I said with a superior air, "for one to think about various matters. It helps to keep one going."

"Eh, I know one thing for sure." Dziunia retorted. "That piece of bread only whetted my appetite."

I felt the same way, but said, "You see? If you thought about other things, you'd forget about being hungry."

"You've always been strange," she concluded, and left. I didn't know whether I should be pleased about what she had said or not.

I was standing near the barracks when Mummy called me. "Come here, we're going to do you over. We'll cut your hair. We have to make you grown-up, because from tomorrow you'll be three or four years older. You have to look it. Neiger's going to come for you as if there was a mistake in your file, and he'll assign you work."

"Couldn't Daddy do it?"

"It's better if it's not him. Somebody might catch on." They started "doing me over." My hair was cut, Daddy came up with a sweater, Aunt measured a skirt and Ziuta brought her coat. They turned me around and looked at me from all sides, but they still weren't satisfied.

Uncle Grünberg wiped his brow, cast a worried eye on me, and finally said, "The figure might pass, but as far as the face goes – she doesn't even look her age, let alone sixteen."

"Too bad," said Mummy. "You can't change the face."

I had no idea how I looked and didn't care, because I was already worried about the next day.

After the morning roll-call, Neiger led me to the *schreibstube* where two SS-men were sitting, and Daddy too – who pretended not to pay any attention. Neiger spend a long time explaining something. They nodded, looked me over like a monkey in the zoo, and ordered Daddy to check the books.

They were surprised that we had the same last name. They ordered me to tell them when I was born. I told them 1927. The OD-man translated. I wondered the whole time if they could see that I was shaking and I was afraid that I would get the hiccups again. I received a work assignment in the brush factory. Neiger led me back to the barracks. It had worked.

I learned that evening that Mummy would be working with me. Her office job had been more comfortable, but she wanted to be with me. She plainly didn't trust me. I had thought that I would manage to be reasonable, and after the "addition" to my age, it seemed to me that I would be able to take care of myself.

Marching to work for the first time and passing the gate I hear *"Aaachtung! Augen links!"* We are marching in step along the road past the villas where our "masters" live. Mummy reminds me not to look around, and to keep my eyes focused in front of me. Curiosity gets the better of me and my eyes dart around. The road leads uphill all the way. On the left, prisoners are pushing carts and repairing the road while several *kapos* with whips stand over them, beating them and hurrying them on. The biggest villa, set slightly back, must be Commandant Goeth's.

"Don't stare like that, you idiot," Mummy hisses. "He likes to shoot from behind his curtains."

We are in the work barracks. The foreman places us at tables and another foreman comes in and begins demonstrating how to make brushes. I am disappointed because I had thought that we would be making brushes out of nice, soft hair. It turns out that those are made only by experts; we will be making scrub brushes with stiff bristles. I have trouble getting the hang of it. I cannot pull the wires through the holes, and when I manage to do so the bristles pop out because they are so stiff.

By dinner break my hands are already sore and scratched, as are Mummy's, too. The soup is as awful as before. When I try to get a little down, I notice that Mummy is swallowing hers with equal effort. Yet you have to eat everything because there isn't and won't be anything better. As I swallow the horrid

90

concoction I wonder what happened to Mummy's happy expression. I did not even notice when that infinite sadness replaced the merriment in her eyes.

Close by sat an even smaller and perhaps younger girl, lovely and dark-haired. There was an attractive red-haired woman next to her. I was amazed that another girl like me was working on these hellish brushes. "Who are they, Mummy?"

Mummy looked up although there could have been no doubt who I was asking about. "That's Reginka Horowitz with her daughter."

"Did they add years to her, too? She's smaller than I am."

"They also seem to have got away with it for the moment."

"Why 'for the moment'?"

"Oh, I don't know. It just came out that way."

We went, ten women at a time, to the latrine and had to do everything in the half-hour break. "Don't look left."

"Why?"

"You're asking 'why' again?"

I didn't say anything because she had already told me so many times to forget about the words "why" and "what for." We were walking near a hill surrounded by a deep ditch. I thought it must be Chuj Hill. Curiosity won out and I glanced left. I could only see several arras and legs sticking out, jumbled together haphazardly. Mummy tugged my hand.

The rest of the day dragged on endlessly and, not knowing whether my hands or my back ached more, I longed for the trumpet signalling evening roll-call. The foreman had already grown angry at how poorly I was learning. The worst thing was when *"Aaachtung!"* rang out and one of the "masters" paced slowly between the tables. He would stop occasionally while the foreman explained that this was a new worker who was learning quickly. At such moments everything flew out of my hands. Just don't let him stand over me! I could see how he stood over a prisoner with his hands clasped behind his back, rocking on his heels, with a smile pasted on his face. At times you could hear the swish of the whip, and you had to accept the blow humbly without touching the place that hurt because otherwise you would immediately get it again on the other side.

Day after day passed like this as the weather turned colder and it became more difficult to rise at five in the morning. You could never get warm because the blankets were always damp and even though we slept hugging each other tight, we were as frozen as ever when we woke up. Trucks drove to the Hill all day and I tried counting the gunshots. It was impossible. They could go on for half the day. Then we had no dinner break. Where did they find so many unfortunates? If they came from Kraków, the whole city must have been dead already.

The Jewish commandant of the camp, Wilek Chilowicz, is completely different from Spira. He is young and vigorous, always popping up everywhere. People say he was a tailor by occupation, but since he wasn't in our Ghetto, he must have come from a different one. He is not a kind person, but they say that, unlike Spira, he doesn't inform. I have heard that he is trying to do good things for us, although I do not know what or how. He shouts all the time, calling us sons of bitches, an expression that is always on his lips.

His wife, commandant of the women's camp, is known as "the Duck". She is a small blonde with very crooked bow-legs and does indeed walk like a duck. She always carries a whip (I have never seen her beat anyone) and calls us "whores".

Chilowicz's assistant is Mietek Finkelstein, even more vulgar than Chilowicz and usually a little drunk. They say he lost his wife and child, but people fear him more than the commandant. Majer Kerner, another of Chilowicz's assistants, is decidedly worse than Spira. A completely evil man, he inspires hysterical fear. He waves a cane around and beats people needlessly. The children have already made up a Yiddish-Polish song about him: "Majer Kerner the bandit, ta-ra-ra-ra-boom, he knows not what he does, ta-ra-ra-ra-boom, if we survive, we'll tear out his eyes." He chases the children with a whip but does not strike them. He must be afraid that people would kill him if he did.

Our work system has been changed. We are on night shift one week and day shift the next. The night shifts are terrible. After midnight, I cannot keep my head from nodding every few minutes and Mummy is exhausted from watching that I do not fall asleep. The Germans have a custom, which they have made into a game, of hunting through the barracks windows for people who dare to nap for a moment. Then there is a shot through the window, or at best twenty-five lashes on the bare buttocks on the *apelplatz*. It is impossible to sleep during the day after the night shift because things keep happening. We have to go out suddenly to the *apelplatz*, or they bring in a new transport, or there is a special inspection of the camp population.

I overheard Mummy and Daddy talking. The night work is torture for both of us because of her anxiety that I will fall asleep. She fears in general that I will not hold out, and if they shoot me she will kill herself. She also said that I must have at least an additional portion of bread. I feel terrible that I am always a problem for them.

***

Daddy has managed to get us transferred to the tailoring workshop. Mummy and I will be mending old German uniforms. New ones are sewn by experts. These uniforms are supposed to have been disinfected, but they are full of lice. We sew up the legs and sew on buttons. Here, at least, they cannot hurry us. We get heaps of clothes and the foreman does not know what needs mending, so we can work on the same shirt or pair of trousers over and over.

Beside me sits a girl I hardly knew in the Ghetto, but whom I always watched because she was pretty and several years older then me. She has turned out to be very nice. So Halinka and I sit together whispering all the time and I am quite impressed by this friendship. Halinka even has a boyfriend here and she says that when the war ends they will marry. She tells me how they met between the barracks and how, when there isn't a *blokszper,* a barracks inspection, he kisses her. I am a little embarrassed but pretend it's nothing to me.

She has taught me to smoke cigarettes, which her boyfriend obtains for her. His name is Zev Szanc. Her mother calls Halinka "my little baby" which drives me crazy. Halinka confides in me because she is convinced that Bubik and I have also kissed. I do not correct her because then she might think I am a "stupid child". I pretend that nothing is new or strange to me.

Through the window where we worked we could now see the whole Hill. We could keep a precise list of how many people were taken there to be shot each day. We were sitting there working when we heard a vehicle driving up the Hill. "That's too quiet for a truck." We edged towards the window. "Why do you think they've driven up there with that woman?" "I don't know. Maybe they like gazing at the corpses." "Look how beautiful she is." Her lovely blonde braids spilled out from under her beret.

The woman walked with two men who were laughing and talking to her. One lingered behind and took out his revolver. When she looked around she started to speak with a look of surprise on her face, but we could already hear the shot. She fell and one of the Germans pushed her body into the ditch as if it were a sack. They patted each other on the back and drove away. I tried to figure out what it could all have meant. She was certainly not Jewish, and it also seemed certain that she knew those Germans. No one ever found out why that beautiful woman was shot just there.

We lost track of Uncle Ignac. Everyone was taken away from the Ghetto prison two days after we arrived at the camp. They were not shot at the Hill. Mummy kept trying to find out, and she consoled herself with the idea that he had been taken to another camp.

More and more often Amon Goeth tormented Uncle Grünberg who, as I have said, was the chief engineer at the camp. Uncle often came back with his face bloody and swollen, but there was no way that he could change jobs. Goeth treated him as his slave.

Bubik sent a mournful card saying that they would be leaving soon, and he asked me to arrange to go to the Ghetto with a work detail. When I mentioned this to Daddy, I almost got a beating.

The camp is being expanded rapidly and barracks are springing up like the proverbial mushrooms after rain. The cold is painful and the *apelplatz* is sinking into deep mud. I have no idea what will happen next. The lice have conquered us completely. I am crawling with them and we cannot even dream of any sort of soap or washing. They are said to be building us a bathhouse but we will rot before it is finished.

It was announced that we were to receive a visit from "dignitaries". They were coming, it is said, all the way from Berlin. The Germans seemed possessed, driving people day and night to get the camp in ideal order. Chilowicz ran around like a madman: all the children had to be concealed. But where, and how?

In the end, he came up with an idea. The windows of a barrack were papered over with signs reading "disinfection" and all the children were shut in under the care of OD-man "Tatele" Koch and another prisoner. They had to sit as quiet as mice, forbidden to make the slightest sound. There was even a proposal to give them sleeping pills, but Koch said he would cope, because, after all, these little children were so terrified and "old".

We got clean uniforms to mend, the barracks were scrubbed, and everything was put in ideal order. We were anxious and told each other that this visit could bode nothing good.

When they arrived, a prisoner stood in the door "on zeks," that is, as a sentry who would give the word that someone was approaching, which people would then pass on to each other by whispering "zeks, zeks." The dignitaries were apparently in the Madritsch barracks, also a tailoring workshop, where dress uniforms were sewn for big shots who even drove out from the city for fittings.

"Zeks, zeks." The sewing machines started humming until the whole barracks vibrated and we could not even hear the *kapo* standing at attention near the door giving his report. My nerves were taut. I could hear many pairs of feet walking in step through the barracks. It was a large group. When they had passed our row, I looked up. There were eight of them, with Amon Goeth towering over the rest. They moved elegantly, stiffly, occasionally stopping to say something to the commandant, who nodded. They finally left. Streams of sweat ran down my arms. The sewing machines were still going like crazy and no one spoke. I wondered why we had to be so terribly frightened of everyone in a uniform. After all, they must be people too.

Amon Goeth, supposedly giving a great feast for his guests, was absent from the evening roll-call. John and Müller, the assistant commandant, appeared instead. Müller was a dried up dwarf and a terrible bandit who trembled grotesquely, had a squeaky voice, and tormented people. Now he was flogging one of the men. I could see that his victim was already on the ground. I don't know what his offence had been, but Müller ordered him to be carried to the bunker for twenty-four hours. The bunker is built in such a way that you can't stand up straight and you are not allowed to sit. You get nothing to eat or drink, and there have been cases where the prisoner was already dead when they brought him out. The longed for word *"antreten"* sounded after three hours of roll-call.

The visit was supposedly intended to re-classify our camp from a *Zwangsarbeitslager* into a *Konzentrationslager,* whatever that meant. People said that nothing good could come of it. The guests had not liked the way that corpses were burned on the Hill. They were supposed to send specialists to build ovens like the ones at Auschwitz.

I renewed nervously my request to be included in a group going out to the Ghetto, explaining that I could have a bath at Mrs. Rottersmann's and perhaps get some clothes from her, since all we had now were filthy rags and it was getting colder all the time. I did not mention that I wanted to say goodbye to Bubik. Several families were still living in the OD house in the Ghetto until the time when the district would be completely cleaned up.

I do not know what convinced my parents, but several days later Daddy said that I would march off with the group going to the Ghetto the next day. Aside from the sentries who would escort the group there would also be an OD-man going along, and he was asked to leave me with Mrs. Rottersmann if that was possible. He would pick me up again when they marched back in the evening.

I lined up to go out with the group. When we heard "antreten," we started off towards the gate. *"Achtung, augen links!"* I had never thought that marching through the streets under escort could be so unpleasant. When we came to the camp, it had been dark and the streets were empty. Now, many people were exposed to the sight of us. How different people's reactions were: there were those who pretended not to see us, while others stopped and shook their heads, wiping tears away. One person tried to slip us a little package. The SS-men had eyes everywhere and shouted and threatened with their rifles. Someone stepped out of a large group of people and approached us shouting, "Brothers! We are with you! Hold out!" This cry made our hearts beat for joy, because perhaps it meant that we were not completely abandoned after all and people were thinking about us.

It was children and teenagers who reacted to us with the greatest cruelty. They might not have known what wrongs were being done to us. Or perhaps this was just their everyday amusement. Several of them were standing waiting. "Here they come! Jews! Jews!" They threw dirty snowballs at us. A passerby caught one by the ear and beat the idea of this kind of game out of his head for a long time. I looked at my fellow prisoners. They were walking with their heads down.

The Ghetto is completely empty except for heaps of furniture and junk where the warehouse was, along with

97

a truck obviously waiting for people who will start to load these "treasures".

Mrs. Rottersmann embraced me warmly and started crying. I asked Raspberry to get Bubik. "I'll make you something to eat and put the water on to boil and you can have a bath. Oh, the way you look! Get out of those rags, they all stink." She fussed over me.

When Bubik came in, I was busy scraping out the pan after eating my scrambled eggs. Mrs. Rottermann laughed, "Take it easy and don't scrape a hole in it. You'll get a proper dinner later."

Bubik stood looking at me silently, as if I were a ghost. "You should see yourself, Stella," he finally stammered.

"The dirt's got under my skin. You don't look so great either." We were both embarrassed without knowing why.

"Take off that scarf. Has your hair been cut short?"

"They had to make me look older so I could work, and aside from that I've got lice," I blurted.

Mrs. Rottersmann opened her mouth as if she was going to say something, but she only pulled Raspberry closer. Bubik also stood there with a blank expression. I always had to come out with something senseless, and this had been my greatest fault since early childhood: talking without considering just what I was going to say.

Mrs. Rottersmann recovered quickly. "Everything will be fine now," she said gaily. "We'll wash your hair, comb it out, scrub you all over and you'll be like new." I felt grateful.

"Tell us what it's like there, Stella. Do they kill a lot of people? Do they beat you?" Bubik asked.

"It depends. There are times when they bring people in and shoot them on Chuj Hill all day."

"On what?"

"That's what everybody calls it. Why do you have such a strange look on your face?"

"Don't you know what that word means?"

"It's alright, Bubik. I'll explain it to her," interjected Mrs. Rottersmann. I later found out that "Chuj" is one of the most obscene words in the Polish language.

"And you ask me if they beat us? It depends. There are people who get it often, but I've been lucky so far."

"You're so thin. Do you go hungry?"

I tried to reply gently. "Not especially. I'm growing fast now and, well, the food doesn't taste so good. When are you leaving?"

"I found out that my parents have arranged Hungarian citizen-ship. I'm not going ..." Bubik went back to his old song.

"Come on," I said, almost angrily. "You should be grateful to your father that he managed to protect you," and then I burst out crying.

"I'll find you, Stella. This will end soon. You're going around hungry and dirty..."

Fortunately, Mrs. Rottersmann cut in: "Come and have a bath, and then you'll look like yourself." That crazy Bubik sat outside the bathroom and played quietly while she washed me. Mrs. Rottersmann smiled and scrubbed me to the sound of the music and then wrapped me in her bathrobe. I lay down on the couch. It was heaven.

Later, Mr. Rottersmann came in and asked me to pass on his greetings to everyone. The liquidation of the Ghetto was almost finished and within a month they, too, would be sent to the camp.

I got another slice of bread and a cup of tea. Bubik brought me a big package full of wonderful things like warm underpants, shirts, sweaters and socks. I had been embarrassed before but now my joy knew no limits.

The bath, the food and the warm room had an effect on me. I do not even know when I fell asleep. I was angry at myself for sleeping, because I had so much to tell Bubik.

Soon it was time to get dressed. Again I put on all the clothes I could. Bubik kept asking stubbornly if I would forget him.

"Don't you remember how you said that everything will come true if we only want it enough? And we want very much to meet again."

I was acting and pretending, knowing that in one more minute I would break down crying. But he broke down first. I couldn't hold back then, and Mrs. Rottersmann joined in and we all wiped away our tears. They went to the gate with me. Bubik held my hand like a child. The OD-man came and said it was time.

As we walked back through the snow my conscience bothered me because I had gone away without a word, without even saying goodbye. I kept tripping, and I lived the whole day over again. *"Aaachtung! Augen rechts!"* I was unaware of having reached the gate of the camp.

After roll-call, they bombarded me with questions. I gave Halinka the warm underpants and socks and she asked if we had kissed. For the first time I felt angry at her. Idiot, I thought, but only said that of course we had, and she was thrilled.

An enormous machine called a dredger stands in the place where our bathhouse is to be. It has a big claw that digs into the ground and then throws the soil off to the side. It turns out that they used this spot earlier to bury people who had been executed, because every so often the dredger spews out arms, legs, or even whole bodies along with the soil. There is already a team gathering up those human remains. They take them to the Hill in wheelbarrows. Everything has to be done on the run. Those bodies are systematically burned along with the newly executed.

They are afraid to burn bodies during the night, supposedly because of air raids. But so far I have not heard the air raid sirens here. The bonfires start at the crack of dawn and burn almost all day. When people who are supposed to be executed are only wounded, not killed outright, they go right into the fire and end their lives in torment there. At times, a horrible screaming from the Hill even penetrates our barracks where the sewing machines make such a din. A German often finishes the victim off with a shot and the voice falls quiet, but they frequently miss in the dense smoke. If the wind is unfavourable to us we have to breathe that specific sweet smoke. The smell cannot be mistaken for anything else and whoever has experienced it once will always be able to identify it anywhere and will never forget it.

They have introduced a new method. The people from the transports earmarked for execution have to undress and pedantically fold and segregate their clothes, all the trousers together, and so on. Before the corpses are burned a detail of our people under the supervision of a *sturmmann* is assigned to walk over that giant grave checking the corpses' teeth and pulling out any gold fillings. There is also a new barrack where they take the clothing of those executed and of the new arrivals from transports. They have to check carefully for dollars or diamonds sewn in the garments. Next to the box where each prisoner works sits a *sturmmann* who never takes his eyes off the worker. A great deal of treasure is found that way and taken every day to Commandant Amon Goeth's villa. He in turn is supposed to send it to the central warehouses, but no one knows if he does so.

***

The liquidation group from the Ghetto arrived today. They say no one is left there except for Spira and his family. Mrs. Rottersmann brought me greetings from Bubik, who had gone to the country called Hungary with his whole family. She had to place Raspberry in the *kinderheim* and is a little heartbroken, although everyone assures her that Tatele Koch is so good to the children that after a couple of days with him they forget about their parents. They are wondering why the Spira family was left behind in the Ghetto. Perhaps they are being sent to a different camp. Nobody believes that they are to be taken to Germany in return for Spira's services as an informer, as he himself boasted.

Daddy appeared following evening roll-call the day after the arrival of the liquidation group. "Come and see. A really big fire is burning on the Hill."

We had heard shots, but only a few – not enough to pay attention to. When we went out in front of the barracks we saw that the flames were burning very high indeed. "What's going on?" everyone asked.

"That's Symcha Spira going on his 'special trip,' He's been paid for his informing. All his kind deserve the same. He sent so many doctors, engineers and artists to their deaths! When we wanted to falsify the records on those outstanding people, that illiterate Spira always sniffed it out and then leaned over backwards to make sure that such-and-such a person was on the list for the firing squad or for Auschwitz. He had an aversion to educated people; if he had wanted to, he could have done a lot of good."

"That's one fire I don't regret," I heard, "but it's a pity about that nice, simple boy who married his daughter." Everyone went to bed without any feeling of sorrow for those from whom the flames leapt so high.

Spring is coming but it can't be seen because there is no grass anywhere that could turn green and even the birds avoid the camp terrain. We can sense the spring because it gets light earlier and is warmer, but our feet stick in the mud worse than ever. We stand for a long time at roll-call. Something is going on in the middle of the *apelplatz*. They are carrying a strange piece of equipment in.

"What is that?" I ask Mummy. In fact, I have been asking fewer questions, since I don't want to upset her any more.

"That's a horse."

"What kind of horse?"

"For flogging people on the backside."

This is new. A prisoner comes running with a bucket, Germans stand there holding whips, and a moment later they lead a man in. They throw themselves on him and tear off his trousers, and while he lies on that horse as if he were hugging it, they tie his hands. Then the beating starts. There is such a deadly silence that every swish and crack of the whip penetrates us as we stand there. I count to ten and start to lose control over myself, feeling that my shakes are going to begin.

Mummy squeezes my hand tightly, a sign that I must keep a grip.

They flog him slowly, with all their might. The man howls like a wounded animal. One of the Germans lifts his head by the hair, pours water from the bucket onto it, and says, *"weiter"*. We can even hear the victim's wheezing breath. It is over. The Germans wipe their faces and pull on their gloves while the recipient of the punishment droops over the horse like a rag.

Several of our prisoners work as Amon Goeth's servants. The best-looking people have been selected for him. His maid is Ala Gut, a willowy girl of splendid beauty with long curly blonde hair. Tall, dark-haired Samek Kempler, with his stunning blue eyes, is Goeth's equerry and gives him riding lessons. When they ride together around the grounds of the camp, Samek looks like a film Romeo seated dashingly on his horse; Goeth, in comparison and despite his massive build, looks as if he is rocking atop a cow, even though all the horses are beautiful.

Adam Sztab, a handsome young boy, runs the kennels. Goeth has only Great Danes, four of them, I think. And then there is Fredek Umholz, the masseur. He says that he is always getting slapped in the face for massaging either too gently or too hard. Each of them, although blameless, is terrified with his job. They could meet the fate of Symcha Spira.

Amon Goeth's mistress is a chapter unto herself. She is a beautiful, petite woman with masses of auburn-chestnut hair. Samek told how once, when Amon wanted to shoot a prisoner from behind his curtains, she went up and embraced him saying: "Not so fast. Let him suffer a little." Samek maintained that in reality this was not why she did it.

Adam Sztab is friends with my brother Adam. He says that evil is hanging in the air; a very large transport is to arrive at the camp, although he does not know from where. He was asked whether he fears being constantly in Goeth's presence, whether the commandant beats him on the least pretext. He said that at first he trembled with dread whenever he heard

Goeth coming, but now he is used to it. Ala Gut is beaten the most, although no one knows why.

One more prisoner is in Goeth's good graces for unfathomable reasons – the stable boy, Grunwald. He is a simple Jew, as big as the commandant, and like Spira he speaks no language properly. Adam reports that Goeth can sit for hours in the stables while Grunwald tells him about horses. Goeth gives him cigarettes and Adam even once saw how, as they walked out of the stables, Grunwald clapped Goeth on the shoulder and said, *"Meinen gite seifele."* Adam said that he almost wet himself in fear at that moment, expecting Goeth to whip out his revolver, but nothing happened.

When Fredek Umholz starts speaking about how he has never in his whole life had the least idea of how to give a massage, you can laugh until it hurts. "You know," he says, "when I start whacking him across that fat arse of his, he doesn't always like it. He rolls over and asks if I'm a genuine masseur. Then I tell him about all the famous personalities I've massaged and in which countries. Of course, I've only seen those countries on the map. Just so it doesn't end badly," he says, turning serious.

Before the war, Fred worked in his father's grain mill.

I haven't mentioned the camp orchestra. It is made up of our people, but of course they play only for Amon Goeth and not for us. The three Rosner brothers perform in the orchestra: Wiluś on trumpet, Herman on violin, and Poldek on accordion. They are excellent musicians. They play in evening dress at the many parties that Goeth throws. They play behind a screen.

At first everyone thought that fortune had smiled upon them, but fortune smiles on no one here. It turned out that they often had to play to the point of exhaustion and were not allowed to take a break even for a moment. A guest once went behind the curtain, saw that they were ready to drop, and "offered" them a stein of beer or vodka by throwing it in their faces. Then the fun started. They had food shoved at them and had to keep playing. Wiluś said that once somebody threw something that might have been a piece of eel at him, and he opened his mouth at the right moment and caught it. Later they were often fed in this way. The Rosners made an art of it and caught the delicacies like dogs.

The construction of the bathhouse is nearly finished. It's high time; the dirt and the lice are helping the Germans to finish us off and there have already been cases of infection caused by the lack of hygiene, if such a word can be used here at all. The *krankenstube* or sick-room, directed by Doctor Gross, a Jew, is also being enlarged. People prefer to avoid the *krankenstube* because there is always the fear that, as in the Ghetto, whenever anything happens, the patients will be killed first.

***

A terrible thing has happened. Two people have escaped from the camp. It was announced over the loudspeaker during roll-call that if they are not found by tomorrow, we will all answer for them. Until then, no one can go to work or leave the *apelplatz*.

I have completely lost my sense of time. I don't know – have we been standing here a day, or a month? We stand and stand, forbidden to sit down or even to squat. The day passes. We have not even been given water to drink. Night is coming. Germans stroll between the ranks; they are everywhere and when they see someone squatting, they pull them out of the ranks and beat them murderously, kicking them in the head. The unmoving silhouettes of the beaten and the dead, lying on the ground, loom in the darkness.

It feels as if each of my legs is made up of several pieces. I can hear the slurping sound of the mud as we shift our weight from one foot to the other. A woman in our row is getting a beating. The whip swishes, there is a moan, and the silence. Night: nothing changes. I won't be able to stay on my feet much longer. Let it end at last. I know it sounds awful, but why do close to twenty thousand people have to suffer because of those two who felt like escaping? My own thoughts frighten me. I hope they make it. But I can't go on. I look up. What am I searching for? The stars are shining beautifully. I had forgotten that stars exist in the sky.

"Mummy," I whisper.

"Quiet! There's nothing I can do to help you."

"Just look, Mummy, how beautiful the stars are..."

She does not even raise her head and I suspect, rather than notice, that she is crying. I touch her face. Yes, she is crying. It always shocks me when Mummy cries because I know that she cries when she is at the end of her strength. Once, at just such a moment, she told me that if it hadn't been for me and for Adam, she would long ago have done away with herself.

"Why don't they finish us all off at once, instead of tormenting us so slowly?" I do not manage to finish the sentence.

I feel a terrible burning and then pain an instant later. I touch my face. It's swelling, and blood is flowing from my lip. I have got it. I have been struck.

"Where's the blood coming from?" Mummy whispers right into my ear.

">From my lip."

"Have you still got all your teeth?"

"I think so."

"Don't talk any more."

I have no intention of talking any more. That blow will probably teach me to stand quietly for a long time. Only thinking is left, but the moment might come when that stops, too.

The place is crawling with Germans. People are letting out little moans. More and more people are being beaten and you can hear the whips at work. A woman faints. I think they are pulling a man out of the ranks and beating him. Somebody howls. I can feel the blood running down my chin and my face hurts too much to touch.

Chilowicz, our commandant, is running around furiously, screaming "Stand still, you sons of bitches." But as he passes the ranks he adds in a whisper, "Hold out, people, hold out!"

He tries to explain something to the Germans and this goes on for a long time. Finally comes the command, "Sit down!" I sit immediately but the pain in my legs gets worse. I do not know how long we have been here – since morning, and now it's the middle of the night. I have wet myself without even knowing when. Spotlights from the towers play over us.

You are allowed to sit, but God forbid that your head should droop for a moment, because you are not allowed to doze off. Mummy still has no chance to relax. She is shaking me because she does not know that I am not asleep, but only dreaming, dreaming of home and of the delicious chocolate-filled croissants that Mania used to bake. I hated cakes and ice-creams, and this always provoked a war at home. Mummy could not understand why I didn't like what other children liked. Mania understood. She liked pastries herself and was always baking those croissants. When I took a bath, Mania didn't wash me. She just sat in the bathroom watching, and when I asked for the towel she said, "Was that supposed to be washing, doll?" Then I knew that I had to do it again more carefully, and when I was finished I asked, "Mania, was that washing?" Then she would take a scented towel and dry me. She would sit beside my bed waiting for me to fall asleep. She often said that she wouldn't give me up to anyone, and that when I got married she would baby-sit for my children. Where are you now, my Mania? You don't even know how hard it is or how hard I am trying. But as I touch my swollen face I think, why am I trying? I am trying to stay alive, but no one can teach you how to do that. What Mummy teaches me is: stand still when they order you to, sleep when they order you to. She always repeats: "Make yourself invisible, that's the only way you might manage to cheat death."

"*Aaaaufstehen!*" howls a German. My dreaming ends. We are standing again. It stinks of urine, it is cold, dawn is coming. Maybe they won't catch them after all, but where can a Jew take shelter? People on the street would turn them in. There are informers everywhere. Is there no place for us, the living? It's getting light. The women have moved me to the middle of the rank.

"You look like you stuck your face in a bowl full of blood," Mummy sobs and wipes at it with incredible delicacy after wetting her handkerchief with her saliva. "You look awful," she sighs, having herself been through a terrible night.

"Look at that," one of our people whispers. "Wouldn't it have been better to put her in the *kinderheim*? The way she looks – to make your own child suffer!"

Mummy answers that it is none of her business.

The day is starting. The bodies of yesterday's victims are already burning on the Hill, and the combination of that sweet smoke with ravenous hunger is terrible. They say that if the fugitives are not found, there will be decimation.

"What's 'decimation'?" I ask Halinka, who is standing next to me.

"I don't know," she whispers back. "It's new."

"Do you want another beating?" Mummy jostles me.

All the dignitaries are now standing on the *apelplatz* and the counting and reporting of the population goes quickly. Fear reigns in everyone; no one knows what lies ahead. I hold my breath and concentrate on being truly invisible, and even close my eyes. Amon Goeth is speaking, orating passionately, and I don't understand everything. But we are to be punished harshly and ten must die for one. I am too tired and nothing matters any more except that I am shaking.

Mummy grabs me by the hand: "Remember, whatever happens, we go together." I nod, but still have no idea what is going on.

There are whispers: "Decimation! But from all the blocks? Nobody knows." There is a strange murmuring, the murmuring of a human crowd driven mad with fear. Germans are shouting *"Still stehen!"* My teeth are chattering rhythmically, no matter how hard I try to clamp them together. A woman tugs me violently and I nearly fall over. Mummy is manoeuvring me into her spot. The women are acting strangely. They are pushing from one place to another and each one is trying to occupy a different spot in the ranks than the one she has now.

Now we know what decimation is like. A German walks slowly along the rank, counting to ten, and he pulls the tenth one out by the neck, using a walking stick with a crook in it.

I cannot squeeze in beside Mummy. They are too close. I decide that if they pull her out, I will step forward myself. Why live without her? There is Daddy, but he still has Adam. I remember how they once talked in hushed tones in the Ghetto, thinking I was asleep. They said then that if one of us dies, we all die. I remember that well. I try to summon up anger at how so many are dying because of the two idiots who escaped, but my thoughts evaporate. We're in such a bad situation, but I want to live, I want to live even though I am hungry and exhausted, even though I am cold. That's all I want – to live.

I am being jostled again. They've got me, I think. No, it is one of our people shoving me aside. There is madness in her eyes and I want to push and stay where I was, but it is too late. *Hauptscharführer* Landsdorfer and his aides stand before us as if they had materialized out of thin air. He is walking along the middle of the rank and slowing down. I close my eyes and it seems that I can already feel the crook of the cane on my neck. I hold my breath. Perhaps I will suffocate first. My heart stops beating. Perhaps I will die right here where I stand. I can hear everything, I hear it so well, and there is such a clamour in my head that it hurts. Without looking I know that he has stopped. Come on, now, now, because otherwise I'll step forward on my own, I can't stand it! Then suddenly, *"Rrraus!"* Someone is tugging at me, but at my sleeve rather than my neck. I open my eyes. It is the woman who pushed into my place at the last minute, and she is still struggling. She is screaming that it's not her place and tugging at my sleeve. I stand motionless. Landsdorfer hits her hand with his whip. She lets go of me, she is dragging her feet on the ground and screaming over and over that it was not her spot.

Tears stream down my swollen face. I am crying because a few centimetres of ground can mean life or death. I am crying for joy that she shoved me away. I am crying because as a result she will die, and I won't.

"It's a miracle, it's a miracle," Mummy repeats with trembling lips.

No, it's not a miracle. It's terror, inhuman terror: she made a mistake in her counting.

When I heard the clatter of the machine gun on the Hill I felt sick and was afraid I would throw up. I would always see that woman's face. I hadn't wanted it to happen. It was my place; she died for me. Did it make any sense? The next day, I could be the one who dies.

The ranks started moving. "Come on, we're going to work. It's not your fault, dear," Mummy said warmly. "Or those who escaped. It's the fault of one madman."

All the way to work, as never before, Mummy talked to me. "Everybody can't be in the same boat," she said. "For now, we're living, but our time will come." Something had broken in her, as well. "And now stop thinking about it. You did nothing wrong."

That was the strangest thing, because before, whenever anything bad happened, I always used to get the blame, whether I had done anything wrong or not.

"Achtung!" We were passing the gate and going to work. The sun was rising, a beautiful red ball. I was a little ashamed, but happy not to be in "that boat".

Work dragged that day because we were hungry and exhausted. Dinner break was torture. Word had spread all over the camp about how I had survived by chance. People came to talk and ask questions. I ate slowly and kept my nose in the bowl to avoid answering.

One woman came up to Mummy and started in Yiddish, *"Jech hole gezukt..."* She caught herself and switched to Polish, "I told you to put her in the *kinderheim*. She wouldn't have seen such things. And you only said 'no, no'."

Mummy was furious: "Everyone does what they think best for their own child. I don't interfere with other people!"

Fortunately, the break ended. The dishwater we got today only intensified our hunger. Too bad – I was hungry, but I was alive! I washed my face in the latrine. It hurt. But even that pain made me joyful – I was alive!

Three trucks, carrying yet another death transport, drove up the Hill soon after dinner. A tight cordon of SS-men surrounded the trucks this time. People jumped out one by one. They were not tied in pairs the way they usually are. Drying blood was visible on their faces. One of them, supported by a comrade, was bare from the waist up. His back was scraped raw and his fingers, twisted out of their sockets and dripping blood, dangled loose as if they were about to drop off.

I had thought that nothing could shock me any more, but I was wrong. Pretending to sew, I kept my eyes on those miserable, defenceless victims. The last one out was a priest in a cassock. He stood in line with his head hanging down and the wind tousling his long, grey hair. The Germans used their bayonets to drive everyone towards the ditch. The bloody man, for whom every step was obviously agony, screamed. This seemed to rouse the priest from his thoughts. He put one arm around the man's waist, stopped, looked up to heaven, raised his other fist in a threatening gesture and shouted in a piercing, sobbing voice: "People! People! There is nothing there! There is no God!"

They converged on him and shoved him towards the ditch. As always, there was a quick series of shots and the beasts drove away laughing.

I spent the rest of the day thinking about how terrible death must have been for that priest. He probably did not fear death, but he doubted. Those last few minutes may have been the worst tragedy in his life. I had often heard that for those who believe profoundly, the drama of death is doubt. I asked myself: Who has the easiest death? Who could answer?

The executions left us all deeply depressed. In the barracks various discussions took place that evening. Someone expressed the opinion that it would be better for us to do away with ourselves before they finished us off. Somebody else reported that Hitler had supposedly said that if, by 1944, anyone could show him even one Jew on the territory occupied by the Germans, he would go up to that Jew and shake his hand. Such reports whittle away at our hopes for survival. I am full of admiration for those who retain their optimism and share it with others. There are several such people among both the women and the men.

***

A completely new development: they are cordoning off a couple of barracks with barbed wire as a *Polenlager*. As Schupke (to whom Daddy reports) said, *"Ordnung muss sein"* and there cannot be any *Rassenschaden,* or contact between us and the Poles. Uncle Grünberg comes to see us after another beating from Goeth, who complained that work was progressing too slowly.

It might be human nature that the past always seems better than the present. Winter was cruel to us but now we cannot endure the heat. Standing on the *apelplatz* for hours without a scrap of shade is difficult enough but the nights are worse. The atmosphere is stifling and the barracks are ruled by bedbugs, not to mention the lice who thrive in hot weather. The bedbugs are strange because they fly instead of crawling. I draw all insects like honey draws bees. Once I even attempted a feeble joke while Mummy was trying to shake the worst infestation off my rags. I said it would be good if those pests had enough strength to fly away with me out of the camp, to freedom. It didn't even raise a smile. I am more and more worried by Mummy's solemnity, because she used to laugh so warmly.

The *aussenkomandos* were given striped uniforms but there were not enough to go around, so the rest had their clothing painted with yellow and red stripes during roll-call. They look as though they came from a circus. The men have been given "lice strips." They have had an even strip shaved down the

112

middle of their scalps, from their foreheads to their necks. In combination with the coloured stripes on their clothing, it looks ridiculous. We women no longer have names. We are numbers. We have been ordered to sew a piece of material bearing a number onto our clothes at breast level. Then they concluded that this isn't enough, so there are rumours that we are to be tattooed.

I dread a tattoo. They are to tattoo those who work outside the camp first. Some people have seized on this as hopeful, saying that if they want to mark us so carefully, it means they are not planning on killing us immediately, and since the Germans are taking a beating on all fronts, we might survive.

These "haircuts," stripes and numbers are supposed to make it more difficult to escape from the camp. The watchtowers are situated close to each other, spotlights sweep the camp at night, and there is a double row of electric fences. I think we watch each other because each escape means a decimation in which many people die. I have heard that there is nowhere to escape to and there is no decent organization to help fugitives. This might be true. Jews have nowhere to hide and people are afraid because the penalty for concealing Jews is death.

There are nights when I dream of food, of freedom, of home. I wake up with the bedbugs and lice consuming me and start to cry – not because of the lice, but because it was only a dream.

The Germans ordered that all gold rings be handed in. Of course Mummy took her wedding ring and the one other ring she had smuggled into camp and dropped them in the latrine. Many women did the same. If the Germans knew about this they would surely force us to comb through the excrement. There are fewer informers in camp than there were in the Ghetto. Even those who would be tempted to make life a little easier for themselves have stopped believing that informing would give them any chance at surviving. They have seen that the Germans are quick to get rid of those who know too much.

Adam still works in the *aussenkommando* and at least he's not hungry because his "free" co-workers in the factory give him a little food. He also has a "strip" shaved through his dense black hair but he's too good-looking for a man, so good-looking that not even the "strip" makes him unattractive. On Sundays, when things are quiet and we are free to go outside for an hour, the girls swarm around him, but he doesn't seem conceited. He might not even know how handsome he has become.

Now I really enjoy going to the latrine. I can't believe how I acted at first. Everything that could be called "freedom" happens in the latrine. No one supervises us there, so we barter, a piece of bread for a cigarette, a pair of underpants for socks. We even have our "latrine poet," as we call Sabcia Sibner, a tiny woman with a huge, crooked nose and beautiful, sapphire eyes, who bubbles with merriment, if such a thing can exist among us at all.

One day when the latrine was full of women and the break was almost over, Sabcia was stamping her feet and waiting for a free place when she began to sing to a lively tune, "Is there a free hole, or are you constipated, or has a field mouse run up your behind?" Ever since, the women have kept Sabcia waiting on purpose, shouting that unless she sings a funny song, she'll have to go in her knickers.

I have already mentioned how Amon Goeth torments Uncle Grünberg. Uncle came to see us for a moment today. "This is the end for me," he said sadly. "Goeth has given me an unrealistic deadline to finish building the sentries' headquarters for the SS-men, who are being reinforced. I can't see how the men can manage. Let him hang me. I've had enough."

Goeth, however, was more perfidious than Uncle imagined. He ordered that Aunt Grünberg and Ziuta be locked up as hostages. He set a 48-hour deadline. If the work is not finished, they are to be hanged as an example. Uncle is going crazy. Many men have volunteered to help, but there is no way that they can finish the work.

Uncle's supervisor is a gentle and completely innocuous engineer with the rank of *Obersturmführer, Bauleiter* Huth. He went to Amon Goeth to explain that the deadline is impossible and to ask for a postponement. He returned several hours later looking downcast; he had managed to gain just 24 hours.

There is no way to pass information to the bunker, where Aunt Grünberg and Ziuta are locked up, to tell them to hold out. But they must believe that people will help Uncle because everyone in the camp admires him. He always took responsibility for all shortcomings. If the Germans caught a worker taking a forbidden rest, Uncle would immediately say that he had given the man permission. Of course, he then got a beating. He was always getting beaten.

The *Bauleiter* had apparently suggested that Uncle be taken to the barracks for at least a couple of hours because no one knew when he had last rested, and there was no way he could hold out. Uncle refused. Daddy said that Uncle had drunk a little "requisitioned" vodka. He never drank because of his bad heart. We were worried about him. Daddy came round at night and I heard him asking Mummy for cloth that could be used as a bandage. Goeth had appeared at the building site and given Uncle a dreadful beating. When Uncle was already down and the commandant was kicking him, *Bauleiter* Huth appeared and told Goeth that he could put Uncle through a meat grinder later if he wanted to, but for now the most important thing was the construction work. This seems to have convinced Goeth, who vented the rest of his fury on others, shooting two people on his way home.

I sat quietly and didn't dare bother Mummy with questions, but I couldn't stop thinking about that man in the SS uniform, *Bauleiter* Huth, who was strangely different from all the others. Why did he stand up for Uncle? Why didn't he beat him like Goeth? Why was it that he didn't seem to see prisoners when he walked past? I was unable to answer these nagging questions on my own.

In the middle of these considerations I found myself asking, "Mummy, why does Huth protect Uncle? Why doesn't he beat him?"

"More boring questions?" Mummy bridled. "The lives of Uncle, Aunt and Ziuta are hanging by a thread, and all you can think of is 'why?'"

"But Mummy," I said on the verge of tears, "I know, I care about them too, I love them after all." Still, I went on: "But that *Bauleiter* Huth is strange..."

Mummy had got a grip on herself and looked at me apologetically. "Remember, Stella dear, or perhaps you can't remember," she paused, "but before the war, Uncle brought you all those pretty things from abroad, an adorable doll that moved, and pretty shoes, the only ones you didn't destroy immediately, because they were from Uncle." She was caught up in the memory.

"Yes, I remember plainly," I interrupted.

"Uncle had been to an architects' conference in Paris. It was 1937." It didn't matter that I didn't know what Paris was. I listened breathlessly.

"Uncle met *Bauleiter* Huth at that conference. They became acquaintances, nearly friends. Uncle even said that he was supposed to come to visit him in Kraków," she said dreamily. "And they met in Kraków after all: Uncle as a prisoner and *Bauleiter* Huth as his supervisor..."

I was hanging on every word: "And he'll save Uncle, and Aunt, and Ziuta!"

Mummy looked as if she had come back from somewhere far away. "Come off it, Stella. They have to pretend they don't know each other."

But I pressed on, interrupting her. "He can get them out of here." My enthusiasm was bubbling over.

As usual, Mummy only said in a resigned voice, "Grow up, dear."

***

116

Aunt and Ziuta were let out of the bunker and Uncle managed to finish the sentries' headquarters on time with everyone's help. I was shocked at the sight of Aunt Grünberg. She had gone completely grey in the course of a few days. I know that she was not afraid for herself, but for her Musiek, as she called Uncle. He was going around all bandaged up but beaming, for his superhuman effort had saved those he loved most.

***

Today we are on night shift. There is an anxiety in the air that no one can explain. It is a beautiful, warm evening and the Germans are roaming the camp. They keep walking slowly through the barracks, very slowly, because they know that we are most afraid when they walk slowly.

OD-man Ignac Kleiner, our work *kapo,* says that when he went to the latrine he thought he saw the silhouette of Goeth with a dog. This is grim news, because the commandant's nocturnal strolls invariably claim a victim. Kleiner keeps walking among the tables urging us on, not permitting a moment's break.

I hear a couple of idiots talking back to him at the rear of the room. "Big-deal OD-man, instead of doing any work yourself, you hop around like a louse pretending you're our master. Maybe you're just another informer like Spira."

"You stupid old whore, if I get my whip out you'll remember who's who," Kleiner threatens. I feel that someone is spying through the window. There is a horrible atmosphere. Suddenly we hear a shot that seem to come from the brush factory. Nobody is defiant any more or has anything to say; the machines clatter like mad.

My back hurts because I haven't straightened it for several hours as I sew buttons on the despised German uniforms.

Groups of ten are being formed for the latrine. I stand with Halina, hoping she has a cigarette. Adam occasionally gives me a drag. Mummy knows that I smoke but turns a blind eye, especially since I sometimes give her a cigarette.

Kleiner's number two leads us to the latrine. There is a horrible stink around the Hill. A *sturmmann* with a rifle is walking there. I didn't even know that a transport had arrived today. I must have been sound asleep all day and not even heard the shots. That idiot is guarding the corpses, or more accurately the corpses' teeth, because in the morning the "cadaver dentists" will arrive. Even diamonds have been found under the crowns of teeth.

It is a calm summer night and as I return from the latrine my heart yearns for freedom. The spotlights from the towers play over the camp and it is so quiet that we can hear the sentries talking up there. If only I could control those dreams about freedom. Most of the time I cannot even imagine what freedom could be like.

We are very tired after a week on night shift. You cannot get more than three or four hours of sleep a day, and it isn't really sleep. The block cleaning detail makes a noise, and then there's the trumpet for dinner break. The only advantage to daytime sleeping is that the bugs are not so relentless.

After the break we learned that the single gunshot the night before had ended the life of the *kapo* in the brush factory. He was Mundek Bloch, and he had supposedly sat down beside one of the workers to chat with her for a moment. So Kleiner *had* seen Goeth after all. Poor Bloch had a good death. Even death can be good or bad.

We decided to try to go back to sleep after the dinner trumpet. But we were not to have any sleep that day. A young OD-man came in all upset and said something to Mummy. I could hear him mumbling about Adam and Daddy. "Tell me what it is you're trying to say," Mummy insisted angrily. "Adam is at work in the *aussenkommando.*"

"They've brought him in, we have to try to save him. I was down below at the gate when they brought a group in from the city... The sentries said they were taking them to the Hill...

I saw Adam... Mietek Finkelstein is with them and I told him to play for time because Zygmunt's son is there..."

The young man in the OD cap stood there helplessly, crying. Mummy did not cry. She dressed quickly. "I won't desert you, son," she said to herself.

I also got dressed but I could not collect my thoughts. "How can we help him?" I asked idiotically.

Mummy looked right through me. "I told you once that I won't leave any of you, and I'm going to him. You..." she paused for a long time, "You stay here, daughter. Maybe you'll make it."

Only now did I realize what Mummy meant. We were also to die. Tears ran down my face; I didn't want to go but I wouldn't stay there. Women were watching and listening to us.

"You're not going anywhere," said the block supervisor, grabbing Mummy's hand. "There's always time, maybe they'll work out how to save him, and there's still Zygmunt."

Mummy had insanity in her eyes and the block supervisor slapped her in the face when she broke free. I listened for shots from the Hill. Was my dear, beautiful brother really going to die in a moment? Would they also search his mouth for gold?

"Leave us alone, we have to go," I said in fury.

Someone had taken hold of my arm – it was Uncle Grünberg. He was gently explaining something to Mummy but I could not concentrate because I kept seeing Adam there on the Hill with his shock of beautiful hair and the stripe shaved through the middle of his scalp.

"Tusia dear, be reasonable," Uncle was saying. "It isn't time to go to extremes yet. Goeth's not there. He went to the city by car. I talked to *Bauleiter* Huth. He's friends with *Obersturmführer* Neuschel, who's in charge today. Zygmunt's there and they're all in front of the sentries' headquarters. They're not going up to the Hill for now, and that's important. You'd only get in the way. Zygmunt is playing it very wisely; he hasn't said that his son is one of them. *Hauptsturmführer* Schupke is there too, and he likes Zygmunt; after all, Zygmunt reports to him. We have to save the whole group. Adam said that he won't leave his friends."

"Did you talk to Adam, Uncle?"

"Yes, dear, for a moment. He's in good spirits. Can you imagine that the sentries wanted to take them to the Hill on their own? The most important thing now is for Huth to be clever enough to convince Neuschel that the sentries were being insubordinate. He might, he just might."

Mummy was more aware by now. "So you say they haven't gone to the Hill, Zygmunt?"

"I give you my word!"

Mummy sat down on the bunk and cried.

"Aren't you going back, Uncle?" I asked.

"No, I'm not needed there now." I suspected that Daddy had asked him to watch us.

We sat for a long time, or so it seemed, waiting for news of the fate of Adam's group. The women were busy trying to convince Mummy that everything would turn out all right and people were helping, so there must be at least a little bit of justice in the world. Finally, a man came up and said that everything had been arranged, but he was furious. He added that the "snot-nosed idiots" would go to the *strafkommando* for a month and would each get 25 lashes on the buttocks. With the threat of death gone, that punishment seemed horrible to me.

The beating took place immediately in front of the sentries' room as a consolation to the SS-men, and perhaps it was better after all that it didn't happen on the *apelplatz.*

We still had no idea what had possessed the SS-men to bring a group back during working hours to be shot. Daddy finally arrived, exhausted. He was both furious and overjoyed as he told us about it. "Those idiots" had beaten up a *sturmmann* for tormenting an old Jew who was working with them. Their group was made up of young boys. "The brats had things too easy and they lost their sense of reality," Daddy said.

"Where's Adam?" Mummy asked.

"Lying on a bunk with a compress on his rear end. Don't worry, Mummy, he's just a stupid boy, and not only him – Emil and the others as well."

"How will he ever be able to work tomorrow?" Mummy lamented.

"The important thing is that he's alive," Daddy urged. "His backside isn't made of china. It'll heal."

***

Fewer and fewer groups are going out to work, and more and more transports are leaving the camp. Adam, Emil and their friends are working in the "metal" barracks and their *kapo* is universally known as "The Mongol." The Mongol took a dislike to my brother from the start and now, like Uncle Grünberg, Adam goes around beaten up all the time, very badly beaten. Whenever he catches him, the Mongol lays into him for no reason with his rifle butt, a stick, a club. Emil says it's starting to look bad. The Mongol might only be waiting for an occasion to beat him to death. Adam will have to be transferred to another job.

The women were all aflutter because the Germans were said to be building a "cathouse." When they talked about it, they had funny looks on their faces. On the way to work they pointed out to each other an exceptionally large barrack under construction, set back from the road. But what was all the whispering really about? I would ask Halinka.

At work everyone was still whispering. "Are they going to take our women?"

"Maybe not."

"Who knows? They call us filthy Jews but for their own comfort they might use our girls and then finish them off as soon as they're through with them."

For a long time nothing had been such a puzzle to me as that "house". What was it going to be? I asked Mummy, but she didn't really know how to explain it. Halinka finally told me

121

exactly what it meant on our way to the latrine. I was so interested in those women that I couldn't wait for the "house" to be finished.

It was said that the women had already been brought in, but to my disappointment they were not allowed outside during our roll-calls or when we were on the way to work. Their barrack was surrounded by barbed wire and the only things that set it apart from the others were flower boxes outside.

A transport arrived at the *Polenlager*. The first prisoners were a pair of newlyweds, the orchestra and the wedding guests. Very curious about these "different" prisoners, I decided to try to go there after the evening roll-call. Halina came with me. We made it because there was only one OD-man guarding them. And there indeed were the bride in a long white dress, the groom, all the wedding guests and a gypsy orchestra. People from the camp gave them pieces of bread because they had not yet got their rations. Some of them were terrified, while others laughed it off, saying they had no idea why they had been brought there but they would certainly be freed.

***

The camp is more and more crowded. *Zugangen* are being brought in. The *Polenlager* is also being filled with people rounded up on the street. These new prisoners are different from us because they have pieces of cloth with a big letter "P" sewn on the front of their uniforms next to their number, and they seem to be treated a little better. Our people, always looking for the bright side, say it's good that our camp is now "mixed". These hopes, however, bear bitter fruit. We have got new *kapos* – German criminals with the letter "V" on their chests. We women are now under the control of *aufsejerki,* German policewomen. Things are clearly going to change a great deal; there is no doubt that our new tormenters are here.

A big gallows has been erected on the *apelplatz*. Fear grips the whole camp, because it is widely assumed that, now that they have put up the gallows, they will be looking for an excuse to use it. The gallows exerts an awful fascination on us as it stands there, massive, intimidating and waiting. You can't take your eyes off it.

The first order from the *aufsejerki* is a prohibition on wearing brassières – on pain of death, of course. The women in the barracks are thinking up different methods, for instance running the straps under their arms. The price of thread and needles has gone up and is now higher than that of cigarettes: a portion of bread for a metre of thread and a portion of margarine for a needle. You can't even borrow a needle for free. Weberka, our latrine supervisor, runs the whole business from her place of work.

Life in the women's camp has become more difficult, worse than before. The *aufsejerki* prowl around like ghosts and seem to be everywhere, even though there are only eight of them.

I watched Mummy in the morning before roll-call. She was putting her brassiere on, of course. I asked her to take it off.

"Leave me alone! Don't interfere."

"And who is always preaching to me," I quoted her, "to stand when they order us to stand and to shut up when they order us to shut up?"

She looked at me and stroked my head. I felt better. She took off the brassiere.

The roll-call goes on and on. It is raining, and we are soaked. The *aufsejerki* have raincoats. I still cannot distinguish their ranks, but does it matter? They certainly won't be angels, that's not why they were sent here. The German women walk between the ranks running their hands up and down the prisoners' backs. They're seething. They have made up their minds to start their work on a lively note and it's plain that they don't intend to be outdone. After we have stood for a long, long time they drag a woman into the middle of the square, beating and pushing her as they go. So they have their victim. Strangely, I sigh with relief. I would never admit to that feeling of relief, but all I can think of is hearing *"antreten"*.

Everybody has become indifferent and people care only about saving their own skin. Daddy looked in during the dinner break. We see him less and less often. I was interested in the woman in the brassiere. "Has she already been shot?" I asked.

"No, she's in the bunker, and during the evening roll-call they're going to make an example of her. They'll bring her out stripped to the waist with her breasts painted with red lacquer. Afterwards we might be able to get her into the punishment company. Chilowicz is negotiating with the *oberka,* but she's a tough bitch, that *oberka."*

This was the first time I had heard Daddy "express himself".

Once in a while, he managed to get a little bread from his superior. If I had thought for a moment, however, I certainly wouldn't have come out with the idiotic question: "Have you got any bread, Daddy? I'm hungry."

Before he could answer, Mummy burst out, "Do you think you're the only one who's hungry? Everybody's hungry!"

"Tusia! Don't be so hard on her," Daddy said quietly.

"Do you think my heart isn't being torn into little pieces? I know without her sobbing that she's hungry, so why does she have to finish me off?"

I couldn't forgive myself. Why had I asked about that bread? I'm hardly any more hungry than I was yesterday or the day before. I feel very bad, because every time I promise myself that I won't speak needlessly, I go and shoot my mouth off.

The trumpet for evening roll-call sounds. A little mound of stones has been made in the middle of the square, next to the gallows. On it stands the offender, stripped to the waist, with her hanging breasts painted red. She is leaning awkwardly forward. Having your breasts painted with lacquer is supposedly terribly painful. Beside her stands what looks like a second woman, but is in fact an *aufsejerka.* She gives the offender a lash with her whip every so often, in a bored way, to prevent her from bending too much. Then the offender stands straight again for a few seconds.

All the groups have to march past her, and then we go to our places. One of the "masters" is talking about the light, innocuous sentence given to the one who broke the rules, because for that lack of discipline she deserved the only just punishment, the death penalty. However, as an act of grace, she will be transferred tomorrow to the punishment company. He rattles on a great deal longer, but I stop paying attention to what he is saying. All I can think about is that I have two more night shifts, and I don't have the strength to hold out all night shutting my eyes and listening for "zeks".

***

There was relative peace for a couple of days and everybody again grew anxious, unable to believe that it could last. Uncle Grünberg came in during dinner break, beaten up as usual with one eye almost swollen closed. It's normal by now for him to walk around like that, a living punching bag for Amon Goeth.

He gave Mummy a cigarette and exclaimed, "There's going to be a big transport but I can't find out where to, maybe to Bełżec and Treblinka, and I don't know if it's to be only men or women, either," and he left quickly.

Daddy came in the evening and confirmed the report. He too didn't know anything definite. The Germans had drawn up the lists themselves and they were in Goeth's office, so nobody knew anything.

We have been standing on the *apelplatz* for a long time today and we know that something is going to happen because there is a lot of movement around the *raportführer's* desk. The block supervisors approach in turn and get sheets of paper, and each supervisor is accompanied by a German *kapo*. They read out names and numbers from the lists. Those who are called line up on the other side of the square. We must have been standing here for seven hours. There is sobbing when a woman sees her husband, son or brother going to the other side, but the *aufsejerki* ensure that no one cries out loud.

Mummy is all eyes and ears. I know she fears for my brother Adam. I'm also worried about him, but I have become more dull and indifferent and it seems that my strongest emotion is my hunger spasms. They are taking only men, but we women know that our time will come.

The large groups of men walk out escorted by SS-men. We go to work.

The *kapo* Ignac Kleiner comes up to our table at work. "Zygmunt ordered me to tell you that Adam is here," he said.

"What do you know about my brother?"

"I don't know anything except that Adam is here."

Daddy couldn't come to see us. He must have been busy copying for his reports the names of those who had been taken away and of those who were left.

***

They thought up something new today. After roll-call, we had to carry wooden beams from one end of the camp to the other with *kapos* and *aufsejerki* chasing us, just so we could carry them back the next day. Those beams were heavy. Daddy came and I heard him saying that his half-brother and Mummy's brother had gone in the transport. Too bad, but I'm so tired that I just lie down on the bunk. All I want is to sleep.

"Time to wake up." I feel Mummy shaking me.

"I haven't even fallen asleep yet," I retort stupidly, unaware that I am already standing and not lying on the bunk. The fact that I can sleep standing up, staggering around, is a great worry for my mother.

On the way to roll-call, Mummy told me that Daddy had failed to pull either her brother or his own out of the transport.

Winter was setting in and we were again sinking into mud from which it was harder and harder to lift our feet, since instead of shoes we had been given wooden clogs that we called "Dutchmen." It was hard to walk in them, and when they were sucked down into the mud during roll-call we had to take our feet out of them and pull the clogs free with our hands.

***

Groups no longer go out on *aussenkommando*. Legends have grown up around one factory where Jews are quartered. This is the *Emalienfabrik*. Its director is a strange, high-ranking Nazi called Oskar Schindler. It is said that Jews are not beaten there and get better food. Everyone tried to get work there, but only a few hundred could be employed. They say that Schindler has told the people quartered with him that he will save their lives. How, no one knows.

This winter is hell for us. We have only our striped uniforms and they offer no protection against the cold or the wind. Freezing and soaked, we have nothing to change into. The uniforms are wet at night and damp in the morning.

I have come down with a chronic bladder inflammation. Mummy asked the block supervisor to move us to a bottom bunk because I constantly wet myself, even in my sleep, and whoever we slept above complained that I was leaking on them. Our straw mattress stinks dreadfully and there is no way to dry it. I also stink, but I can't hold it in. Doctor Löw gave Mummy the name of a medicine that could help, but there is no way to obtain it. Since one group from the *Polenlager* still works outside, Mummy asked Uncle Grünberg if he could arrange for the medicine to be smuggled in, but he hasn't managed so far. People are afraid because the workers are searched painstakingly when they return. It doesn't even bother me anymore that I stink, but the pain is constant.

We can't keep each other warm during roll-call any more, because we have to stand an arm's length apart. The *aufsejerki* watch closely to make sure we're not too close. Now, every violation of the rules leads not to an individual lash of the whip, but to a real working over.

I can hardly believe it, but Uncle Grünberg has asked *Bauleiter* Huth to help get the medicine for me. He says that if it weren't for Huth, Goeth would have murdered him long ago. The *Bauleiter* no longer cares about anything besides the construction of the camp. Uncle says that when they talk, Huth always repeats, by way of apology, "I'm only an engineer."

***

I do not know how we made it through the winter. We are still alive. A lot of transports have gone out and others have come in and there are new German "V" *kapos* who are now probably the greatest threat to us. My memory is starting to play tricks. As I stand at roll-call I try to recall old times, the good times, of course, but by now I hardly remember them. When did I really begin to remember things? It must have been four years ago, when we were fleeing, in 1939. Only four years, and it seems like centuries.

"What grade would I be in now?" I broke the silence when we were standing at roll-call.

"What grade? I think you'd be in high school,"

"It seems to me that I don't even remember how to write."

Mummy did not allow herself to be drawn into a conversation. She is increasingly silent, increasingly tired. She often divides her bread ration in two and forces me to eat. When I refuse the bread she offers, there are tears in her eyes.

The roll-call ended quickly today. We march near Goeth's villa, trying to make as little noise as possible with our clogs so that he won't come to the window.

At work a whisper goes around, *"Zeks, zeks awojdym!"* I do not know what those words mean, but I know that they are a warning.

They're coming! *"Achtung!"* I hear from the door. We are working as hard as we can. I do not know who has come in. I can hear slow footsteps. They stop, start again, and pass us. My heart stops. It is Amon Goeth with his Great Danes Ralf and Rolf, and he is wearing his field cap, which is a bad sign. Beside him walks Hujar, a shrivelled little man with a neck like a turkey, the opposite of Landsdorfer. They are walking so slowly because they know that we stop breathing when they approach. I hold my breath almost to the point of suffocation, which is the only way to avoid the hiccups.

They're gone. They're gone and nothing has happened, which is the most frightening thing of all: Amon Goeth in his field cap, with his dogs, and not a single blow, not a single shot! We keep listening until the dinner break, and there is not a shot fired. Experience teaches us that in such cases what comes next will be worse.

The trumpet plays the wake-up call, but differently. This trumpet means: the living to roll-call, the dead, to be written down and counted for the *raportführer.*

"What's the date today?" I ask Mummy, stamping my feet beside her in the crowd of drowsy women.

"The fourteenth, I think." The fourteenth of May, a beautiful morning. It will be warm.

We are already lined up. There are whispers and rumours every-where: decimation, a transport? Has there been an escape? SS-men are filing into the *apelplatz,* two hundred of them, perhaps five hundred; this has never happened before. They surround us and we stand there horrified. Are they going to shoot us all?

Something new and dreadful has been prepared in total secrecy, and neither Chilowicz nor Pemper, who works in the *schreibstube,* has had the slightest inkling.

Now it's no longer a secret. There is going to be a liquidation. The question is – all of us? The whole camp is on the *apelplatz,* including the staff. The *aufsejerki* are there, the "V" *kapos,* the SS-men, the OD-men, all the "dignitaries" and Amon Goeth with his dogs.

The SS-men are standing in a tight cordon aiming their guns at us. The *aufsejerki* act as if they're not in camp at all. They're sharing a funny story and laughing like horses.

"Eins, zwei, drei." They are testing the loudspeaker. There can be no doubt that it will be something terrible. But what? Is this day in May, 1944 to be the last of our lives? The sentries with their dogs and levelled rifles stand at precise intervals.

Goeth is there with his whole court. I recognize a few and remember their names. *Hauptscharführer* Müller and Landsdorfer are there Amon Goeth is standing on a platform. Two open trucks have driven up in the distance on the road outside the camp perimeter.

There is deathly silence and the sun begins to beat down on us. The *oberka* and her unit of eight *aufsejerki* stand stiffly, tensely, as if it were hard for them to control their enthusiasm. The whips in their hands keep twitching like living things.

The atmosphere is so tense that no one dares look around, although we can hear the sound of marching feet. It is the children from the *kinderheim,* marching behind Tatele Koch. He is leading the children onto the *apelplatz* in even rows of five. His face is bloodlessly pale. He leads his group to the desks where the "masters" are standing. There must be more than a hundred children. Tatele's voice breaks as he reports to Goeth. The commandant waves his whip dismissively, as if he wants to show that it isn't important any more. He lays the document that Koch hands him casually on the desk, without even looking at it. He summons the trucks with a wave of his whip, and they immediately drive up and stop near the children who are standing there motionless, in perfect order.

A wave runs through the whole *apelplatz.* Sobs burst from the breasts of mothers and fathers. Several Germans jump out of the trucks. >From the throats of the children, who have been standing there terrified, as quiet as mannequins, there now issues in unison a plaintive shout. Already being shoved by the Germans who have surrounded them, the children are screaming and calling for help. "Mother, Mummy, Daddy, Tatele, save me! I don't want to go, I'm afraid, get me out of here!" A tiny child tried to crawl away on all fours. As if they had been waiting for this moment, the *aufsejerki* lash at him with their whips, pick up his limp body by the arms, and toss him like a sack onto the truck.

No! This is unbearable! The whole *apelplatz* is howling, the whips are flying, the dogs barking. I cover my face and ears with my hands. Mummy roughly pulls my hands away from my face. I am standing straight again, trembling. I look at

130

Mummy's face. She is staring straight ahead as if she is blind, with no expression at all. At that moment, music in waltz rhythm begins to play from the loudspeakers: *"Mama, komm zurück."* The trucks drive off towards the camp gate as the children call shrilly, trying to shout over the loudspeakers, their hands stretched out in despair.

Women are throwing themselves on the ground, ripping their clothing, tearing out their hair, clawing at themselves, crawling towards Amon's desk. The efficient whips of the *aufsejerki* and the *kapos* drive them back to the ranks.

The trucks full of children have disappeared beyond the gate, but the howling goes on. The cordon of SS-men and snarling dogs closes in. The music plays on. The whips crack. So far, not a shot has been fired.

Commandant Goeth sits unmoved behind his desk, surrounded by his whole merry court. With a bored look he issues an order to Hujar, who walks around the cordon giving instructions, and then all the "masters" get into their cars and drive away.

We keep standing there, waiting to be dismissed. Mothers crawl to the cordon, begging to be shot. The *aufsejerki* kick them away, drag them by the hair, whip them back into place.

The sun beats down mercilessly. We have been standing there so many hours. My throat and ears are parched. I tremble as if it were below zero. I think – but how is it that I can still think? – of how my Mummy foresaw things, of all the unkind words she had to put up with, about how she was forcing me to suffer by making me work with the adults when I could have been among those children who only occasionally had roll-call. Mummy seems to read my mind. She keeps touching me as if she wants to make sure that I am beside her. My legs start to disobey me. A whisper runs through the ranks: "Ignac Kleiner has gone crazy, Ignac is laughing like a madman. They took his beloved little Marek. They are beating Ignac, but he won't stop laughing." I stand there numb. It is twilight, and the howling has not stopped. The numbness helps me survive. Not much gets through to me. Only a tug from Mummy's hand makes me aware that the ranks are moving towards the barracks. The first steps cause terrible pain in my deadened muscles. To take a drink and sit down are all I dream of. I do not dare feel sorry for myself; I'm alive, I'm walking.

I began to come out of my numbness at the block. Something is going on. The women are aroused. I listen carefully. A couple of children supposedly hid in the latrine and have been pulled out half-covered in faeces. Whose children are they? The latrine fills with people. The *aufsejerki* are slinking suspiciously around the camp terrain, walking between the barracks like ghosts. One of the children is supposed to be little Jerzy Spira, around ten, and the other is Juluś Cinz. The women are wondering how to get them out of the latrine, how to clean them up and where to find clothes for them, and where to hide them in safety. They will have to stay there until tomorrow. Weberka, who watches over the toilet, is assigned to feed them and make sure that nobody sees them. Fortunately, no *aufsejerka* ever comes near the latrine; they avoid it religiously because of the stench.

We have been given no food today. Mummy pushes a piece of bread into my hand; she is always farsighted enough to save a little piece overnight as a reserve. I try to explain that I'm not hungry at all. She gives me such a look that I quickly grab the stale chunk and hide on the bunk so that she can't see how I devour it.

***

I do not know if I fell asleep, but it seemed that it wasn't a dream, and I was hearing the trumpet for roll-call again. The block supervisors are going crazy, the *aufsejerki* are beating people and driving them out of the barracks. The torpid women drag their aching feet in the heavy clogs. We are back in our rows of five, marching to the *apelplatz*. The sun is setting like a big red ball. We have our camp superstitions: if the sun sets red, it will be a bloody day. But then, do we have any other kind?

I must have been thinking out loud, because Mummy asked, "What 'other kind' are you talking about, Stella?"

"Nothing. Just to myself."

"Try to be more adult," she whispered. I could still see the children being taken away. Perhaps they wouldn't be killed, I thought, perhaps there's a special camp for children, although deep down I knew I was only deluding myself.

We lined up. Mummy was always repeating: "If you want to live, then stand when they tell you to stand, sit when they tell you to sit, and be quiet when they tell you to be quiet." I do not know when she acquired that camp philosophy. She had always been impulsive and wild. How she had changed! Now, she stood there quiet, preoccupied, following me with her concerned gaze. She brightened up whenever Adam appeared. My brother had grown up, becoming thinner and more serious. In the short periods when we were able to meet, no one said anything. We only looked at each other in mute apprehension and worried over whether we would see each other again.

We were standing surrounded by the guards, not as many as in the morning but still silent and threatening. There were whispers and rumours. Perhaps they had found out about the hidden children and there would be decimation or a transport.

No, this was completely different. The sick were trudging out of the *krankenstube,* led by Doctor Gross. Once handsome, he was now a stooped, old man. They were being marched out by a special execution squad carrying rifles. A car drove right up to the desk and the chief physician, Blanke, got out. Hujar, Landsdorfer, Müller and what looked like all the "V" *kapos* walked on to the *apelplatz* carrying whips, so loud and cheerful that they must have been drunk.

Doctor Gross went up to the desk and handed over a list, then stood at attention beside the patients. The stronger ones were carrying others on stretchers. Landsdorfer signalled with his whip for Gross to withdraw. At that moment, the execution squad pounced on the patients like wild beasts. Shouting and beating them with their whips and rifle butts, they herded the unfortunates towards the Hill. The patients hobbled bravely up the hill with their eyes raised, looking at the sky as if they

133

expected aid or a miracle. Those on stretchers were shot first and left behind, with their bodies strangely twisted.

Suddenly, there was a murmuring among the ranks. What was it? They were praying. The prisoners were praying for those about to die. They thought it would help them on their last journey. Nothing will help them, I whimpered quietly, nothing. There's nothing there! Nothing! Mummy gave my shoulder a painful squeeze to head off a possible attack of shakes or the hiccups. It helped, and I fell silent. There were shots, not the usual salvo but individual, deliberate shots. That is why the Germans had all come, so that there would be a little "recreation" for each of them. The shooting ended and we were ordered to march back to the blocks. Now the privileged ones were gone: the children who had had better conditions and the sick, who had likewise been better off in the camp hospital.

I remember how Daddy had come a few days earlier with a piece of bread. He often did that. He always said he had got an extra portion. He was so thin that I did not believe him; like Mummy, he must have been going without so that Adam or I could have more. I swore that I would accept no more bread from either Mummy or Daddy. In any case, he had said that I looked very exhausted and that it would be best to put me in the *krankenstube* for a few days. After all, he knew the doctors there. Mummy answered that that was an idiotic idea, and Daddy let it drop. Now that scene kept running through my mind.

Wiluś Rosner blew the goodnight signal, and it seemed that the trumpet wept. I looked around to see if anyone else was crying. All I saw were grey faces, faces without life, without expression. Or rather, they had an expression: terrible, hopeless despair.

The next day brought nothing new. As usual, a few trucks delivered people to the Hill to be shot. As we worked we heard the opening bars of the Polish national anthem, cut off by the roar of rifles. The next transports did not sing: the prisoners' mouths were taped shut. We could hear only the rifles.

Important commissions visit the camp frequently. Rumours say a crematorium is to be built. Others reply that this is impossible, it wouldn't be worthwhile. Auschwitz is near, and the crematoria there are large enough for everyone. Before I heard about the asphyxiation of people in gas chambers, I had most feared death by hanging. Now, when I hear the grown-ups talking about people being suffocated in chambers with some kind of 'cyclone' from which you allegedly don't die immediately, I get short of breath. At times, I can turn this to my advantage. When I have an attack of the hiccups, which are an additional torment for Mummy (more than once I've got it across the back from an *aufsejerka* during such an attack), thinking about death in the gas chamber takes my breath right away.

Mummy has been having a hard time since the children were transported out. Many women look balefully at me and Mummy can't help noticing. At such times she tries to make me inconspicuous. She doesn't allow me to talk to anyone. I'm to sit on the bench and mind my own business. One night, I dreamed about the gas chamber and cried out in my sleep. Mummy hit me, then hugged me and started crying. It also happened that one of the women whose children were taken away came up to me and, without saying anything, lay a piece of bread on my bunk. She must have been in the habit of saving it for her child, and it choked me at first. But now I devour such bread, swallowing it without thinking, ravenously and quickly, so that I don't brood on it.

Zugangen, transports from Hungary, Czechoslovakia and supposedly even Russia, are arriving. The prevailing chaos signals nothing good. The camp is bursting at the seams and people are saying openly that there will be transports leaving. Chuj Hill burns during the day. They are incinerating corpses and that's horrible, unmistakable smell clings to the camp, penetrating everywhere and everything. No birds ever appear over the camp. I pointed out to Mummy once that nothing flies here and she said, "The birds smell death."

Doctor Blanke has come by car to the *apelplatz*. So we know that there will be a selection. But where will they be taken? Will they be finished off on the spot like the sick, or taken elsewhere?

Mummy leans my way and whispers, "Listen carefully. Remember. Remember," she repeats distinctly, "if..."

I can sense that she has to pause. I can sense it, even though I cannot look around because the *aufsejerki* are walking back and forth between the ranks, enforcing the silence, stalking their victims.

"Remember," she repeats after a moment, "if they pull me out, you just stand there calmly, shut your eyes and don't move."

I've got goose-flesh from head to toe. I had never admitted to myself that such a thing could happen. And yet it might. What do they care that we are one whole? We're not the only ones.

"If they take me, Mummy, you do the same," I whisper.

"Don't be an idiot," Mummy hisses.

She's pretending to be tough. I know this – when she's terrified, she pretends to be tough.

Now I remember that people have been talking recently about transports to other places besides Auschwitz. I have heard names like Stutthof and Flossenburg, and also that our women are taken away and drowned in the sea.

I was at the seaside once. What was the place called? I dredge up the name: Hel. There was a lot of water, and I thought the world ended where the water met the sky. We were there with Aunt Grünberg and Ziuta. I kept getting spanked all the time. I was supposed to make sand castles, but I kept running into the water. All I wanted was to get to the place where the world ended. Mummy kept saying she would never go anywhere again with such a wild child who constantly tormented her. Later, Uncle Grünberg joined us. To save my bottom from further punishment, he played with me at the water's edge all day long. Thanks to him, I think, I did not end up hating the sea, to the edge of which they would not let me go. What a long time ago that was.

The *aufsejerki* are moving slowly, lethargically, along the ranks. That is the most dangerous. They have innocent little canes in their hands. They catch women behind the neck with the canes, drag them out of the ranks like dolls and lead them to the desk where Blanke is sprawled in a chair. The women have to strip instantly and stand at attention. Blanke barely looks at them. Young or old, he waves his whip to order them to the other side. The *aufsejerki* cannot deny themselves the pleasure of putting their canes behind the women's necks again and lashing them on their way with the whips.

Panic grows in the ranks. None of us can figure out how the *aufsejerki* are selecting their victims. Mummy is terrified and moves me behind her. I always stood in front of her so she could keep an eye on me. Whenever I fell asleep standing up or started to squirm, she would poke me to bring me back to order. And so it was a surprise to find myself behind her.

The *aufsejerka* Orłowska, whom we call "Big Fellow" because she resembles an overgrown man is strolling along the rank. The selection is still going on. They have finished with our block. The men are standing quietly and evenly, but they crane their necks to check for their wives, sisters and daughters among those selected. The group of women on the other side is growing rapidly, the whips are cracking, the *kapos* and the *aufsejerki* are having a hard time maintaining order. I hear calls, "Husband dear, son, brother, goodbye!" There is one shot, over there where the selected women are going mad with fear.

I am trembling all over and I have the hiccups again. A jerk on the arm from Mummy does no good. Lined up in fives now, the group is walking towards the camp gates. It's a little better. They're not taking them to the Hill, and who knows if they won't manage to survive. There is dead silence on the *apelplatz*. The gate closes behind the women.

We stand there. Blanke is sitting at his desk surrounded by the *aufsejerki*. We can hear their laughter. Yes, they are laughing like madwomen. One *aufsejerka* pulls another one with her cane, imitating the way they were pulling women out a few moments ago, mocking. I stand there unthinking and numb, with a feeling of utter defeat, hopelessness and fear. One thought goes around and around in my head: today it was them, tomorrow it could be us.

Our generally calm block supervisor is going crazy and chasing us to the barracks without even allowing us to go to the latrine. She is angry, cursing. By morning, she has to compile a list of the numbers of those who were taken from our block and of those who remain.

Those children who hid in the latrine during the liquidation are now in the *krankenstube*. It is not a pleasant place, but since the Germans have a frantic fear of sickness, they seldom go there.

The *zugangen* from Hungary are a lot of trouble. It's bad enough that we cannot communicate with them; they are also totally unaccustomed to camp life. They have had no ghetto "schooling" in the progressive degradation of human beings. For instance, they decide to go to the latrine during *blokszper*. The block supervisor grabs them and tries to hold them back, but they go out anyway, so many of them are killed or beaten. I often think that if they are bringing Hungarian women here, then Bubik's family must not have managed to escape.

I am covered in lice and my skin seems to hang loose and move with them; I cannot sleep, stand at roll-call or work in peace. They must come from those horrid uniforms we mend. I am angry at being so lice-bitten, but at the same time I am glad that those Hun murderers on the front lines have them as well.

Our food rations keep getting smaller. Mummy and I have a running battle. She used to pretend that the portion of bread we get was too much for her. Now she's starting to push her soup on me. She stirs it in simulated revulsion and says she can't swallow anything so disgusting. I often manage to resist this enormous temptation. I say, "Neither can I, Mummy. It just won't go down. Please give it away," and try to keep an indifferent look on my face.

Mummy, poor thing, looks at me for a moment and then, as hungry as I am, sighs and raises the spoon to her lips.

A terrifying change has come over Mummy since the children were taken away. She won't let me go to the latrine alone. This might sound stupid, but I used to meet my friends in the latrine and we could fool around for a moment and even laugh. We really forgot where we were. And now Mummy goes to the latrine with me. Whenever we're not working or at roll-call, she stands over me and makes me go inside the barrack. And when we're not allowed to lie down, she orders me to hide in the far corner of the bunk and just sit there. At times I wonder if she still gets offended at me like she used to. I asked her about it today. She looked at me with her eyes brimming with tears and said I was mistaken. Then she hugged me violently. I'm worried about her and would rather she got angry.

***

A truck drove up the Hill again today. As is usual lately, the people who jumped out had their mouths taped over. They had to fold their clothes up precisely after they got undressed. Then they stood over their grave. There were two children in this transport: a boy of about ten or twelve to judge by his height, and a girl who couldn't have been more than four. The boy undressed first, as fast as he could, and then he undressed the little girl. He hugged her, pressed her head to his stomach, and stood over the grave. They all stood in a straight line in the last seconds of their lives. The little boy's shoulders were shaking visibly.

At such moments, the sewing machines in the barracks roar at a mad pace. You can hear the hammering of the rifles. One German walks vigilantly along the edge of the ditch and there are individual shots as he kills off the ones who were only wounded. As usual, the Germans are loud, laughing, amused when they get into the trucks.

I wonder to myself if these people – because they must be people, they have heads and arms and legs – have families, have any relatives. Are they capable of suffering, loving, being afraid, anything else? I'll probably never live long enough for anyone to be able to explain it to me. I can't understand this appalling hatred for all of us who are imprisoned and defenceless. I keep seeing that little boy embracing the tiny girl. Fighting with each other –that's how I imagined war. I don't like that, either. Everything in me wants to cry, but without tears, because you're not allowed to cry. That too is forbidden.

Wiluś's trumpet sounds mournfully for the dinner break. I do not feel like eating. I feel like throwing up. These internal convulsions will probably stay with me until I die. And what kind of death will it be? And when? Forever? But how long is forever? I join the group going to the latrine, and Halinka says she has a piece of cigarette. I have already decided to give it to Mummy.

Halinka's beloved Zev works in the "V" *kapos'* kitchen. Thanks to his job he can toss us a cigarette or even a couple of boiled potatoes now and then. I do not really know why, but Halinka always shares everything with me, even though she has her mother. Her mother still calls her "my beautiful baby". Those "baby's" get on my nerves, but Halinka loves it and beams at her mother, as if she were one of her admirers. She really does have a pretty face.

I do not know how she manages, but she often acts as though she were completely unaware that each moment could be our last. She is planning for her future. When we get out of the camp, she and Zev will get married and go to America. His father owned a big restaurant in Bielsko before the war and supposedly left a lot of money with his acquaintances. I imagine she tells me all about it because I pretend to be interested, but in fact half the time I feel like giving her a whack on the head to bring her to her senses. Then I think that it may be better for her this way because she doesn't get the hiccups or the shakes. I'm really terrible; she shares her thoughts with me and I encourage her.

Mummy told me once that it's a very bad trait of mine that I analyse everything and everyone. I did not even know what the word meant. Mummy laughed and explained that it's like a cow grazing: it swallows its food and then lies on the grass and chews for a long time. That was a long time ago, but Mummy knew how to explain things to me. I had always liked animals, and whenever we went on holiday they always had a little peace if there were animals for me to look at. Whenever we went to the zoo in Lasek Wolski, I would end up crying and trying to tear away and go back inside when it was time to go home. And then, if Mania wasn't along, I would get a big spanking.

I do not know how long I had been sitting in the latrine. Mummy was standing over me. "Are you ever going to act like you know what's going on? Have you fallen into another dream about the past?" Everybody else in the latrine had already finished and gone back to the barracks; there was going to be a *lagerszper* in a moment.

I looked at Mummy resentfully. "All right," she said, "as long as you understand that I'm very worried about you."

"I won't do it any more, Mummy." I felt guilty as I trudged back with her.

As usual, I sat down on the corner of the bunk as soon as we got back. I could hear women talking animatedly about how we were going to be transported out gradually and the camp slowly wound up, since the battles at the front were getting fiercer.

A period of merciless *lagerszper* has begun. We are not allowed to go alone to the latrine after roll-call or to move freely among the barracks after work. It's a pity we are in a different barrack from Aunt Grünberg and Ziuta. Some of the women in our block are nice. Rózia Kornhauser has been in the next bunk for a while now. A transport arrived from Montelupich prison a couple of months ago and by some miracle, I don't know how, a dozen or so people from it managed to survive, among them Rózia.

Rózia has taken to Mummy and shares her bread with her. They have decided to organize underpants for the "little one", that is for me, before winter. This can be arranged only with those who segregate the clothing of the murdered people, and only for bread. At times I feel like telling them to forget it and eat their starvation rations, because we are not going to live anyway. But I fear speaking up, even though they must think the same thing.

We have barely any contact with Daddy and Adam. The women's camp is sealed off with barbed wire fences. Only a few of the OD-men have access to us. Daddy is also an OD-man, but an ordinary one, whose job is making up reports on how many transports have arrived and departed and how many people have died. I have heard words to the effect that he sometimes puts the living before the dead, which is supposed to be dangerous, although I have no idea what it means.

Mietek Pemper, the head accountant of the camp, often told Daddy, in secret of course, about planned transports. If the Germans ever found out, he would have an agonizing death. Pemper had to be terribly careful. He alone had direct access to all the camp documents.

Ignac Kleiner never recovered his equilibrium after his son, Marek, was taken away. He is said to have attacked a *sturmmann,* wrestled his bayonet away, and perhaps wounded him, although no one knows for sure. In any case, the *sturmmann* shot him. I think that he might have wanted it that way.

Hanka Kleiner bore all those tragedies more easily. There had been rumours for a long time that she was in love with Emek Langer and that her husband knew about it and suffered. Emek is an OD-man who would never harm anyone, a big mountain of a man. I feel revulsion towards Hanka. She lives two bunks away and is pretty and sweet. But I always avoid her. My arrogant reactions to people whom I dislike for any reason have not left me, even in this hell. Mummy tells me that I should not act this way living in a crowd, that I cannot just shrug my shoulders at people and turn away. She says

I have always been like this and could not change even if
I wanted to, but perhaps I don't want to.

***

We have *zahlapel* almost every day now. At the sound of the
trumpet we have to line up on the *apelplatz* at a breakneck
pace. The clogs impede our progress since they fall off our
feet and somebody often picks up another person's. We run in
two right clogs or two left ones, anything to make it in time
and avoid a blow from the whips of the *kapos* and *aufsejerki*.
The worst *zahlapels* are the ones held after we've been
working all night. Mummy jerks me and pulls me but still
can't wake me up. At times I'm so unawake that I rush out
barefoot, and then she runs along carrying my clogs or pulling
at my arm to try to wake me up. Afterwards I always feel bad.
She has so much more trouble because of me.

We worked last night, too. I'm still half asleep and run to the
zahlapel among a group of women who push me in every
direction. I stumble. In the end, we line up in even ranks like
well-drilled soldiers. I look around. In camp, I have learned to
look around without moving my head. When an *aufsejerka*
comes near, you have to look vacantly straight ahead, with
your eyes neither too sharply focused on anything nor
completely dull. Nobody ever knows what kind of facial
expression will provoke a blow from the whip.

This time, there are two tables in the middle of the *apelplatz*.
I start to get afraid. I am used to one table, but two is a new
development, more threatening, I see Doctor Gross and the
other Jewish doctors from the infirmary. I wonder if anyone
has informed on the children in the infirmary. Doctor Blanke,
who has often been on the *apelplatz* recently, drives up. What
will it be today? I have the shakes. Mummy puts me behind
her. She is afraid that I am tired, without sleep after the night
shift, and will not be able to control myself.

143

A whisper runs through the ranks. Without turning around, Mummy says, "Stop shaking, damn it! They're only going to tattoo the ones who still go out on work details."

There are two women doctors in our block, Doctor Filipowska and Doctor Löw. Mietek Penner comes by to see his mother and two sisters. He is an OD-man and a fine, merry fellow. He often brings a little vodka, which is treated as a priceless medicine, in his mess-tin. Mietek laughs and says he is a silent partner in one of the Germans' offices; the German drinks a lot and Mietek has made a duplicate key to his cupboard. Doctor Löw asked Mietek's sister Wanda if he could give me a few drops of vodka from time to time, because "the little one's resistance is fading and we have to do something". I cannot say that it tastes good, but it really helps at critical moments.

There are *zugangen* almost every day. The camp is more and more crowded and confused, and the *kapos* and *aufsejerki* are more rabid. We can hear the whips at work like never before.

Mummy's behaviour terrifies me. She is silent and sits on the bunk with her head down. "What is it, Mummy? Are you sick?" I ask in the evening, stroking her hand.

"There's nothing wrong," she says, although I do not know if she is talking to herself or to me. "There's nothing wrong. When you had the measles in the Ghetto, Doctor Schwarz promised me, he solemnly promised, that he would get me cyanide. He tricked me!" she shouts. "He tricked me and I can't go on. If I could only finish it for us both."

I know what cyanide is. It's a terrible, quick poison. In the Ghetto I heard about whole families poisoning themselves with it. What's happening to Mummy? I cannot utter a word or even move, and the tears stream down my face.

Doctor Löw comes to our bunk but I cannot follow her conversation with Mummy. She has brought a little mess pan full of vodka and makes Mummy take a sip. She sits with her for a long time, trying to talk her into something. At last,

144

Mummy embraces me convulsively and I cannot help bursting into tears. I do not dare look at her sad face and her burnt-out eyes where every trace of the old merriments is gone. I want so badly to be nice and comfort her, but my voice is choked.

At night I cannot fall asleep. In my memory I hear her laughter and remember how people used to say, "Even when Tusia is serious, her eyes are smiling." I swore that I would give Halinka my bread so that Zev would bring Mummy a whole cigarette. I couldn't think of anything better. What else was there?

***

Summer is ending. It is clear and dry. Far beyond the fences, I can see trees that are still green and a solitary grey house that constantly draws my gaze. There lies freedom. What a foreign, unreal word: Freedom. What could it look like? My fantasies are no help; I can imagine neither freedom nor the death that lurks in each passing second. There is only emptiness, and fear. I have stomach spasms from fear and hunger, and if we live until winter there will also be spasms from cold.

Those devout fools pray all the time. At work, they put on a sort of white scarf. The Germans stand outside the windows just waiting for this, and then they shoot them. But more keep doing it, and they die for their prayers. I am afraid even to think about such things.

Once, when they shot a man who was praying, I could not help pestering Mummy. "They're complete idiots. They just speed up their own death, and there's nothing there!"

Mummy answers, "Be quiet, dear. Maybe it's easier for them to live and die that way. There are times when I regret that you weren't raised in the faith and never learned to pray."

I was amazed. "Do *you* believe, Mummy? Do you pray?"

She turned away. I had upset her again, but I hadn't wanted to.

145

We sit over those lice-infested uniforms at work. The *kapos* are brutal when they come into the barracks. They beat people with clubs for no reason. They drag one of us into the middle of the room and throw down a heap of those filthy German uniforms. They command her to pick up a garment in her teeth and bring it to them on all fours to the accompaniment of beating and kicking. They yammer in broken Polish, "Fetch that sacred clothing, you whore, you're not fit to touch holy objects with your rotten Jewish hands!" The ones who arrange such sport are mostly drunk; generally speaking, they're drunk all the time.

I found out only recently that there had been an uprising in the Warsaw Ghetto. As I handle the lice-filled underwear I think of how I hate these German clothes that we have to mend. Joy sweeps over me when I come across a garment, for example a shirt, stiff with dried blood. I examine it meticulously, trying to determine from the bloodstains if its wearer could have survived or not. Not even Mummy understands why I always root around and choose the shirts from the heaps of clothing. She remarked once, "The trousers are smaller and lighter. They'd be easier for you."

"No, I like the shirts because I can figure out from them how many Germans will no longer be able to harm us."

Perhaps she knew what I was thinking.

That uprising in the Warsaw Ghetto obsesses me. How I would love to shoot and kill even one German! I heard that the children fought there. Why doesn't something like that happen here? Were the Jews there different from us?

"Achtung! Alle antreten!" I snap back to reality. I hear Wiluś's trumpet and I stand up. Is it dinner? No, it's too early. We are lined up in ranks and marched out under escort, not to the *apelplatz* or the Hill. They are leading us between the men's and women's camps. All the barracks are marching ahead of us at intervals. In the distance, on horseback, I can see the enormous silhouette of commandant Amon Goeth. Near him stand two prisoners holding sticks between which a banner, an enormous piece of cloth with something written on it, is stretched. As each block reaches Goeth and those

prisoners, it halts, stands for a while, and then marches on. I have no idea what it all signifies. In any case, such a parade is a complete novelty in the camp.

The *kapo* stops and screams, *"Aaachtung! Augen links!"* The group turns obediently to face Amon Goeth and the men holding the banner. I catch snatches of what he is saying: that for lack of discipline, for dissent, each will die this way. I stand dumbfounded, understanding nothing, digging my fingernails into my palms. The bodies of Wilek Chilowicz, his wife, Finkelstein and several others are laid out evenly in front of us. It's really them, dead. I cannot take my eyes off the flies crawling into the nostrils and open mouths of the corpses. Goeth's voice booms in my ears and I am stupefied. Mummy pokes me and we march on.

I cannot understand why. There were people who hated Chilowicz, but I don't think he was so bad to us. He ran around screaming and waving his whip, but by contrast with Finkelstein, I never saw him beat anyone. He yelled and shouted and brandished that whip, but they say he tried to help us. I heard that he amassed great quantities of delicacies, cognac and sausages, all for Commandant Goeth. "The Duck," his wife, could be brutal in the women's camp and always called us "you Płaszów whores," as if she were not one herself. But we had it better under Chilowicz than in the Ghetto with Symcha Spira.

Now they lead us onto the *apelplatz*. The gallows stand waiting for a victim. Who will it be this time?

"Remember," Mummy whispers, "if you start shaking or get the hiccups I'll give you a spanking when we get back to the barracks."

Already trembling, I whisper, "It doesn't matter anymore, Mummy." But it does.

Amon Goeth is still on horseback. I notice now that he's in his field cap, which means something special is coming up. Goeth and the other Germans gather around the gallows. The *kapos* drag a terribly beaten man towards them and another walks on his own with his hands tied behind his back. I blink several times, unable to believe what I see. The one walking under his own power is Adam Sztab, a tall handsome boy who went to school with my brother and took care of our commandant's beloved Great Danes. Ralf and Rolf are terrible dogs, trained to attack people. Adam supposedly crossed Goeth once, and Goeth tried to set the dogs on him. He wanted to shoot Adam then, but his mistress Majola stood up for Adam and saved his life.

Now that handsome boy is standing in front of the gallows. I close my eyes because I am not going to watch Adam die. I knew him well. He and my brother used to take me on wild outings to the park. I can see him throwing me a ball and I hear his voice: "You're a butterfingers if you don't catch it, Stella." They're going to hang him? For what?

I feel a painful burning. I have got it from an *aufsejerka*. She stands looking at me with a hostile stare. I do not raise my hands to my face, but she hits me again. I open my eyes wide. They're hanging there, Adam and the other one. Adam's body seems to be quivering.

Amon Goeth goes on and on about how there was a conspiracy, and how the other rebels will meet a similarly harsh fate. I cannot take much more. I am ready to vomit. Mummy jerks me from behind. I feel like dying; I've had enough.

Mummy and Doctor Löw haul me back to the barracks. My jaws are clamped shut and my tongue is bitten and bleeding. I can still feel the blow to my face. Doctor Filipowska, Doctor Löw and Mietek Penner's sister are standing over me. They pry my jaws open and pour a little of the medicinal vodka into my mouth. Mummy is explaining something to Doctor Löw. She is saying she can't take it any more, a fourteen-year-old girl should be able to control herself. Doctor Filipowska gives me another sip of vodka, hugs me, and mutters in her broken Polish. She speaks Polish in the same funny way that Bubik used to. She's a German and she's not even Jewish. She came here with her Jewish husband, who was her whole world. She wanted to stay with him, to die with him, and now she's alone.

"He died, dear. He died, I'm alive and I don't know why."

I cry on her shoulder and she goes on talking.

148

"He kicked a ball around," I whimpered through my tears.

"I know, dear. Every boy used to kick a ball around."

One of the women from the next bunk comes up. "More problems with that little brat?" she asks maliciously. "Thanks to "her, we'll all end up in the *strafkommando*. Anybody could tell she's not sixteen."

Another one joins her and whines: "That cry-baby should be transferred to a different block because she's nothing but trouble. She's late for roll-call, she loses her shoes, she holds up the ranks, wets her bunk and her mattress stinks."

These women had seemed so good and solid in the midst of our abject life, and now they're full of hatred. I can feel Doctor Ilza's shoulder's sag. She stands looking at them in bewilderment, as do Mummy, Doctor Löw, and Wanda. The little group of women is going berserk. They tear the mess tin full of vodka out of Wanda Penner's hands.

The block supervisor is suddenly among them, screaming, "You whores! You lice-ridden whores! Get in your bunks immediately or I'll report you to the *strafkommando*! What do you want from that child? What do you want? I lost mine, too," her voice breaks, "but I don't take revenge just because another child is still alive."

That helps. They move back.

What am I supposed to do with myself? I'm in despair. It's true that I wet myself, but I've been calm and quiet for a long time now. Why is there so much anger and hatred even among these women? Löw, Filipowska and Wanda are sitting on our bunk. I stare down at the ground.

"Just forget about what they said, dear," Mummy speaks up. "It's nerves. Everyone reacts differently. Lie down and try to get a little sleep."

"We'll switch your mattress tomorrow," adds Löw with forced cheerfulness. "Don't pay any attention to their stupid talk."

"Thank you," I manage to murmur. "I'm sorry."

"You don't have anything to be sorry about. You didn't do anything wrong."

149

I lie on the bunk but I can't fall asleep. I keep remembering different things, the way it used to be. I remember how Mummy once promised to take me to the circus on the Błonia. We met Aunt Tusia, Ziuta and other friends with their children. It promised to be great fun. A man all painted up and dressed as funnily as our men in camp came into the ring. He turned somersaults and acted silly. Then a trainer came out, holding a stick and forcing animals to do tricks. He commanded dogs to jump through hoops and walk on two legs. That was too much for me. I started to scream terribly about how he shouldn't torment those animals. Of course this caused a scene. Mummy had to drag me outside, where she gave me a good hiding and promised never to go anywhere with me again. Fortunately, Aunt and Uncle came out and defended me. Aunt and Uncle Grünberg got me out of a lot of jams in those days.

For the next few evenings after the circus, my Mania came from her servant's room to mine when my parents were asleep or had gone out. I kept waking up crying, or I shouted in my sleep that the animal trainer was hurting the animals. Mummy pretended not to know what was going on in my room.

Mummy came up beside the bunk. "Are you awake, dear? I asked you to try to go to sleep."

"I can't sleep. I keep thinking about that circus."

"What circus?" she was confused.

"You know, the one we went to with Aunt Tusia."

"Ah," she said softly, placing her hand on my forehand. "Have you got a fever?"

"No. Certainly not."

Mummy sighed deeply and lay down.

***

We crowd into the bathhouse; there are more and more of us. Sanitary conditions are getting worse. Mummy is struggling to reduce the lice population on my head.

Borrowing a fine-toothed comb is an expensive undertaking; it costs half a portion of bread.

We once had such a comb and lent it out free, but it was stolen. My hair is terrible, matted and infested. Some are in a worse condition: their hair is falling out and they are losing their teeth, which supposedly means scurvy. Others have running sores called phlegmona.

Those who go outside the camp on work details now have more difficulties smuggling medicine in, because the searches at the gate are more thorough. When a smuggler is caught, the whole group is flogged and the "offenders" sent to the *strafkommando* where their lives are in the hands of the *kapo* Ivan and his helper Willi *"Mörder",* as he is called. When I first saw Willi at roll-call, I thought he would be good to us. But the tall, slender blond with a gently smiling face turned out to be an exceptionally sadistic murderer. Our people say that he had been in a German prison for killing his mother. That's the kind of *kapo* we have now, and in the *strafkommando* they make quick work of our people. When Ivan and Willi lead their group out for roll-call, the prisoners are always carrying several corpses and the rest are so badly beaten, that it is difficult for them to shuffle their legs. I said that the prisoners' lives are in their hands; no, their deaths are in their hands.

And so we crowd into the bathhouse. That's a funny name for it. In prison language it is called the *waschraum.* On the way in, we have to strip naked in a sort of vestibule. The uniforms are sent to be deloused, and we walk in single file into a narrow room. The block supervisor slaps a dab of foul-smelling paste, allegedly soap, from a bucket into each person's outstretched hand. Then we crowd into another room that has several openings in the ceiling, allegedly showers, from which dribbles water that is sometimes lukewarm, sometimes cold, and sometimes boiling. The pushing and shoving starts, because each woman wants to catch at least a few drops. Dirty bodies rub against each other, wiping away the small traces of evil-smelling pap they call soap. The pandemonium ends quickly. They herd us out into the corridor where, after perhaps half an hour, they dump our uniforms that have come back from delousing. Then the real hell starts. You have to find the uniform with your number on it as quickly as you can. The women are aggressive, hitting each other over the head, jostling, knocking each other down. Unabashed, the lice go wild.

It's worse in the winter. Sweaty and overheated more from the struggle to find our own uniforms than from the bath, we are driven immediately onto the *apelplatz* and kept standing there for hours until we freeze. So the baths make a quick end of many women. Any method is good, as long as it kills quickly.

***

Mummy called me to the bunk today. Into my hands she put a magnificent piece of bread with butter, and a large, fragrant pear. I was overwhelmed. Mummy was close to delight. She divided this real bread into portions, saying to herself, "This is for my little son, this is for Daddy, this is for Aunt and Ziuta, and this is for Uncle."

"Mummy, it's a miracle. Where did you get it?" I asked in a hush, so as not to draw anyone's attention.

"It's a long story."

"Please, please tell me." I kept turning the bread over in my hands, unable to get enough of its smell.

"Well, then, an old acquaintance is a prisoner here in the *Polenlager*. At the very beginning, before they got their food rations, Daddy was able to give him something to eat. Now, he goes outside on a work detail. Long ago now I hid a diamond ring away. I thought to myself that, if they transported us out, they would get the ring anyway. So recently, with Uncle's help, I managed to give the ring to that Pole, so that he could exchange it for a little food."

I had had no idea that Mummy was so brave. I knew that when they ordered us to turn in all valuables, under pain of death, of course, soon after our arrival, she had thrown her wedding ring and a beautiful emerald ring into the latrine.

"That acquaintance told Uncle," she went on, "that he got so little because they're not allowed contact with any people except the ones who bribe the sentries. What do they call them?" She thought for a moment. "Hyenas."

"And did that acquaintance get a cut, Mummy?"

"No, he wouldn't take anything. Come on, eat, eat."

I ate the glorious bread and butter.

"But we'll split the pear, Mummy."

"No, go ahead. I can't stand pears."

Sitting on the corner of the bunk, I luxuriated in it. What a shame it was gone so soon. The juice ran down my chin and I caught every drop on my fingers and licked them clean. I thought that never in my life would I enjoy a pear so much. That "never in my life" made me a little sad, because I immediately started wondering how much of my life was left.

As long as I can remember, I have slept well on a full stomach. It was like heaven, with no hunger pangs. As I fell asleep I thought half-consciously what a wonderful mother I had, and how disgusting I was to have ever wished that she would be run over by a tram.

***

We have been standing at roll-call for a long time and whispers are going around that there will be a transport. Everybody, absolutely everybody is on the *apelplatz* – all the *aufsejerki,* the *kapos,* the dignitaries. The *aufsejerki* and the *kapos* begin strolling among the rows of women. Without any lists, they are separating out people from different blocks. With the help of their whips, they are chasing the selected women onto the road that leads to the camp gates. I can see that they are dividing the blocks in different ways, half a block here, a quarter of a block there, as they please. I dare not even dream that they will pass our block over. Why should they? As long as we stay together, so that they don't separate us. Their wild cries are closer now.

"Abmarschieren, schnell!" Off we go. Mummy and I are marching in a group of women towards the road, to a transport. Where? What kind? Auschwitz, Treblinka, Bergen-Belsen, Oranienburg? Or will they murder us immediately?

I try to catch sight of Daddy or Adam, but I am too scared to look around. I don't want to be beaten and tortured before my death. There is a long column ahead of us, in rows of five. I cannot hear any crying or shouts. I just don't want to die. I really don't. But who would, idiot, I say to myself, who would want to die?

Mummy is acting strangely and keeps mumbling, "Together. As long as we're together."

"We are together, Mummy. We're walking together," I whisper.

She has a terrifying look in her eyes, and though I dread using the expression, she looks like a madwoman. She clutches me convulsively by the hand.

The shuffling of the clogs is louder and louder. A whisper passes through the ranks. Then we hear the shout of the guard nearest to us. I am trying not to listen, but it comes through clearly: "Grünberg Berta! Grünberg Róża! Müller Berta! Müller Stella!"

"Antreten, los!" the *aufsejerka* snarls.

We are just in front of the gate. I can see that they have taken Aunt and Ziuta out of the column. Mummy acts as if she isn't there. Now I'm the one who pulls her by the hand, because I haven't gone crazy and I have distinctly heard our names called out. The *aufsejerka* prods us aside with her whip: we have ruined the order of their ranks. My heart is in my mouth; I can hardly breathe.

How arduous it is to walk across the *apelplatz* which is now so vast, through the crossfire of observant, hostile gazes. Just as long as I don't trip and can get back to the ranks as quickly as possible. Aunt Grünberg and Ziuta are already back in place, and now Mummy and I are too.

In the distance, I can see Uncle Grünberg standing beside *Bauleiter* Huth. Neuschel and many other dignitaries are also there. It must have been poor Uncle, continually beaten and tortured, who got us out of the transport – what courage that must have demanded! We are standing in our block ranks, which have been reduced by half, and the whole women's part of the *apelplatz* is greatly thinned out. Half of the women are gone. The gate closed behind them as if they had never been here.

On returning to the barrack we checked to see who had been taken from among our friends. We usually knew more or less where it was safe to stand on the *apelplatz* but this surprise transport, which not even Mietek Pemper had known about, caught us unprepared.

Mummy hugged Rózia Kornhauser, Wanda, Doctor Löw and Doctor Ilza. They stroked my head and all tried to talk at the same time.

"We thought it was all over for you until we saw your brother-in-law Grünberg go up to *Bauleiter* Huth. We watched anxiously. Huth went to Müller and Schupke, and then they all approached Amon Goeth. We saw the transport starting to march out," they kept talking excitedly, "and we could see Goeth flicking his whip against his boot-tops, which meant that he was thinking it over. And the rest you know."

The joy of our companions in misery was genuine. Even the block supervisor came and told Mummy," Come on, I'll give Stella a cleaner straw mattress."

Mummy sat down and put her head in her hands; her enthusiasm had passed.

"What is it, Tusia? Aren't you happy that we're all together?" asked the women.

"I'm happy, but I'm worried that my brother-in-law will pay a terrible price for this."

"Well, it wasn't just for you. His wife and daughter were there, too."

"Yes, I know. But Goeth won't forget that he used Huth's intervention. He'll torture him as soon as he gets the chance. He's already in such bad shape. I remember how, after one of those horrible beatings, he asked Goeth at the roll-call just to shoot him, and Goeth hit him with the whip and said, 'Oh, not yet, Grünberg, I still need you.' You can see for yourselves how he always goes around all beaten up."

"Tusia, don't worry needlessly. Your brother is so brave and it might not be as bad as you think. He's already made it through worse moments."

We did not know how many women had gone. Somebody said six thousand, and somebody else said only half that many. After registration the next day we would learn the bitter truth about how many had gone, but as for where they had gone, we would probably never know. Many women were rooting around in the vacant bunks. Those who were taken might have left bread.

"What are you rummaging for?" the block supervisor snapped.

We felt foolish, and perhaps it was impractical of us, but we weren't looking for anything. The supervisor grabbed something from Hanka. They started tussling and Hanka explained that she needed it for her "baby." This infuriated the supervisor, who smacked Hanka in the face. Löw and Filipowska, for whom all the women have a touch of respect, intervened and tried to calm down the supervisor. She shouted, "I'm sick of hearing about her 'baby.' That little whore always has more bread than we do. Is it my fault that the runt doesn't grow? She's seventeen years old, and all we hear is 'baby'."

Hanka started to cry.

***

There was an air raid alert last night and the sirens howled as they had at the beginning of the war. Everyone's heart pounded for joy because something was finally happening. The spotlights on the towers were extinguished and there was total darkness everywhere. We listened on tenterhooks for aircraft, but nothing broke the silence.

There was terrible confusion on the *apelplatz* in the morning. Several men had supposedly escaped when the lights were out during the alarm. We were horrified and no one was permitted to go to work. On the one hand there was joy that someone had managed to escape and on the other dread over what would happen to us, and particularly to the men. Women whispered in the ranks, "If only they make it!" These were mostly the ones whose husbands and sons had already been taken on transports or died. Others cursed the beasts and swine who had exposed so many to suffering and death.

I wondered how long we could keep worrying about each other to the point of madness and distraction. Daddy and Adam must have gone mad the day before; now it would be Mummy and I.

I knew that Mummy was trembling as she thought about Adam. Things had been good, if they could be good at all, while he was going on *aussen* to Bauminger's. Since he started working at the camp, he was constantly being beaten. The *kapo* Ivan had it in for him. He hit him over the head with a metal rod or heavy tool one day and would have killed him if another *kapo* hadn't saved him. No one knew why Ivan hated him so; perhaps it was because Adam was very handsome and Ivan was so ugly that everyone called him "The Mongol". With the help of Mietek Pemper and others, Adam finally succeeded in getting transferred to another job.

What would happen now? Decimation, flogging? Things could be worse. Perhaps no one had escaped from the block where Daddy and Adam live. I knew that made no difference. Everyone was responsible. I tried to chase away the grim thoughts.

Every so often, sentries ran in great agitation up to the desk where the Germans were gathered. They went away, came back again, and kept looking towards the camp gate. What where they trying to spot? Perhaps a *zugang* was coming. I felt like beating my fists on my head just to stop thinking, even for a moment. My ears were ringing from the unbearable tension and everything was swimming before my eyes.

157

A truck drove onto the *apelplatz* and six SS-men jumped out. They tossed two badly beaten men down like sacks. The men lay there, not even trying to get up. We could see the shaved stripes on their heads. Amon Goeth pulled on white gloves, a sure sign that something appalling was about to happen. He struck the human rags casually several times, almost unwillingly. *Kapos* tugged at the prisoners. They stood, staggering. More blows fell. One man crawled to Goeth's feet and in the terrible silence we could hear him begging to be shot. Goeth and his whole court burst out laughing. They doubled over with merriment. No, this was not human laughter, they must have been mad, but not even the mad laugh that way.

I looked around carefully: there was no one at the gallows, so they were not going to be hanged.

I heard a whisper from behind: "Switch places with me in a moment."

Amon Goeth summoned the *laufers,* the messengers, who hopped on their motorcycles and drove off towards where the Germans lived. I had been standing in Mummy's place for a while, time passed, and I became aware of whispers going around. A *sturmmann* led Goeth's two horses onto the *apelplatz.* Another brought in the Great Danes, Rolf and Ralf, who ran eagerly to their master. He patted them affectionately and pointed his whip at the poor prisoners. The dogs' hackles came up and they lunged at the unfortunates.

Now, SS-men tied the prisoners to the horses. Amon mounted one and Hujar the other. The madness began. They galloped around the *apelplatz.* The men screamed as they were dragged along and the frenzied dogs kept lunging at them and tearing away pieces of their bodies. When they galloped past the desks, the Germans urged the dogs on. The dogs snapped and the men being dragged along the ground moaned. The Germans thought it was hilarious.

I stood there pressing my eyes shut. It was a matter of indifference to me whether I was beaten or not. I heard two individual gunshots. The poor men had been finished off, although it was hard to tell whether they had still been alive after their torture. I had neither the hiccups nor the shakes, and I did not want to live. Here, however, there was no wanting or not wanting anything. You died when you wanted to live, and lived when the desire for life was gone.

"Antreten!" We turned away and marched to the barracks. I sat, as usual, in a corner of the bunk and there was a dull, hopeless silence in the block.

Wanda came up with her little mess-tin. "Tusia dear, do you want to give Stella a sip of vodka?"

"Drink, dear," Mummy says.

"No."

"Does it hurt?"

"No."

I could tell that it was an effort for her to even talk to me.

How can you live when everyone around is a murderer? I thought. Human murderers, dog murderers, horse murderers! Would I be capable of going out where the Germans were sitting now and just murdering them? Probably so. I was losing my mind. My head was exploding with pain.

Filipowska came up.

"Stella, dear, have you got a headache?"

I hadn't been aware that I was holding my head.

"No," I shouted, "No! Go away! Nothing hurts, I just have to face it myself!"

"Go ahead and cry, child."

"I'm not a child any more and I'm not going to cry. I'm never going to cry. I want to kill!" I burst out in dreadful sobs that racked my insides.

Ilza said in a gentle, soothing voice, "After the war, dear, everyone will be good and smiling, and nobody will hurt anybody else, and there won't be any bad people..."

"After what war?" I asked stupidly, sobbing.

"Well, after this one," Ilza answered.

"What do you mean? Isn't this war going to last until the end of the world? After all, it's been going on so many years, I was small and now I'm grown up and nobody has tried to help us."

159

"In the first place," she said, stroking my lice-infested head, "you're not grown up, you're still a child and it's harder for you than it is for us adults. The war will end before long."

"But we won't be around, we'll be dead!"

"You're not going to die because you're a good, brave girl."

Mummy was sitting opposite looking stunned at how, not for the first time, Ilza was able to cope with me so easily.

"Ilza, when the war ends will I be able to carry earthworms from the pavement to the grass again so that nobody steps on them?"

"Of course, Stella dear, because that's the way you are. Only now, remember, you have to be strong and not give up. You know they're just waiting to break people down. You're good, adorable girl."

"Me? Adorable and good? Not a cry-baby?"

"No. You can trust me. I know people."

I myself could hardly believe what a soothing effect Ilza had on me. Doctor Löw, Wanda, Rózia and Mummy calmly sat there watching. How is it that one person can do so much evil, while another soothes and calms to the point of serenity, as Ilza did with me? Not long before I had witnessed a ghastly murder – was it really possible that evil people would disappear and only the good be left? And those murderous dogs, would they also be gone? I felt more sorry for the dogs than for the human murderers. I could not sleep, thinking about how such splendid creatures could be taught to murder.

When I was little, to the distress of everyone at home except for Mania, I used to run up to every dog I saw and hug and pet it. No dog ever harmed me. Mummy had told me about an incident I did not remember. When I was four, we went to visit my grandparents in the country. There was a huge Alsation there called Lord who disliked children, and especially me. I sneaked up to his kennel and ate from his dish. He never did anything to me, but just sat there growling while I urged him to eat together with me because it would taste better to him that way. Once, I crawled inside Lord's kennel and went to sleep. This was a story I had heard many times. Grandfather had a fish pond nearby and he called out the whole village to

160

drag the pond with nets, thinking that I had rolled in (I was a very fat child then) and drowned. Mummy fainted and they had to call the doctor. Grandfather was beating the farmhands and servant girls for not keeping an eye on me. In the end, an uncle noticed that Lord was in front of his kennel whimpering. When they went to let him off his chain so that he could help to search for me, the uncle saw that I was sound asleep inside, smeared with Lord's food. I have a vague memory of what happened next. Grandfather locked himself in a room with me and I got such a whipping with his belt that Grandmother had to make compresses for my behind and I spent several days lying on my stomach. Afterwards, Grandfather made a long leash and kept me tied to the fence or a tree.

Perhaps it is a good thing that my marvellous Grandfather died so young. I remember that I was five when he died. I felt ashamed when I remembered such silliness.

***

Uncle Grünberg came to the work barracks this morning and asked our *kapo* if he could have a few words with his sister-in-law on a very urgent matter. One of the prisoners would have to be posted on *zeks* watch. The *kapo* could hardly refuse since everyone liked and respected Uncle so much. His face was bruised as usual, and he had two black eyes. They seemed to confer for hours. I was both curious and anxious about what news Uncle could have that was so important, and it was impossible for me to sit motionless. One of the women even said, "Sit still, Stella. You're sticking your neck out like a goose and somebody's going to notice."

They talked for a long time, until Wiluś blew the trumpet for dinner. They finally came out from behind the pile of clothing. Uncle kissed me on the run and Mummy's face was flushed brick red.

"Let's go to the latrine, Mummy. What did Uncle say? What's going on?" My inquisitiveness and apprehension got the better of my hunger.

"Oh, be quiet," Mummy said. "I have to get in touch with Daddy, I have to." Her eyes were darting about.

I did not give up. "But has anything happened to Adam or Daddy? Or maybe to Aunt Grünberg or Ziuta?"

"Let me think, dear," she hissed. "I'm all mixed up."

The stubbornness came out in me. "You know, I've also got a right to know. I'm not a doll. I'm still alive!" I almost screamed.

"Yes, yes," she looked at me more awarely. "My poor dear, I'm sorry, you're right. I'll tell you everything but not right now. Just calm down. Nothing bad's going to happen."

We walked amicably to the latrine and she even let me take a puff from her cigarette. She had known for a long time that I would eagerly do so whenever I had the opportunity.

Mummy worked as if she were in a trance for the rest of the day. On the way to evening roll-call, she told Mietek Penner's sister, "Wanda, if you see Mietek, tell him that my husband should contact me. It's very important. Mietek is clever and he'll think of something."

I was still in the dark.

Just so there would be a little entertainment after roll-call, the *aufsejerki* ordered us to carry planks and beams from one end of the camp to the other. Then, to the accompaniment of the whips and their shouts, we had to go to our barracks on the run. This had happened before.

We were finally back at the block. Mummy paced around the bunk like an animal in a cage, and sighed, "He won't come. He's not clever enough."

I could see how agitated she was, but she was in a better situation than I was. She knew why she was upset, and I didn't. Unable to hold back, I grabbed her uniform. "If this mystery concerns me in any way, Mummy, please tell me. I'm not a child. It will be easier and better."

"It concerns you, dear, it concerns you, but my head is bursting over whether or not it will be good. I still have no idea what it means. But whatever it is, we have to trust Uncle Grünberg because he certainly wants the best for us. But how can we ever be sure here, Stella, that the good isn't bad?"

162

Daddy didn't come. Mummy finally gave in and started talking. She didn't know how to begin. "They're going to liquidate the Płaszów camp, understand? There will be transports out, one after the other, and the people will be liquidated."

"So they're going to kill us?"

"Sit quietly," she said impatiently. We were both turning our untouched bread rations over in our hands.

"You've heard of that enamelware factory in Zabłocie where a certain group of Jews is quartered and the owner, or whatever the hell, is an SS-man called Oskar Schindler?"

I was agog. "Yes, yes, I've heard things that are quite unbelievable!"

"They're making a list," Mummy went on. "This Schindler is trying to get permission to take his Jews to an ammunition factory in Czechoslovakia. Uncle told me that it's called Brunnlitz."

"So why are you so upset, Mummy?"

"Why? Why? You and your eternal questions. Because Goeth won't let Aunt and Uncle Grünberg go. Uncle will stay until the liquidation is complete, and you know what they do with people after liquidation. Uncle wants to use all possible influence to get us on that list of Schindler's. The number of places is limited. And in any case, I'm afraid it could be a trick. Why would an SS-man want to save Jews?"

When Mummy had told me all this, I also started wondering. But I trusted Uncle without reservation, since he loved us just as much as he loved Aunt Grünberg and Ziuta. "Remember how wonderful the Holzingers were when you worked there, Mummy? They were Germans, too."

"Oh, my dear, that was completely different."

"But you said yourself that they wanted to take us out of the Ghetto and hide us."

"Yes, I remember, but we knew them."

"Mummy, maybe this Schindler is also a different kind of German."

"Don't torment me, dear. I have to find out, I have to talk with Daddy."

Daddy didn't come that evening; it must have been impossible. We whispered long into the night. How had Uncle found out about the transports and that list from the enamelware factory? Certainly from Mietek Pemper and *Bauleiter* Huth. Yes, that *Bauleiter* was another strange SS-man. As far as Mietek Pemper went, his information had always been reliable.

In the morning, to our astonishment, we found a lot of *zugangen* on the *apelplatz,* men and women both. In the confusion we managed to learn that these were people from Tarnów, Bochnia and Trzebinia.

The confusion increases each day. Transports are leaving and new people arriving. I hear about Stalowa Wola and many other assorted names. This is often accompanied by beatings and there are more gunshots. We have stopped getting our rations every day and we have to set aside some of our tiny portions for later, just in case.

Now there is theft in the barracks. Women hide their pieces of bread under their straw mattresses, regardless of the lice and bed-bugs that march over them. Such bread stores have been looted. Fights break out and the thievery is always blamed on the new arrivals from the *zugangen.* The block supervisor occasionally joins the battles, at times brutally.

One can feel that the situation is abnormal. More and more German cars have been pulling up in front of the clothing store-house, where there are piles of things taken from the *zugangen* and the murdered. The Germans load up haphazardly with furs, dresses, boots and even bedding confiscated from the Hungarians and Czechs. Goeth watches over the valuables, which are taken straight to his house.

With all this turmoil, perhaps the war is ending. We stick solidly together in our group, sharing every crumb of hoarded bread, keeping each other's spirits up, and supporting each other because this is the only way we can make it. Deep inside, however, I wonder whether we can really help each other, whether we have a chance. They could lead us up Chuj Hill and it would all be over. There are times even when I am surprised that they haven't done so already.

Lately, that thought has obsessed me. I went to Ilza's bunk one night. "Ilza, why are we still alive? They've screamed so often about how the world will be clean and wonderful when they've killed off every last Jew."

Ilza laughed with genuine amusement. I thought that I had made another stupid remark, since Ilza was very patient and always answered all my questions. Now, once she stopped laughing, she said, "You silly child, we're their cover, their defence. If they killed us all off, they'd have to go to the front, and they're just a band of malingerers."

"Oh, Ilza, you've made it all clear to me now. I was trying and trying to figure it out." I hugged her. "It's so simple, and I couldn't understand why they hadn't just killed us. You know, Ilza, you don't speak Polish very well, and when the war is over, I'll teach you. I already had one friend in the Ghetto, he was German, too, and I taught him how to speak properly."

"Yes, yes, we'll learn together."

"Of course, you really don't have to learn anything because you're a doctor and you know everything. But me?" I pondered sadly.

"Why are you so gloomy, Stella dear?"

"Because I don't know how to do anything. I'm going to have to learn how to write and even how to read."

"Right now, dear," she stroked me, "all you have to think about is being brave and strong. There will be time for everything. If only there's time," she added quietly.

***

Zugangen arrived every day, and transports went out. Many workshops had already been liquidated. We were still mending those lousy uniforms. Daddy came to our work barrack one day and pulled Mummy behind a pile of rags. They didn't talk for long.

He confirmed that Uncle Grünberg had placed us on the list going to Schindler's factory in Brunnlitz. Uncle had told him that this was the only glimmer of hope for survival. Uncle was optimistic. He was counting on help from Róża, their faithful cook with whom they had miraculously managed to keep in touch. With the help of *Bauleiter* Huth, Róża was preparing an escape and hiding place for the Grünbergs. Uncle insisted that we go with the transport because there was no way that Goeth would release him.

Then came the horrible day in August or September, I do not remember, when a huge transport arrived on its way to Gross-Rosen. All the Jews from Schindler's enamelware factory were in that transport. That evening, Mummy went mad with despair.

"Adam, my little son," she kept repeating. "Adam, Zygmunt and all you innocents with your good Oskar Schindler! He's just another bandit and malingerer and everybody knows he's sent them to their deaths in Gross-Rosen!"

Doctor Löw, Ilza and Wanda Penner kept Mummy under constant guard. "Tusia, stop and think," they urged her. "Your brother-in-law must have heard encouraging news, because he would hardly send his wife's brother and his son to certain death! You know him better than that. Don't you trust him?"

Natka Feigenbaum, who had recently been assigned to our block along with her daughter Janeczka, about eighteen, came up to Mummy. The two of them had previously worked in the enamelware factory. "Listen, Tusia dear," she said forcefully, "This is not a trick. Oskar Schindler is no fraud, and we worked for him from the beginning. You have to trust him. He'll get them out of Gross-Rosen and to Brunnlitz. You know, my husband and son are in that transport."

"Don't be an idiot, Natka. Do you believe that SS-man, just because he didn't beat you and hang anybody? They'll give the bandit a medal for getting so many people to board the transport without any fuss."

No arguments could undercut her despair. "If only I could let myself be deceived like Zygmunt. He's so wise but he let himself be taken in. I know he wanted the best, but he just stopped thinking. It would have been better to die here together."

The women shrugged their shoulders helplessly. Mummy's state petrified me. I saw her completely broken for the first time in all our sufferings. For several days she had been behaving as if I wasn't even there. I never let her out of my sight. I knew that when she wiped her brow she was thinking, calculating, but I didn't know what. That only made me more frightened.

Several days later, Uncle came to see us again. I heard how Mummy lost control and begged, "Zygmunt, you have to fix it so that Stella and I can stay with you, and we'll all be together. What happens, happens. That whole list is a swindle."

"Tusia," Uncle urged, "he'll get them out of Gross-Rosen. How can you think for a moment that I would send your Zygmunt and Adam to...? Just because I've been hit over the head so much doesn't mean I've lost my senses. It's as if you thought I could send my own wife and daughter to death."

Uncle explained things to her for a long time, and in the end she calmed down. As long as I can remember, Uncle had always had great influence over Mummy. They came out from behind the rags. Uncle hugged me and pushed a piece of bread into my hand. "You're such a big girl now, Funny Face," he said.

I used to hate it when he called me that, but now I put my arms around his neck and hugged him. He had once been a beautiful man, and now he was just skin and bones. I wiped the tears that were running down my face against my will. He kissed me and then he was gone.

I wanted so much to believe that he was right. Mummy seemed to be a little more sedate and did not sneer when Natka explained that Schindler was not an SS-man, just a Nazi party member who had co-operated before the war with wealthy Jewish factory owners.

To be on the safe side, Mummy added, "All right, but that doesn't change the fact that he could be a fraud and a malingerer."

Aunt Grünberg and Ziuta managed to get to our barracks. I loved my cousin and my aunt very much (as I have already said, Uncle and Daddy both had the same first name, and so did Mummy and my aunt). How they had changed! Aunt had once been a lovely brunette but now she had lots of white patches in her hair and her round face (Uncle used to call her Funny Face, just like me) had become as small as a child's, although it still had its charm. And Ziuta was now completely grown-up, a lovely young lady.

Aunt Grünberg took me on her knee and tried to cheer me up with jokes. "How did it happen that my dear little second daughter is almost as tall as I am, and you've got those long, skinny, stick legs that used to be so little, fat and round? You've grown so."

"Auntie," I whispered in her ear, "have you come to say good-bye?"

Pretending not to hear my question, she asked "Do you remember Uncle's favourite song?" and began to hum the tune.

I remembered the words. "Hurry to Bonerowska Street and you'll find Tusia Müller. Hurry along to number four, her beauty is a thrill. Golden Tusia is waiting for her loving husband, with Aunt Mindzia, and Aunt Malcia, Uncle Zygmunt and the servants."

"Yes," she sighed, "we'll meet again on Bonerowska Street. And you won't run away from your piano lessons any more?"

"No, I won't, Auntie. I was little and silly then."

A *lagerszper* was coming up and the block supervisor was hanging around nervously, but she didn't say anything because she recognized Aunt and knew she was Mrs. Grünberg. We kissed wordlessly and we were all weeping but nobody could come right out and ask whether this was to be our farewell. We knew that it was.

Over the next few days, *zugangen* of 500 to 600 people came in, and transports of 1500 people each went out among the shouting and the screams.

We could sense from morning on that our time had come. The block supervisor ran around and the *aufsejerki* counted the ranks over and over again. Certain groups of women had already been marched off to work, and all the men had been marched away. We stood in ranks while the whips cracked around us and the *aufsejerki* kept working out their frustrations.

Mummy whispered, "I'll never let myself be taken away. Let them shoot us here."

I had no idea how it had happened, but I, who had always been the one with the teeth chattering in fear and the hiccups, who had to be watched all the time so that I stood in line, was alert and tense today. I focused all my attention on Mummy so that she wouldn't do anything wrong, although I didn't know exactly what.

We could hear that they were counting us, and women were being added from other blocks. Women from our block were sent elsewhere. There were now a lot of strangers among us. Where they the ones from the enamelware factory? It took many, many hours. I held a crushed, sweat-soaked piece of bread in my hand and kept thinking: should I raise it to my mouth or not? I suspected that I wouldn't be able to swallow it, I was so thirsty.

"Mummy, we're moving." I had to pull her by the hand.

We marched to the rhythm of the *aufsejerki's* screams and the swish of the whips. I was afraid to look around, but from the shuffling of the clogs it sounded as though there were a lot of us. The most important thing was that Mummy was moving along peacefully. She had a vacant look on her face, it's true, but she was walking. After being counted at the camp gates, we were surrounded by SS-men pointing their guns at us. It intrigued me how they could keep a straight face, pointing their guns at a group of miserable, weak women trudging with difficulty in heavy clogs. I looked at our group and then at those brave soldiers and had a real urge to burst out laughing.

169

Maybe they're just playing soldiers, the way I once played with little boys? More likely, they must be malingerers. I really liked that word.

We were outside the camp terrain. I wanted to see normal, free people. But there was no-one in sight, and perhaps it was better that way because I might have started crying. As we walked along, I remembered where we were going. "Mania?" "What, angel?" "Where are we going?" "We're going into the unknown." How I loved those walks with Mania into the unknown.

It was not far. We could already see railway tracks and cattle trucks. It must have been the siding. All the doors were open, like jaws waiting to swallow us up.

They started yelling and shoving us with their rifle butts, just to cause confusion and fear, and give them an excuse to beat us. How were we supposed to get in? It was so high. How were we to get in the right way, without giving them an excuse to hit us and push us? We were helping each other, and I could see hands reaching down to help people up. They were pushing a hundred of us into each wagon. It was my turn. Mummy pulled me up.

"Oh, I've lost a clog. What a shithead."

"Don't be vulgar," Mummy scolded me.

Somebody handed me the clog. Mummy said, "Don't let your-self be pushed back. There won't be any air there. Try to stay near the wall, near the door."

Our wagon was loaded, though they were still pushing people into other ones. We stood by the open door.

"Look, Mummy, there's a beautifully dressed woman running along the tracks at the front of the train. I imagine she's a German. She's got a large bag and a fox stole. Maybe she wants to travel in luxury like us. She's got such bright, blonde hair..."

"Stop leaning out! Won't you ever learn? One of those sentries could get the bright idea to start shooting at the heads that are sticking out."

I withdrew, but couldn't stop wondering about the beautifully dressed woman.

"Mummy, now she's talking to one of he sentries like a fool and waving her hands around. Either they're arguing, or she doesn't speak German."

"Stella!" Mummy was getting angry. "What do you care about some German bitch?"

But she couldn't help taking a look herself, and a moment later I heard her say, "This is impossible! It can't be Róża!"

Still gesticulating, the woman vanished along with the sentry. Mummy sighed, "I think I'm imagining things because of your craziness."

"Mummy! Mummy! She's walking along the wagons hand in hand with a sentry. It really is Róża!"

"Don't talk nonsense." But she leaned out further.

Róża had spotted us. She had never had a beautiful nose, but now it was swollen from crying and looked like a potato. She wore a false smile as she nervously pulled bread and bottles of vodka out of her bag and handed them to us, talking about having bought herself this son of a bitch as a temporary boyfriend, meaning she had bribed the sentry. He kept looking around nervously.

"What are you doing here, Róża? Mummy asked.

"I got news," she panted, "and I've been coming here at dawn for the last few days."

"Róża, quick, we need water. Water for Stella."

Róża caught the sentry by the arm and said, *"Komm, komm Liebling"*

It was a comic sight. She was practically dragging him along, stumbling every few steps in her high heels. We lost sight of her. Unfortunately, she did not make it back with the water before they closed the wagon.

There was a sharp jerk and we were moving. At first we were wrenched forward and then backward, and at last it settled down into a rhythmic rumbling.

Rózia Kornhauser spoke up with forced cheerfulness. "Come on. Tusia, give us a bottle. What fun. Real fun. It'll be

171

better to die plastered." She hummed, "Drink, drink, drink brothers" and handed me the open bottle.

"What are you doing?" Mummy screamed at her.

"Oh, Tusia, stop trying to educate your daughter now. We're on a transport to Auschwitz." Mummy said no more. I took a healthy swig from the bottle. It didn't taste very good, but it was wet.

The women showered Mummy with questions about how Róża had been there by the tracks, and who she was and where she had come from. Mummy explained that she was Uncle Grünberg's housekeeper, very attached to her employer, and had even managed at times to send us packages while we were in camp.

Not everyone drank, and there were a lot of those bottles. I felt sleepy and wanted to pee. Too bad, you had to do it where you stood. Before long, there was a terrible stench in the car. The women decided to take turns standing and sitting. So we sat in the pee and the excrement. A woman began to sing one of Sabcia Sibner's old songs in a drunken voice: "Beyond the barbed wire it's grey twilight, and the cemetery gates are open." The train stopped often, and we held our breath and listened.

We stopped again. We could hear Polish words. We started knocking. "Tell us where we are. Where are we heading?"

At last, a voice from outside answered, "To Auschwitz."

"Give us water."

"I can't. The doors are sealed and the windows are too high to reach. They've got wire over them. Germans are running around like rats. I'd help you, poor things, if only I could..."

The cars started moving again. Dawn. The women lifted me up so I could look out the barred window. Nothing, just fields, and here and there a farm building.

The rhythm of the wheels was drumming one question into my mind: Straight to the gas or not? Mummy was right. We had been horribly cheated by that splendid friend of the Jews, the one from the Nazi party, the great Oskar Schindler.

3

Auschwitz-Birkenau

It is already bright and the train has stopped. We can hear dogs barking nearby. *"Rraus!"* There is more room in the car because we are huddled tightly together in fear. After that hellish vodka, my tongue is glued to the roof of my mouth. To think that you could want anything so badly a moment before you die – but all I'm dreaming of is drinking a large quantity of cold water. The doors open with a crash and the daylight blinds us.

"Rrraus!"

We jump out as quickly as we can without stumbling. Whips are lashing around us. Although we line up obediently and according to instructions, they are hitting us with rifle butts and whips wherever they can and dogs, beautiful Alsatians, are lunging at us.

We are lined up straight again, under escort. The wet soil sticks to our clogs. We march through a gate with the inscription *"Arbeit macht frei"* on it. There are lovely high trees and behind them a building or buildings with tall smoking chimneys and there is that smell that you can never mistake for anything else once you've smelled it. Are we going to turn towards those beautiful trees? We all hold our breath for a moment. We go straight, and so we have escaped the crematorium, at least for now.

We are walking into abject misery. Human skeletons, with no expressions on their faces, stand in front of the barracks not even looking at us. We can see a single gallows, different from the one we had in Płaszów.

They line us up near a grey building. The *aufsejerki* approach.

The first one holds her head up proudly and the others follow her every movement, so she will be the *oberka*. Block supervisors or women *kapos*, I can't tell which, come running with rods in their hands.

We stand evenly but they hit us wherever they can.

"You Płaszów whores!" they shout. "You're in Auschwitz-Birkenau, and there's order here! Discipline! This is no brothel!"

Brothel? Is that a camp? But I don't ask. I don't want to give them a pretext to beat me. I know one thing: This is bad, and it couldn't be any worse. Or could it? After all, in the Ghetto we also said "it couldn't be any worse."

First they count us, and then they make us do endless deep knee-bends. One woman is punished with a duck-walk that ends in a fearsome beating. They pull her aside, and perhaps there is one fewer of us.

The *aufsejerki* walk between the ranks looking us over carefully and at their leisure. A small, thin *raportführer* with a bulging Adam's apple approaches with a *kapo* for an escort. He is carrying papers. They count us again. Nothing else matters to me now except getting something to drink because since yesterday, no, the day before, we haven't had a drop of water in our mouths.

Many of the skeletal women walk near us, but none look our way. They must no longer even know if they are alive or not.

The *kapos* are driving us towards that grey building with iron doors. Could it be another crematorium? There is a corridor, an entrance to a larger room, doors here, doors there. We know nothing. Men in striped uniforms are scurrying around. Somebody says this is a bathhouse and somebody else says that they are going to gas us. A woman who must come from Tarnów and has a fat daughter with her keeps repeating, *"Oy reboyne, oy main kindele."*

174

"Mummy, why doesn't somebody give the one that's whining a slap in the face? Her oy-oys are enough to drive you mad."

"Quiet. It obviously helps her."

I can't believe that my mother has become so understanding.

They're shouting again, these block supervisors or female *kapos* or whatever, calling us "whores" and "Płaszów scum." They order us to strip, even to take our clogs off. I hear one say, "Why the hell do they order us to waste our time on this carrion?" She is referring to us.

I must have looked bad, because Ilza summoned up courage and asked for water. She was thinking of me, poor thing.

"Water, you whore? You'll get water in a minute."

I did not know why they started laughing. They grabbed Ilza by the hair, roaring all the time, and sat her on a stool. They started shaving her head and every place where hair grew. Then one of them took a rag soaked in something out of a bucket and slapped Ilza several times across the face and on her shaved head.

"How do you like the taste?" They were still guffawing.

I could see how Ilza covered her eyes, so it must not have been water. A pile of hair grew on the floor. It was my turn. I sat down. They worked the electric clippers brutally, not so much shaving as ripping the hair out. I could not control my tears. The men in striped uniforms were going back and forth all the time and I felt a little ashamed. Those men did not look as starved as the others. I was finally shaved, and then I got a taste of that "water." They hit me with a stinking rag that made every shaved place burn, whatever it was, carbolic acid or something.

I stood next to Ilza. I did not want to see Mummy's blonde hair falling. Ilza took my hand. "Don't cry, dear. As long as the head is there, the hair will grow back. Do you know how beautiful you are? You've got a lovely, round, even head and with those big black eyes you look like a doll. Just don't cry."

"I'm not crying. It's just, you know."

"Touch it," Ilza said. "Your head is perfectly round. And do you know how beautifully your hair will grow back now?"

"Ilza, is Mummy finished?" I was standing with my back to her.

"Yes, here she comes."

"You know dear, it just struck me that if we were going to the gas, they'd hardly shave us." She tried to smile.

I pretended to listen but I was thinking of how thin she looked.

She had had a very full head of hair and without it she seemed to have only a quarter of her face left.

"First group to the showers!"

They started pushing us into that larger room without giving us any soap-like mush. The iron doors opened. We stood waiting for the water to flow. Nothing. Women started going crazy and one shouted, "Do you smell the gas? I'm suffocating!"

Mummy hugged me so tight that I really couldn't breathe. I broke free. There was shouting all around. I felt a hand digging into my arm and couldn't shake it away. A woman fell, scratching my thigh.

"Mummy, Ilza," I found my voice. "There's no gas." But I was choking. "The stink is coming from us." I wanted to say that it was coming from our heads, from that stuff on the rag, but I couldn't. Why don't they calm down before they kill each other?

"Hysteria! There's no gas! Calm down!" shouted a couple of strong voices.

A moment later, boiling water spurted onto us. We danced around and everyone tried to find shelter against the walls. The iron doors finally opened and they drove us outside naked. We immediately formed ranks, and many of us looked terrible, all scratched and bruised. It was drizzling. We shook, we shook from cold, hunger and thirst.

The *aufsejerki* came. The *oberka,* in a raincoat, looked closely at us. She did not touch, but only pointed with her whip. Then the ones with the rods moved in and pulled the victims out. This must have been a selection. I could see from the corner of my eye that most of the ones they pulled out were older and skinnier. I stood behind Mummy, looking at her upright, graceful figure, and at Ilza, too. She was taller than Mummy but not as thin, or perhaps I only wanted to see her that way.

There were fewer of us. They drove us back inside to give us clothing. Two of those men in striped uniforms were passing out clothes and clogs. We lined up. They tossed each woman a striped uniform and two clogs, without caring whether they gave two left ones or two right ones.

It was my turn. "Hey, little one," I heard, "if you want underpants and a shirt, come over here into this room." They were both laughing.

I hesitated, thinking they might really give me additional clothing. But Mummy, Doctor Löw and Rózia immediately surrounded me.

"Remember," Mummy admonished, "whatever a pig like that promises, don't go with him. They're usually perverts."

"All right," I said, although I would have liked to know what that word meant. There was no time to ask for an explanation.

It was already dusk. A block supervisor divided us into two groups. We marched to the barracks. At the door, a block supervisor with a rod handed out one bowl for every five women, and gave each of us a spoon and a tin mug. The barracks were horrible. There didn't seem to be a floor. A bulb shedding no more light than a candle (maybe it was better that way) hung from the ceiling and there were no straw mattresses on the bunks, only a kind of grey rag resembling a blanket for two people. Shouting and cursing, continually holding those rods, they showed us our places. I dreamed of being on the bottom because I was having trouble with my bladder again.

We got the second level, but fortunately Doctor Löw and Rózia were under us. "Don't worry," they laughed. "You can leak on us, and if it gets really bad we'll swap places later."

Mummy and I climbed up on the bunk and discovered to our despair that we had a broken window right beside our heads. A shiver ran through me; our existence at Auschwitz-Birkenau was not beginning particularly well.

Then the block supervisor screamed about the regulations and informed us, "lice-infested shit", that we did not yet have work assignments. I thought that was bad. She finally croaked, "Four fall out, to the kitchen for coffee."

Rózia Kornhauser jumped forward. "Rózia," said Doctor Löw, "stay, I'm stronger."

With an almost joyful look on her face Rózia said, "No, I've got to go and start spreading the word because my friend Bronia might still be here. We were together in Montelupich."

When they had left, Doctor Löw shook her head sadly. "Poor, naive Rózia. She believes that her Bronia could have lasted this long in this hell, that she's still alive."

They finally came back with a pot full of cold ersatz-coffee and no bread, nothing, But as I stood in line with my mug I danced with joy anyway, because at last I would be consuming something wet. The assistant block supervisor was doling it out .The vile thing didn't even give me a full mug. I drank it in one gulp and still felt thirsty. I was sure there must be a lot left in the pot. I went back and asked timidly, "Could I get seconds?"

She looked at me in amazement. "Sure, you lice-infested shit," and threw a whole ladle-full in my face.

I cleared away as fast as I could because I was afraid it could end worse.

"Idiot," Mummy commented. "You wanted to be independent. But I haven't finished mine. Look, there's still a little left in my mug for you."

I felt so bad, because I knew Mummy had wanted to drink more, too, and now she wouldn't.

The block supervisors threw us rags and ordered us to wipe the long table running almost the length of the barracks with the rest of the coffee.

"Until it shines," they added, "you Płaszów maggots."

Just in case they didn't leave the coffee in the pot, but poured it onto the table. Then they left. We noticed that they had a separate room near the door.

I dreamed of lying down, even on those hard boards, but that was out of the question without permission from the block supervisors. They were back soon with thread and a couple of needles. They ordered us to line up. Each of us got a rectangular piece of material with a number and the Star of David on it. This was to be sewn on evenly, economically and quickly.

"It's a waste of thread on you, anyway," they added.

Why did they hate us so? They acted as if they weren't Jewish, or weren't even prisoners. Yet we could tell that they were prisoners.

I got number 76372. It was 22 October, 1944.

Natka Feigenbaum was good at sewing, so we lined up in front of her. Fortunately, she really did sew them on as evenly and as well as was possible. After a while, the block supervisors started checking the quality of the sewn-on numbers. It was then that we found out why there were bricks laid evenly in a corner of the barracks, and a bucket containing a small quantity of crushed brick beside them.

This is what the brick penalty consisted of: depending on the offence, the block supervisors sprinkled out a little of the crushed brick and the offender or victim, again depending on the type of offence, had to kneel with her bare knees on the crushed bricks and hold one or more bricks above her head, with her arms straight. They first applied this penalty for badly sewn-on numbers. I did not then realize how bestial it was.

They finally announced lights out and allowed us to lie down. We could hear squeals and laughter from their room.

I was too tired to fall asleep. There was a draught from the broken window on my shaved head. Mummy tried to cover my head with the blanket, but then my feet stuck out. We couldn't warm up, and we were racked with shivers of cold, hunger, and fear of the next day.

Then I fell asleep. I was roused by a strange squeaking noise. I touched Mummy.

"If you want to pee, get down from the bunk."

"No. Mummy, do you hear that squeaking and that pattering?"

"Are you imagining things?"

A moment passed, and then Mummy sat up so suddenly that she struck her head on the bunk above us.

"Stella, dear, could that be... mice? Rats? Rózia! Ilza. Are you asleep? Don't you hear it?"

"Yes," Rózia answered. "There are rats as big as elephants running around."

"Aren't you afraid?"

"Yes, you fool, I'm so afraid of rats that I'm about to mess myself."

Down below, someone kept banging the floor with a clog all night long. So one more plague was visited upon us.

In the morning, and it couldn't have been later than five o'clock, the block supervisor shrieked, "Get up, you lazy whores. Fold your blankets in even squares. If not, you'll fold them with your teeth."

We were more tired after that night with the rats than we had been after the transport.

"Outside! Line up!"

For this, we had been trained. She read off the numbers and counted. We stood for a long time in silent, even rows. We could see human shadows on their way to work. We stood for at least two hours. It was drizzling, and our striped uniforms grew more and more damp.

The *aufserjerki* came along and the block supervisor reported, "Full count, no deaths." When they had gone, she screeched, "Four to the kitchen."

Rózia was first. The poor thing was still searching for her Bronia, who had certainly gone up in smoke.

They returned with coffee and bread. At last, a piece of bread. It took a long time before they set out the bread divided into portions, along with some kind of a can. This was unbelievable, it was a can of marmalade. We stood like puppets with our hands stretched out in front of us as the rules demanded. One block supervisor gave out the bread and the other one followed behind digging dollops of marmalade out

180

of the can with her fingers. I got my bread. I held the bread out for the marmalade. The block supervisor holding the can gave me a fierce look. "Oh, you elegant whore," she hissed. I got the marmalade right in the face and it stuck to my skin.

We received coffee. I used a couple of drops, although it seemed a shame, to wipe my face a little. Mummy was upset and I was afraid I would get in trouble.

"Couldn't you tell, you genius, that if they put the bread in your left hand then the right one was for the marmalade?"

The women cut off the flow of her reprimand. "Did you notice how that shit cheated us? That was no portion of bread. That was half a portion at most. What should we do? Can we complain?"

Rózia was full of optimism and said that she had now asked the second shift in the kitchen to help her find Bronia. If they just told her that Rózia from "Monte" was looking for her, she would know.

We could feel the lice moving in our wet, striped uniforms. There were hordes of them and the moment was coming when we would gladly tear off our only garments, and our skin as well.

So that we would not sit around idly, the block supervisors gave us brooms and ordered us to clean up. To tell the truth, I don't know what we were supposed to sweep up, since there weren't even straw mattresses here. Afterwards, we were to sweep in front of the barracks. Again, it was hard to tell why, since there was only mud there.

Only then did I notice that, as far as the eye could see, there were naked corpses in front of each barrack. Once they had been women, but they were now lifeless bodies and, what was worse, they were being gnawed at in broad daylight by enormous rats that were not bothered in the least when people walked past. They did not even try to hide. I watched the loathsome rodent feast as if hypnotized. A hard blow from the block supervisor brought me back to my senses. Would it end with one blow? It was my first day and my second warning. I had better be careful.

Dinner break. Rózia went stubbornly to get the kettle full of soup. The block supervisors ordered us to line up with one bowl for five people. I had become used to unpalatable food long ago, but what they poured into the bowl surpassed my worst imaginings. It was stinking dishwater with nothing, absolutely nothing floating in it, not even a trace of a potato or turnip. The five of us stood around the bowl, which Rózia was holding. We looked at each other. We all felt like vomiting, but there was nothing to bring up.

"Well, my dears," said Ilza, "unless we come up with a better idea, we'd better get it down. Otherwise, the rats will soon be making a feast of us."

"Aren't those lousy trollops going to lead us to the latrine?" I asked. "Or perhaps they don't have any latrines here?"

We were completely lost. We didn't know where anything was.

In this state of disorientation, in weather that was getting colder all the time, in stinking, striped uniforms that never dried out, we passed several nightmarish days.

We found out about the latrine. It wasn't holes in a board, one next to another, but just a pole along a sewer ditch, encrusted with excrement. The same building contained a washroom, a laughable term. A sort of tin trough full of stinking water ran the whole length of the latrine, with a big sign over it reading, "Water not suitable for drinking – risk of typhus." But even those few drops of water full of typhus often led the women to shoving contests and outright fighting.

Our state of hygiene and appearance were in rapid decline. It was impossible to find even a scrap of material with which to wipe our stinking bodies. Women started getting eczema with running sores. There was a selection at practically every roll-call. The open sores made it easier. Since we had to strip naked and a large ulcer was easy to spot, the ones with ulcers had no chance at all.

Ilza and Doctor Löw checked our little group every night, although I do not know why. Even if it turned out that one of us had developed an ulcer, what could they have done?

The block supervisors mistreated us. One day they took away our coffee because of alleged disobedience during roll-call. They emptied out both containers and we had to wash the barracks with that foul but life-sustaining liquid.

Rózia kept going stubbornly to the kitchen. She heard that there was a *szrajber* named Bronia in the *krankenstube*. We said nothing, since wasn't necessarily "her" Bronia. Rózia said that Bronia would come, she'd come for sure. I had no idea what Rózia expected from her meeting with Bronia. Perhaps she had delusions that Bronia would set us free, or change our living conditions.

You can often see a cart being pulled between the barracks by horses or people. It collects the corpses. More will be lying there the next day, with constant additions. It seems to us that they are always the same ones, because those twisted remains of what used to be women are so similar to each other. The rats nibble frenziedly at them.

We lost all sense of time. Sundays were like any other day. We had a bath and delousing this morning. *Aufsejerki* and *oberka* Mandel stood among the block supervisors and male *kapos.* After taking off her striped uniform, each woman had to walk up to the *oberka,* stand still, and turn around. From time to time, the *oberka* simply gave a signal with her whip. The block supervisors then leapt forward and led the woman to another room. Today it was not only the ones with open sores that went, but also those whose bodies were sagging the most. It was a selection, pure and simple. Even if they went out peaceably, the ones picked by Mandel received a furious beating with canes. It was as if they wanted to say to us, "Don't think that just dying is enough. When you die, you have to remember until the last second exactly where you are dying." No one has yet been taken from among our friends, but how long will this luck hold?

A cart loaded with rotten potato peelings passed the barracks today. A few pieces fell to the ground and a couple of women scooped up as much of the rancid garbage as they could and stuffed it in their mouths. Doctor Löw saw it and lamented, "Those madwomen are going to get typhus."

She was right. The groaning started two or three nights later. We made a pledge to each other that none of us would ever reach for potato peelings, even if we were dying of hunger. Various thoughts raced through my mind. What was the difference? Whether you died from a potato peeling or from another illness, in this place you had to die eventually.

In the morning, the block supervisor was screaming, "Nurses from the infirmary are coming and whoever needs bandaging or is sick should report. They'll get medicine and help."

Two prisoners-nurses did in fact come after roll-call. They kept their heads down. Several women stepped forward. The block supervisors walked among the ranks. "Come on women, if anything's bothering you, speak up and you'll get medicine." The invitation was exceptionally polite.

Rózia managed to whisper to one of the nurses about Bronia. She looked at her, but the line of those needing aid was waiting. They left. Those who went for medical help never returned.

I woke up sobbing at night. I had sworn that I would never again cry, yet I could not control my sobbing. I clapped my hand over my mouth so that I wouldn't wake anyone up.

"What is it?" Mummy shook me.

I couldn't get a word out. My sobbing had woken up the women on the lower bunk.

"You haven't got a stomachache, have you? What is it?" asked Doctor Löw in a matter-of-fact way. She checked my pulse.

"Nothing hurts," I stammered between sobs. "I had a dream."

"Stop!" Doctor Löw was upset. "Stop or you'll get a smack in the face. What's wrong with you? Such a big girl!"

"It was a horrible dream. I won't get out of here, I'll die here..."

184

"She's suffered terribly from nightmares since she was a child," Mummy said. "God, I don't think I can take any more."

I gradually calmed down. We were lying in the bunk and Mummy asked me what I had dreamed.

"That you were going away in an open wagon, Mummy, without a roof, and I was running after it in a velvet dress. You put out your hand but it speeded up, you were trying to grab me. I couldn't run any more, my hair came undone and I was almost out of breath when you grabbed me by the hair, but I knew in the dream that I didn't have any hair.

Mummy lay silent for a long time and I thought she had fallen asleep, but then she said in a forced, joking way, "So you see yourself, silly, that it was only a dream. But it turned out all right. We went together."

She was right, of course. The most important thing was the ending. But the feeling of fear and anxiety kept me awake. I don't think Mummy slept either, but only pretended.

Day after day passed the same way, except that the cold and our increasing hunger were signs to us that we were in a bad way. Women were getting sick; many had already come down with pneumonia. The sick people that reported to the infirmary never came back. Once, we asked a nurse what happened to them. She replied hesitantly that they had been temporarily reassigned to another block.

The delousings were agony. They wiped our heads and all the shaved places with those stinking, burning rags each time.

I could see that some of our women's scalps were already turning dark as their hair started to grow back. I didn't even have any fuzz. "Mummy, is my scalp getting darker?"

She looked carefully, "No," she said warily, but then smiled. "You always dreamed about having lighter hair. The only way we could ever give you a shampoo was by promising that it would be blonde afterwards. Maybe now it'll grow back that way?"

"I suppose I must have been really unbearable, Mummy."

185

"No, you weren't unbearable at all. You were just very lively, not like other nice little girls."

"Would you have wanted me to be that way?"

"Not at all. I would never have changed you for a warm little dumpling. Only, I don't know, I guess I never took the trouble to analyse your behaviour."

"If you could go back to those days, would it be different?"

"I think, Stella, that if I had known what I know now, it would have been different. And would you have loved Mania more than me?"

That was a hard question, but I answered with Mummy's own words: "If I had known what I know now, certainly not."

"You clever little thing!" she laughed. "Do you know what? I was jealous of Mania at times."

We often had such night-time talks in the bunk. They allowed us to turn our minds to something other than gloomy topics like the rats on the floor.

One day, new nurses came from the infirmary.

"Anyone sick?" one of them asked. "And is there a Rózia here?"

Rózia was already standing beside them, wild with joy. "Bronia told you!"

The nurses looked around apprehensively to make sure there was no block supervisor near. Rózia put her hand over her mouth too keep from squealing with delight. "Tell me where she is and what she is doing!"

"She's a *szrajber* in the *krankenstube,* for the chief. It's serious work. The chief is Doctor Mengele, very dangerous," they said quickly. "She can't come and go as she pleases."

They handed Rózia a big piece of bread and a rag. "Hide that quickly or the block supervisor will take it." And they were gone.

We declared a holiday in our little group. Rózia had found Bronia after all. We treated it as an extraordinary event.

The situation with my bladder had become catastrophic. I wet myself all night uncontrollably. Our group decided to save up bread to get me some underpants.

Today, they sent us to the *kartoffelkeller.* "You whores will finally do a little work," said the block supervisor. As if it had been up to us!

It was terrible work. We rooted around in rotten potatoes and turnips with rats and mice running over them. Yet it was better than standing at attention in front of the block. While we were sorting that decayed mess, there was a terrible incident.

Janeczka Feigelbaum must have found a relatively fresh turnip and popped it in her mouth. The women *kapos* saw her mouth moving. They attacked her with their rods and beat her so fiercely that we thought they would kill her. Janeczka's mother begged on her knees that she be spared and promised them a week's bread rations, which helped. Yet they must have hurt Janeczka badly because on the way back she couldn't walk and we had to help her.

An unusual occurrence: the *raportfuhrer* with the neck like a turkey came during the morning roll-call accompanied by a whole troupe of *aufsejerki* and several higher-ups. They all kept coming to attention in front of one of them, and we could hear *"Jawohl, Herr Doktor," "Zum Befehl, Herr Doktor."* There was no way that this could have been a good sign, but we watched with curiosity. We supposed it must be Doctor Mengele himself. Older prisoners from Birkenau had told us that he was the worst of the murderers, and that he performed awful experiments on inmates and then killed them. I kept thinking about what I had heard, that he tore the tendons out of people's legs to see if they could walk afterwards, and burned off their organs. I didn't know which ones, but everyone said it was true.

It's terrible to look like a *muzulmanka,* a skeleton woman, but it's also terrible to try to look passable. In order to appear less pale, some of the women scrape off brick dust to make rouge for themselves. In the daylight, that caked brick on their cheeks is grotesque.

My heart is pounding: There's going to be a selection, there's going to be a selection. Four prisoners from the infirmary with white scarves on their heads stand among the dignitaries. I can feel instinctively that one of them is Bronia because she has a bundle of paper files under her arm and those of us who are in on the secret can see that she keeps looking in Rózia's direction. They all confer for a long time until "Turkey" takes out a sheet of paper and starts reading off names, in reply to which the block supervisor immediately supplies the numbers.

I am shaking terribly. Why is he reading names? Is that good or bad? The ones who are called out go immediately to a different line.

"Feigenbaum, Janina," we hear. Janeczka tries to walk as well as she can. She has been limping since her beating.

"Feigenbaum, Natalia!"

He continues reading and carefully observes those who step forward.

"Löw, Matilda!"

I can see a lot of our women in the other line, like Grüner with her "baby" and Reginka Horowitz with Niusia.

"Müller, Berta! Müller, Stella."

I am afraid that I won't walk straight. Then we are in the new line. The woman in the white scarf, who must be Bronia, is facing Rózia and they are staring at each other.

We have been formed into a new group, and we march away. Where to? The fear is heart-stopping again. Would it have been better to stay there? What are they going to do with us? I look instinctively at the tops of the chimneys and the smoke rising from them. Are we getting closer, or not?

***

"Halt, you piece of shit!" They were new block supervisors, but the style was the same. As if we could expect anything different. They counted us and poked us with sticks, some more than others. I got a beating with a stick on the way into the barracks, but not very hard. My left thigh hurts; it hurts all the time now, itching and burning. I have a sort of pimple there but I don't say anything because why should I worry Mummy about trifles?

The block supervisor who attacked me with the cane was horribly ugly and misshapen, so we contemptuously nicknamed her "Gargoyle." She gave us even more trouble than the *aufsejerki.* Whenever she walked around the barrack she had to hit somebody, just like that, even if there was no reason.

We were assigned bunks and this time we got a bottom one. There were straw mattresses and we had no broken window over our heads. I wouldn't have to worry about wetting myself, but the rats would be regular visitors. Luckily, we all ended up close together. The mother of Mietek Pemper, our exceptionally decent head *szrajber* from Płaszów, was with us.

We had a flicker of hope now. The women from the enamelware factory crowed, "You see, Tusia, you sceptic, that almost everybody here is from Schindler's list. We're together."

The block supervisor brought us back down to earth. "Attention," she cried. *"Ruki dolu!"*

"What's that? What language?" An hour of standing as punishment, and no dinner.

They prowled doggedly around the barracks, taking the stick to anyone whose looks they disliked. "You can go to the infirmary twice a week. If anybody craps in the barracks, they'll lick it up!"

We got one dish for every five women, a spoon and a mug.

Janeczka could barely walk and complained of a sharp pain between her back and her hips. Löw and Ilza examined her, manipulating and prodding. They told her that she had a deep bruise that would go away in time. But I wouldn't have been myself if I hadn't overheard what I wasn't supposed to, even by accident. I had developed that kind of ear. So I listened to Ilza and Doctor Löw saying that they suspected a serious bone injury and could do nothing. They did not even tell her mother. I felt very sorry for Janeczka, who was so quiet and peaceful, never did anyone the least harm and never used a dirty word, which was more than I could say for myself.

Mummy had changed visibly and all the women noticed. They joked that she had recovered a bit of hope after our transfer to the new block.

After one of Gargoyle's outbursts, I said that the bitch deserved a smack in the chops. Mummy got angry: "What are you going to grow up to be, if you use that gutter language? You're downright vulgar!"

Rózia laughed. "There you go again, Tusia, teaching your daughter manners in Auschwitz." But such remarks were never malicious, and we liked each other very much.

There was frost in the mornings, and before long the temperature would be below zero. Perhaps they would give us more clothing. Standing for hours in nothing but our striped uniforms was awful, and we shivered day and night.

My thigh hurt worse and worse. The straw mattresses became a torment and seemed to move by themselves, there were so many lice in them.

We had been lying for a long time in the bunk. My head felt hot, and I was trembling all the time. "Mummy, isn't my hair ever going to grow back? Everybody else has at least a little bit, but whenever I touch my scalp there's nothing."

"It'll come, dear. Maybe it's taking longer because of the cold."

"But all of you are cold, and yours is growing back."

After a pause, Mummy said, "Are you asleep? Why are you trembling like that? You're warm." She touched me. "You've got a fever! What hurts, dear? Where?"

"My leg hurts a little, up high on my thigh."

"Doctor Löw, Ilza, come here."

"What's wrong, Tusia?" They were there in an instant. Are you in pain?"

"No, it's Stella. She has a fever, a high one, I think."

They told me to get out of the bunk.

"Yes, it's a fever. Have you got a sore throat? Maybe it's a cold. It's a miracle she's gone so long..."

"She says her thigh hurts, that she's got something there," Mummy interrupted.

They were afraid to go out into the middle of the barracks under the flickering light, so they took turns touching my thigh.

"She's got an ulcer there. It might be open and it's full of pus," they said anxiously.

I wanted to reassure them. "It's nothing. I heal quickly. When I was little, I was covered in scabs, right, Mummy?"

"That's right, yes. You've been scratching all the time lately. Why didn't you say anything?"

"What was I supposed to say?" It had started as a small sore and later, on the straw mattress, it hurt more and more but I thought it was only lice.

Before morning roll-call, the two doctors examined me carefully. They were horrified. "It's an open wound full of millions of lice."

"Rózia, you've got to notify Bronia. We've got to get disinfectant."

"I'll try. In the meantime, clean it out with this." Rózia gave them her rag.

My fever rose and it was hard for me to stand up straight at roll-call when they counted us. A couple of days passed. There had been no chance to communicate with Bronia. Fortunately, she came on her own.

She and Rózia wept with joy over finding each other alive. Bronia lived in the *krankenst.be* and could not leave without special permission. She was the chief *szrajber* and kept the files on the people used in experiments. That was secret work. Carrying a file just in case she met the *oberka,* she had been able to come because her boss was away for the day. She had some bread and a little margarine for us.

Doctor Löw and Ilza butted in on their reunion, and Rózia also got down to business. "You've got to help us, Bronia, because our little one has a fever." I was almost as tall as

Rózia. "She's got an ulcer on her thigh with lice in it and you've got to try to get some disinfectant. You've got to."

Bronia wiped her forehead. "I'll certainly try, and I'll think up a way to send it here." She looked at me. "How old is she?"

"She's supposed to be seventeen, but she's really fourteen."

"Keep an eye on her. She's just the type that bastard likes to pick for his experiments."

She hugged Rózia and left.

In our neighbourhood, if I can use the expression, I noticed deep ditches between the barracks. I wondered what they were for. I heard in the latrine that they were filled with water in the summer, but I did not know if they were to drown yourself in, or for fire prevention.

By their combined efforts and after much saving of bread, the women got me underpants. Mummy rinsed them in the washroom and dried them on her own body, so I could start wearing them as soon as possible. But the underpants didn't help. The gland in my crotch was as big as a pear.

Janeczka and Mrs. Pemper were also sick. One day, for a large payment in bread, Ilza, Doctor Löw and Wanda Penner asked the block supervisor to let us stay in the barrack. Gargoyle took the bread. I was no longer capable of standing at roll-call. Violet streaks ran up and down from the growing, running wound. Bronia had supplied a liquid that burned but did not help.

We stayed inside. Then Gargoyle entered with a shout. "Out you go, you lazy whores!"

I started moving awkwardly around on the bunk, and suddenly my breath was taken away by a series of fearsome blows on my back, head, everywhere. I could not lift myself. She kept hitting me, and I could not stand.

"Go ahead and kill me, you whore. They're going to kill you, too," I croaked involuntarily.

That made her stop! She simply stopped beating me, and said, panting, "Crawl outside, you maggot, before I get the *oberka*."

I dragged myself along the barrack. I don't know how, but I made it. We were standing in our rows and when the women saw me, they could figure out what had happened inside. We were being counted. I only made it through the roll-call because the women helped me up.

We went back inside. Janeczka and Mrs. Pemper told about how Gargoyle had battered me with the stick. They lifted up my striped uniform and I heard, as if through a wall, "She hacked her to bits. She'll pay for this."

I was beyond caring.

The women kept watch over me at night. The rats could smell the pus and whole herds of them ran around the bunk. They were dangerous and did not fear blows from clogs. They stood on their hind legs and emitted a hideous panting or hissing. They were enormous, or perhaps they just looked that way to me.

I heard a noise. The women were rousing Gargoyle out of her room to give her the blanket treatment. They threw a blanket over her head and pummelled her with their clogs. The other block supervisor came in and threatened to report us to the *oberka*. Our women said they would denounce both of them as perverted and say that they held orgies in their rooms at night.

That was the end of the matter, except that Gargoyle went around with a smashed face. I was drifting into oblivion. I snapped out of it every so often, wet and sweating. I was covered with many blankets; the poor women had given me theirs. Scenes from my childhood kept coming back and flitting away again.

I felt something pulling at me.

"Gargoyle, you whore."

"Forget that, dear. Wake up, it's me, your Mummy. I've got soup for you. Sit up and drink a little."

I can't. I want to sleep."

Someone was shaking me again.

"Stella, take a drink. Your Mummy's here," Ilza mumbled. "She cleaned the latrine to get you soup. Just a few sips."

I came to. I wanted to drink that soup, but I smelled the horrible odour of faeces and the latrine. To be nice to Mummy I drank a little, but immediately I threw up. I lay there and heard them talking about me. Nothing mattered.

"Tusia, you have to face the facts," I heard a voice that seemed to come from a cracked megaphone, now louder and now quieter. "She has *erysipelas,* she's infected, and without help she'll soon die. Do you hear me, Tusia? She'll die. She has to go to the infirmary."

Was that my mother crying? My mother sobbing?

"Let her die here in my arms and let me go right after her, but I'll never give her up. Never."

Why were they tormenting me? Why couldn't they let me sleep instead of shaking me.

"It's night. Leave me alone!" I seem to be screaming.

"Stella, dear, we're going to help you. The nurses from the *krankenstube* are here."

"Not that!" I was wide awake.

Doctor Löw and Ilza were pulling me and I clung to the mattress, the only thing that could save me. "Mummy! No! Mania! I'll die there! The rats will eat me! I'm afraid!"

Nobody came to my aid. Mummy stood there covering her face with her hands. I was being taken away by women I did not know, and along the way they were collecting sick women from other barracks. Now and then, one of them snatched me by the hand so that I would not remain behind. I looked around, unable to understand how it was that Mummy was not coming along. I was sure she would catch up with me.

We passed through a gate in a barbed-wire fence. This must have been the infirmary. There was a little room, white smocks, a German, another smock, a nurse, a desk. My striped uniform and underpants were pulled off. A big face in glasses said," *Weg mit die Scheissel"*

That must have been me. They led me out. A door opened and they shoved me inside where it was full of bodies, a whole mountain of bodies, and it stank. Something or someone moved now and then but most of them were motionless.

The door opened. Mummy? No. They threw a body on top of me and liquid was running out of it. Excrement. Excrement was simply streaming out of it. I tried to get out from under that body. I was smothering. I couldn't because something was holding on to my ankle, and I stopped struggling. All my strength was gone. The door opened. I rolled into the concrete corridor with other bodies. Something was still attached to my leg as I tried to crawl.

"Look how she's struggling, Stefka," I heard a voice, "Wait, I'll help you." A hand lifted me up. "Stefka, knock that hand off, a corpse has got hold of her leg, it wanted to hang on to something at the last moment."

Who were those women? Were they going to kill me now? They pulled another person out from under the pile of corpses. I was a little more conscious.

"Maybe someone else is alive in there," I mumbled.

"Mind your own business. And stay ahead of us. You're covered with shit, walking typhus."

They led me into a hallway in the same building. "Climb into that tub."

I looked. It was a big tub, like a laundry tub, and the water in it reeked.

"Go on, get in."

I climbed into the cold, stinking liquid, thick with filth.

"Come on, sit down and wipe yourself off with the rag." It burned like the stuff they deloused our heads with. "Get out!"

I was shaking. They threw me a rag similar to a blanket.

"And my striped uniform?"

"Uniform?" They were puzzled. "You won't need one any more. Lie down here!"

They led me to a bunk with no mattress.

"Now what?" I asked.

They both stopped. "Now you wait."

"For what?"

"For your turn," they said in unison.

"And a bandage?"

"Bandage!" they laughed. "What an idiot! Are you completely new?"

195

They were gone. I looked around. On the bunks lay women with tiny faces and big, expressionless eyes. I had the shakes. I seemed to feel a hand and I pushed it away, I was hitting children because they were catching butterflies but I couldn't reach those children, and Gargoyle suddenly appeared. I called to Mania for help but she was also laughing. I heard a voice, perhaps it was Mania's or perhaps it was Mummy's, saying, "Calm down."

Liquid was being poured into my throat. I choked. "It's all right. Swallow."

This was not a bad voice. I felt somebody touch me. Those were not bad hands. Could I have died? Then death wasn't so bad.

That voice again: "You're alive, you're alive."

I tried to open my eyes. "Did I say something?"

"Yes, you've been chattering practically non-stop."

"So you can talk in heaven. You're an angel and I'm in heaven. And I never believed in such things."

"Open your eyes wide and drink. You don't have to be afraid of me."

I opened my eyes. A woman was standing over me. She had white hair, a young face, kind eyes, and a white smock over a striped uniform. I stared as if she were a ghost.

"Come on, drink a little more." She held my head up. "And don't look at me that way. You can touch me. I'm as alive as you are."

"Where am I? And who are you? How long have I been here?" I asked in astonishment.

"One thing at a time, little one. You've been unconscious, completely unconscious."

"Since yesterday?"

"You've been here more than two weeks."

"How long? Two weeks? What about my leg? It must be completely rotten."

"It's healing beautifully. Now try to go back to sleep."

"Not yet. Who are you?"

"Me?" She thought for a moment. "I'm a prisoner, a doctor, and I'm a very unhappy person, a mother who lost her

196

daughter, perhaps a little bit like you, and that may be why I couldn't just watch you suffer." She was talking to herself, not to me, and tears rolled down her face. "You have to go to sleep now," she said, wiping her eyes.

"Only tell me one thing. Has my Mummy been here?"

"Have you got a mother in the camp? Nobody is allowed in here. This is the epidemiological ward, and thankfully not even the *aufsejerki* come in because they're afraid of catching something."

"So why did you save me? Do you think I don't know that everyone is supposed to die here?"

She didn't say anything, but stood looking at me with despairing eyes. I was so exhausted that I fell asleep crying.

I was awakened by the sound of a thud on the floor. I lay there listening.

"What's your problem? It weighs no more than a child."

I turned my head warily. I had heard that voice before. I could see two women carrying corpses to the back door.

"Stefka, go up on top. There was one more Greek, and I think she's dead now, too. Why the hell do they put them up there when there's room at the bottom now?"

The other one climbed up. "You're right. She is."

Then there was that sound of a body falling, again.

"That's enough for today. We'll do the rest of the bunks tomorrow," one of the women said. "Let's go."

They stopped beside me.

"I can't figure out why the doctor has taken to this one. She hovers over her like a fool."

"You know they gassed hers."

"As if this one will end up any differently."

"But see how she's taking care of her. The fever has broken. It would have been better for her if she had stayed unconscious until the end."

"Forget it, Stefka. She helped me, too. It'll be a year now that I've been carrying these corpses out, because she said I was strong."

"Do you think our time's up?"

"I don't think about it. Maybe something will happen."

"Let's go, you moron. Something, indeed!"

If they hadn't been talking right beside my bunk, I would have started howling. From despair. I recognized the voices – they were the ones who had put me in the tub to wash.

I was wet. The sweat was running down my face and I wanted to get up and run away. But I was wrapped in the blankets and too weak to disentangle myself. I sat up and the whole barracks spun around me.

The doctor came in. "You're sitting up? Why did you uncover yourself? It's below zero. Why are you looking at me in that way?"

How I hated her at that moment. Why hadn't she let me die? I wouldn't even have known when it happened. The one called Stefka would have carried me out.

"What is it? Does it still hurt? Speak to me!"

"Go away, you doctor, you! Why did you have to bring me back to consciousness? Is it easier to die that way?"

"Oh, my poor little thing, forgive me. I couldn't do anything else, it was stronger than I was." She was crying and tried to hug me.

Behind her I could see those enormous eyes staring at me, still alive but already dead.

"Why don't you save her? What did I do to you?"

She turned around. "There's nothing that can be done for her. They need something to make them stronger, and there's nothing to give them. She's going to die today. There was a transport of Greeks, and they had no resistance at all. They've been dying like flies in winter."

"What is it that she's holding in her hand and licking?"

"A crust of bread. She can't even swallow it. She'll die with that crust in her hand. If only I could help them somehow... You have to lie down. It's cold and you're weak."

My anger passed. "What's your name?"

"Mira."

"And what was..." I couldn't say it.

She understood. "Her name was Elżunia, but she called herself Unia when she was little and it stayed that way until the end. We called her Unia. What's your name?"

"Stella. Promise me something, Mira, swear on your Unia, I know you can do it."

"What am I supposed to promise?"

"Just promise."

"All right. I promise."

"No, say the whole sentence, that you swear on Unia to fulfill my request."

She did what I asked.

"Now tell me what you want."

"If they're going to take me to the gas, you'll know when. I heard them saying that there's no other way out of here except to the gas. So you must, you have to give me some poison, because I'm so terribly afraid of the gas. You have promised!"

"Oh God, oh God, how could you?" She covered her face.

"But you promised!" I shook her.

"I'll save you." Now she was crying.

"You can't save me. There's no way out of here."

I had already seen various forms of despair in the face of death, but I would never have believed that anyone could despair because they were alive. Yet I was in despair. I lay there numb. My head was bursting from all the thoughts which crowded in. Was Mummy still alive? Or had the transport left? After all, they had read out our names and transferred us to another barracks.

They brought *muzulmanki*, living corpses, to the barracks every day, and carried out the ones who had died. It was quiet. No one even moaned. Whenever I dozed off, I woke up terrified. I kept feeling my scalp but it was still smooth, with no hair. As if that mattered any more.

Mira came in, bringing bread with margarine and hot water with sugar.

"Where do you get sugar?"

"It can be arranged. There's a repair crew from the Polish camp and they smuggle it in. Medicine, too."

I ate and drank. Mira took something out of a little bag hanging around her neck under her striped uniform. "Swallow this pill."

"Is it night or day? It's always dark in here."

"It's evening, after roll-call. How old are you, Stella?"

"Fourteen. No, seventeen."

"You don't have to be afraid of me, silly. I thought so. My Unia would be fifteen."

"How old are you?"

"Thirty-seven."

"More like twenty-eight, I thought."

"When I was twenty-eight I was one of the happiest women alive. I had a delightful daughter and a wonderful husband."

"Did he die too?"

"I don't know. I hope and believe that he's alive. If I didn't believe it I couldn't go on. They brought my parents and me here with Unia. To this day I cannot understand why I was saved from that transport, I and about fifteen others. Many of them are dead now, but I'm still alive. I often ask why," she said quietly, as if to herself.

I didn't want to interrupt, but the words just flew out of me: "Mira! You have to find out if the transport for Brünnlitz has left yet."

"What's that?" she asked absently.

"I don't know exactly, but that's what it was supposed to be called."

"What was the number of your barracks?"

"I don't know. First there were two barracks, then they transferred us, and then I got sick and lost track of everything. Will you find out?"

"Yes, I'll try."

"And you'll bring me the poison in the morning?"

"Yes, but now you have to sleep. I'll just clean your leg and you should go to sleep."

She brought a little cup full of ointment. She moved like a cat and had such delicate hands that it didn't hurt at all. I touched my thigh.

"What's that hard thing you put on it?"

"Something special so that nothing gets into the wound, and there are no lice in these blankets, at least I hope there aren't."

I wanted to keep her there.

"You know, Mira, when I was little I never got sick. Once I caught cold and Daddy brought a doctor in a cab because he thought I had pneumonia. The doctor was furious because Daddy hadn't even let him get dressed. He threw his fur coat over the doctor's pyjamas. I remember how that doctor yelled that every doctor would end up in the insane asylum if there were more parents like that."

Mira laughed. "Your Daddy must have really loved you."

"He still does. I'm sure he's alive. He's wonderful, he always stood up for me whenever I made a mess of anything and he would say, "She didn't mean it, it just happened.""

"Tell me more."

"My brother Adam got scarlet fever. A nurse came to see him and before she went into his room she put on white gloves so she wouldn't have to touch the doorknob. I was jealous of all the fuss over Adam, and I wanted to have scarlet fever, too. I sneaked into his room once. You should have seen his face! I jumped on him and started kissing him, even though we were always fighting. Then I made him drink out of a cup and I took that cup and licked it and I was sure I already had scarlet fever. The nurse came in and made a horrible scene. I got a terrible spanking, but I didn't catch scarlet fever. Mummy called the same doctor that had been going to the insane asylum. He liked me a lot and stroked my head and said I was free to go into Adam's room because, knowing me, I'd never get scarlet fever. I was very disappointed. But I really didn't get infected then. And now all these problems from a silly leg."

Mira laughed until she cried, and then she turned serious. "You know, it's the first time I've laughed since..."

"I know, Mira."

"In your own way, you were a little terror."

"Maybe I was, but now I would act differently. I would want to be good to my Mummy for all she's done for me, but it might be too late. Have you got the poison?" I came back to reality. "Have you really got it? Surely you don't want me to suffocate in that chamber?"

"No of course not. Now go to sleep. You're exhausted. I'll be looking in on you, so you can sleep soundly."

Mira left. I couldn't fall asleep because I kept reliving the memories and the longing for home and for my childhood. I looked around the bunks. There were only heads, shaved and identical to each other, and those enormous, dark eyes staring into the distance. I could not stop looking at those eyes.

I woke up anxiously every so often that night. I wondered whether it was autumn or winter. The light bulb in the ceiling threw a dim light. I decided to stand up, get out of the blanket, and go to the latrine. I wasn't sure what I wanted, but I had to get up. I struggled with the blanket for a long time, for an eternity. I was worn out and perspiring but in the end I got free. I tried to take step and my legs folded under me. I went back to the bunk. This helplessness drove me to despair. How far was it to the latrine? Five or six metres. I had to make it. I threw the blanket over me. It was heavy and I was shaking with cold. Again, I tried a few steps. I finally made it. I didn't know what I had expected, but I was disappointed. There were two holes and a tiny window very high up the wall. If I had stood on the board I might have been able to make out where I was. But the window was too high. I sat down on the board in desperation and started to cry. That was how Mira found me.

"What are you doing, girl? Why are you sitting here? Why are you crying?" She led me back like a drunk and wrapped me in the blanket. "Do you want to catch pneumonia?

"I just want to die. You said the fence was nearby. I thought it might be electrified."

"Have mercy on me!"

"Like you had on me? Why did you save me?"

"Maybe something will happen." Mira was heartbroken.

"You mean that a miracle will happen – like when they gassed your Unia?"

"Watch yourself."

"Mira, forgive me. I'm horrible. I didn't mean to say that."

"Yes, I know. I'm not angry."

"This fear makes me so loathsome."

"I know, dear, I really do understand."

"Mira, has anyone ever left this block except to go to the gas? Not counting those corpses they drag out of the door like sacks? There's a whole pile of corpses out there. When will they take them away?"

"There aren't so many transports now. They say the war will end soon."

"But when will they take those corpses? And how do they take them?"

"A horsedrawn cart comes. Stella, you're terribly upset. You have to trust me. I'm thinking all the time about how to get you out of here, maybe to a different part of the infirmary. You just have to control yourself."

"I know, I know. But who am I to you, that you shall go to all this trouble?"

"Don't talk that way. You have no idea how much will to survive you've given me."

"Don't be angry. I've always said things I regretted." I threw my arms around her neck.

The next day brought nothing new. Stefka and the other women took out several corpses and threw a couple of barely living women on the bunks.

They stopped near me, and I again pretended to be asleep.

"See, she doesn't look anything like a *muzulmanka*. Her head's as bald as her knee but her eyelashes are so long they curl up, and she's sleeping well."

Whenever Mira came she brought something worth eating, either a better soup, or water with sugar, or bread.

"I must be taking the bread out of your mouth. You give me so much that I'm not hungry any more."

"Don't worry about it. I want you to get up and try to walk across the barrack by yourself."

I took a couple of steps. "What's going on, Mira? Please tell me why you're ordering me to walk. I promise I won't get excited whatever it is, just as long as you tell me!"

"All right. Have you ever heard of someone called Bronia?"

"Yes, that's Rózia's friend." I had to sit down. "Was Bronia here? What did she want? Did she bring news from Mummy?"

"You promised not to get excited."

"I won't, but tell me!"

"She asked about your condition, because the transport might be leaving."

"The transport? Will they leave without me? Mummy won't go! She'd die all by herself, and me by myself. She wouldn't go without me, I know."

I sat taking in the depressing possibility that the transport might have left already, and that Mira only wanted to save my feelings.

"Stella," she said, "I don't know if you can, but try to remember... No, I'll find out," she said to herself.

"What do you want me to remember?"

"Your camp number, the one that was sewn on your striped uniform."

"Wait a minute," I said feverishly. "Let me think. It'll come. I've got it. The number is 76 372."

"You're a wonderful girl. Throw a blanket over yourself and walk as much as you can. I've got to do something."

She went out. I practiced walking as if I were in a trance. I sat down, walked some more, and wasn't even frightened when rats ran between my legs. I bumped against a hand hanging out of a bunk and touched it; she was alive, the fingers moved slightly. I stroked that hand. The sweat was running down my face, and I was thinking of nothing except walking. My bare feet were frozen.

"Have you lost your mind?" Mira was back. "I didn't say you should walk until you dropped."

"But I'm getting better at it."

"Climb right under the blankets. You're like an icicle."

She gave me two pills to swallow and went to work on my legs.

"Mira, your hands are shaking."

"Did you say something?"

"No."

"I've already got a striped uniform with the number sewn on," she said to herself. "It'll work. It has to work."

"What has to work?" I asked stubbornly.

"I don't know exactly, but it'll work, for my daughter's sake, you just might..."

With so much evil around and so much hatred, here suddenly was goodness without limit. How was I supposed to make sense of all this in my silly head? How could there be so much goodness and love in this horribly wronged Mira?

"You know," I said, "it's going to be hard for me to leave you, too."

We were suddenly very close to each other and there was so much I wanted to tell her.

We barely slept all night. Mira ran to the door ever so often. I tried to tell her about how I felt, but she wasn't listening.

"Are you waiting for someone?"

"Yes, Bronia was supposed to come. She should have been here before roll-call. Stand up and let me check whether you've got a rash anywhere." She looked. "There's nothing wrong, except that leg. I'll wipe away some of that white ointment. The wound looks too big. The gland is still swollen. Maybe you walked too much." She was terribly nervous.

"Tell me why Bronia's supposed to come now."

"She has to see if it will work."

"If what will work?"

"Putting you in the transport," she blurted.

My legs felt suddenly weak. "Is the transport leaving today?"

"Today, today. Just keep control of yourself. You're not allowed to cry and you have to be sure that you're absolutely, completely healthy. I know you can do it, I know you now like

I knew my own..." Her suppressed tears seemed terribly painful.

"Where are you from, Mira?"

"From Lublin, from Bełżec, from the ghetto."

Bronia arrived out of breath and perspiring, looking as if she had run kilometres. She had a white band around her head and a white apron over her striped uniform.

"Let me see her." She was watching me through the door. "Oh, Jesus," she moaned. "She has to stand naked in front of the doctor. Naked, you understand? What can we do with that leg? Rip it off or cover it up? I've already faked her file. I searched for it all night by candlelight. I wrote that she had a slight throat infection. If they find out, they'll kill her and me both." She stood with her head against the door, exhausted. "I wrote a different block number."

"Bronia," said Mira, "so much has already been done. Pull yourself together. I've put a uniform with her number on it in the dressing room. She can hold her blanket against her left side while you distract him. We've gone to far too back out now, understand."

"What do I say when they ask about her striped uniform?"

"Say it was infested with lice. She'll be better in a blanket. If she took off her uniform that leg would show immediately. It's time now, Bronia. Take her to a different block, at least. They'll be coming for the corpses in a minute. There's going to be an inspection here."

I stood rooted to the floor like a post. I felt sorry for those women, but I could only stand there and wait. For one second I wanted to cry out, "Go, leave me here," but no, the power of hope pulled me towards life.

"They're already lining up for the transport," Bronia whispered to herself.

"Bronia!" Mira jerked her by the arm. "Do you hear that? They're driving up to the back door. In a minute it will be too late!"

"Come on! Walk in step behind me."

Barefoot and wrapped in the blanket, I followed her. The ground was frozen and I moved as if I was in a trance, just trying to keep up. I wanted to turn around and look back for Mira, but I was afraid of falling out of step.

"Listen to what I say," Bronia panted.

"Slower, because I can't keep up!"

"You have to! When I tell you to take off the blanket, hold it against your left side and don't let it drop. When he asks to see your throat, show him immediately. Stand up straight and don't show any fear on your face. We're almost there."

Violet spots danced in front of my eyes and millions of bells rang in my head, in my ears and in my heart.

We entered an outer office and Bronia disappeared behind a white door. An *aufsejerka* came in. I thought: Stand up straight and don't sway. Another moment and I would go crazy.

The doors opened. There was a rough voice: "Come in!" It was Bronia's voice.

A German stood up from behind the desk. He looked enormous. Was he the one from the selection?

"Take off the blanket!"

I took it off and held it against my left side. I looked him straight in the eye. What colour were his eyes? I have no idea. He was the lord of life and death.

"Turn around!" Just as long I don't get tangled up in the blanket. "Turn back around! Throat! Close your mouth!" All of this was in the same sharp tone.

Then Bronia said smoothly and quickly that I was a trained skilled worker still strong enough to be of use, and that with me the transport would be complete.

I stood there like a plaster statue that could crumble any second. I kept looking him right in the face. It might have only seemed to me that the lord of life and death wore a somewhat bewildered expression.

"Put the blanket on. Out!" Bronia gave me orders as if she were angry, but I think she was pretending.

Bronia picked up the document that he had signed and laid it on his desk. He still had that strange look on his face, as if he were considering something, but I might have been imagining that part.

We left. Would I be able to keep walking? After a moment, Bronia slowed down.

"It worked, understand?" Now, she had a different voice and a different face. "It worked," she was choked up. "Just hold out a little longer. You've been very brave. Such a chit of a thing, and so brave. Now there's just the dressing room and the *raportführer.*"

Nothing at all was registering in my mind. We went inside somewhere and there were women stammering about something. I stood against the wall in fear. They were crying and laughing. They dressed me, putting on underpants, a shirt, a sweater, stockings, socks and finally the striped uniform. Somebody tied a scarf around my head and kept saying, "Birkenau will never forget this, never."

Bronia was impatient and tried to hurry things along. She tied the laces on my big boots.

I kept standing there like a dolt. Bronia pulled me by the hand and I gradually became aware of what was happening. I gasped out, "Tell Mira I love her! Don't forget!"

We entered a vast hall or block.

"Stand here."

It wasn't empty. There were lots of women around and every one of them was crying. Why were they crying? What was going on? Bronia stood before the *raportführer* for a long time, showed him the document, explained something, and then it seemed that they were arguing. He finally took the document out of her hands. Was he going to tear it up? Instead, he picked up a notebook from the desk and roared, "Müller, Stella! Fall into place!"

I walked and walked. When I got there they turned me around and everyone touched me. A hand gripped me like a vice. I looked and saw an old, injured face with almost all the skin torn off one side, on a crippled body.

The female *kapos* and the *aufsejerki* were shouting that we should form rows of five to leave. Was it possible? I would

208

wake up any moment on the bunk among the dying Greek women. And what about that hand gripping me? We were marching.

"Stella, dear, can you walk?"

I didn't have a fever. That was my Mummy's voice! What had they done to her? That ruined, crippled woman was my mother!

I wanted to look around and see if all our women were there, but I was afraid. No sense tempting evil. The *aufsejerki* and a couple of SS-men were walking beside us. I felt that I could not endure a single blow, I was too weak. Doctor Löw was alongside as always, and Natka Feigenbaum and her daughter were ahead of us. Janeczka was trying to walk straight, but I could see that it was costing her a great deal. The motion of her hips was unnatural.

It was quiet now. We must have been passing the crematorium. The smell seemed stronger than before, but I did not care about the crematorium. The only thing that mattered was continuing under my own power. My legs seemed to be getting shorter and sinking deeper into the ground, yet the ground was frozen.

We reached the gate. So Schindler had helped after all. But were we going there? It didn't matter where, as long as we didn't stay here, as long as we got out of here.

Dogs were barking. The siding was surrounded. The *aufsejerki* were going mad, hurrying us along with their whips, unable to forego the pleasure of a farewell flogging. I was worried about getting up into the high railroad car. My legs were aching. How would Janeczka make it? They counted us off by hundreds, so there were three hundred of us. And the others? There had been at least fifteen hundred of us. Were they still alive?

There was no time to think. I had to concentrate on getting in. The women in our group were quick thinkers and the tall Doctor Löw and Ilza were already up and deftly pulling the others after them. Anything to deny them an excuse to beat us. Janeczka was in.

"Give me both your hands, Stella."

I flew up like a bird without seeing or feeling anything, and was inside. Mummy stood beside me holding my hand tight. We looked at each other without saying anything. We might both have been afraid that it was a dream, and that at the first word we would wake up and again be separated.

The wagon was full. They closed it. That was good. We waited for the jerk, it didn't matter in which direction, just as long as we got out of there. Then we were moving. We flew against each other, and it was too tight to worry about falling. I found myself in Mummy's embrace. She sobbed piercingly. I was afraid to touch or cuddle her because she was so badly hurt. I had no idea what had happened, but I could see that it was bad.

The wheels were thumping evenly. The whole car had come alive and more and more women were talking. Some were shouting from one end to the other. Only Mummy and I had not yet said anything.

"Don't look like that, Stella." It was Doctor Löw's voice. "We're already moving, do you hear? Yes," she said with unnatural vivacity, "we didn't think she would get you to us."

"Mira?" I ask.

"What Mira?" Doctor Löw looked disoriented.

"Who then?"

"Bronia. Who's this Mira?"

"It's a long story." I suddenly felt animated. "Do something about Mummy's face before she gets an infection."

"How, and what? We haven't even got any water."

"Ilza, take this shirt off me. I've got a clean one underneath. Some women dressed me. Wipe Mummy's face a little."

"You leave that shirt on," Mummy spoke up.

"Well, then at least tear a strip off it, please!"

Nothing mattered more to me at that moment then delicately to bandage Mummy's face. I tried to tear off a piece of the shirt, but I couldn't. Either it was too tough, or I was too weak.

"Help me," I blubbered.

"All right, we'll tear it."

"Because if Mira hadn't bandaged me," I sobbed, "I would be dead now."

"Stella, you must still have a fever."

"No. Who beat up Mummy like that?"

Had my mother lost her mind? Holding the strip of my shirt in front of her face, she started to laugh. I was stunned. Ilza, Doctor Löw and Rózia laughed, too, but they had embarrassed looks on their faces.

"Well, here's what happened," Rózia began. "When we learned that there was going to be a transport, your Mother said she wouldn't go. She kept repeating stubbornly, 'My child is going to die, and I'm going to die, too.' It didn't help that Bronia promised to do everything humanly possible to get you out. The truth is that we didn't know what kind of shape you were in."

"Or even if you were alive," Ilza added. "We lied to your mother. We told her we had news that you were better, but in fact we didn't learn anything until yesterday. So we decided to keep an eye on her. When the *raportführer* called out her name, we tried to push her to the other side. And she really fought against going. She stepped back when she heard her name. We pushed her, and maybe we pushed too hard, because she landed face first on the concrete. Then the *aufsejerki* let her have it for being clumsy. And it wasn't easy to hold her in line until the moment when..." Ilza paused, unable to go on.

"Until the moment when Bronia brought you in," Rózia finished the story.

"How long was I gone?" I still could not figure this out.

"A long time, you poor thing."

"If not for Mira, I would have died there."

"Who are you talking about?"

"Like I said, she's a doctor who lost her own daughter. She took care of me so doggedly that if it hadn't been for her..." And I burst out crying again. "If only she were with us. She's so wonderful."

"Now, dear, you have to get a grip on yourself. Such is fate."

"It's not fate. It's Mira."

"But think, Stella, what about Rózia, and Bronia? If it hadn't been for them, we wouldn't be together now."

My poor, dear Mummy, such an old woman now.

"Let me take off this sweater so you can put it on." I didn't know any other way to show her my happiness.

"Dear, we're together and that's all that counts. If it turns out that we escape from this hell, nothing will be more important in life than for us to be with each other."

"Let's stop feeling sorry for ourselves. For now, we're moving, and as for the rest, time will tell," Wanda said. "We have to decide about the order: which half sits down first."

Mummy and I squatted by the wall. Our enthusiasm gave way to reflection. What would happen next? Were Daddy and Adam still alive?

"Tusia!" Rózia joined us. "How should I do this? Bronia gave me a piece of bread." Wanda Penner squatted with us, too. "There's not enough to go around. There wouldn't even be one bite for everyone."

"I think," said Mummy, "that we should give it to the youngest ones."

"How many are there? There's Niusia Horowitz, Janeczka has to get some, then there's 'Baby' Grüner, and Stella..."

"I'm not hungry. Mira kept me well fed."

"You be quiet, you have nothing to say about it."

I hugged Mummy cautiously, mindful of her face. "Does it hurt?"

"It doesn't matter. The pain is a joy to me. Take a nap, Stella."

"I'd rather not, Mummy. I have to get used to believing that it's not a dream and we're really together. Do you remember that dream of mine, Mummy?"

"Yes, I remembered it all the time. I pulled you into the wagon at the last moment. I had stopped believing it could come true."

"I didn't believe it either. I asked Mira to give me poison, and she promised she would."

"You really wanted to take poison? You shock me."

"How could I not want to, when I heard in the block that there was no way out of there."

"Poor dear, you've been through a nightmare."

"But Mira was so wonderful, Mummy, such a good woman, and she suffered so because of me. She told me that I had to live, and kept repeating that I had to live for her Unia. That was her daughter. Her name was Elżunia."

"If we make it and survive, I would like to meet this Mira of yours."

I couldn't stop talking about her. "Do you know what she said, Mummy? That I had given her back the will to live. I would give anything for her to be with us."

"I know, dear. She is an exceptional woman."

Mummy was tired, but I had to keep talking.

"She's not allowed out of her barracks. It's epidemiological. If she could get out, she would have a chance to survive. Supposedly, Mummy, the war is ending."

"You see how it's ending. They haven't stopped killing us."

"It's cold. What month is it? It must be December already."

Sometimes we went fast, and sometimes we slowed right down. It stank in the car. We stopped after many hours. We heard voices outside, speaking neither Polish nor German.

"What language is that?" I asked Rózia.

"I think it's Czech."

"Are we there?"

All the women stood up. Now what? Were we moving backwards?

"They're switching us to another track," Ilza said.

The train stopped again. There was total silence. After an hour, or perhaps after many hours, we heard movement outside. We knocked. That was risky, because what if it was a *sturmmann*? Our nerves couldn't take the silence. After a few moments, there was a voice.

"Ano, ja sem tu."

"Where are we?"

"Československo."

"Why aren't we moving?"

All we could understand was that there was no locomotive.

"How did we get here if there's no locomotive?"

"The Germans took it for the army." And then silence.

We stood for a long time. The panic-mongers started saying that we were going to be taken out and finished off. Ilza and Doctor Löw hushed them. Women started praying, and the wailing in a language I could not understand drove me mad.

"Ilza, I beg you, make them stop."

"I can't, Stella. I haven't got the right. It gets on my nerves, too, but it helps them."

Then the wagon gave a jolt! They were coupling the locomotive, and then we would start. I could not quite explain to myself why it was such a joyful thing to be moving off into what was, after all, the unknown. But it was joyful indeed.

Rózia shared out the bread in little pieces, two bites each. The women were getting hysterical again.

"We made it out of there and now we're going to freeze to death on this train, without water or food."

"Calm down over there before I smack you! Everybody's cold and hungry."

Time was playing tricks. We had lost track of how long we had been travelling. One day or two? At times there was a dim gloom in the car, which meant that it was day, and at other times it was totally dark. The train had stopped again.

We stood up. There was a strange voice: "Anybody in there?"

"We're here," almost everybody screamed. "Why have we stopped?"

"They want to take you back to Auschwitz."

We went crazy. Anything except that. Let them kill us here.

The hours dragged.

"Mummy, I'm going to take off my sweater and you put it on for a while at least."

I knew in advance that she would refuse.

"No, dear. Let's press our backs together and we'll be warmer."

We heard someone speaking Czech.

"Hey!" we called. "Do something! Give us something to eat, or a little water!"

"I can't."

It was quiet again. We could hear the heavy footsteps of the sentries. The women started conferring, just to have something to do, about designating one corner as a toilet. But they only wanted to talk, because in the first place it was too late, the car was already filthy, and in any case, how could you get to a corner through a hundred women?

We were moving. It was grey outside again. Were we going back, or not? It was well below zero. Doctor Löw and Ilza didn't allow us to sleep, ordering us to keep waking each other up.

Natka Feigenbaum, who was usually so quiet, kept repeating obsessively: "If Schindler doesn't save us, that means he's dead himself."

Somebody said, "Shut up about Schindler, Natka. He took as much money from the Jews as he could, and that's the last you'll see of him."

Mummy was quiet. I knew that the unattended wound and the dried blood were making her miserable, although she didn't complain. I wanted so badly to help her. I felt guilty again: it was all because of me.

The praying started. Wanda, Rózia and Doctor Löw, who had been calm so far, screamed: "Stop moaning, you cretins! You know what you can do with your prayers!"

They too were losing control of themselves.

"And you, Natka, stop blabbering about your wonderful Schindler and try to lay Janeczka down where she's comfortable. Can't you see how she's suffering?"

Natka seemed not to hear, and just kept repeating, "God will help, God will help."

Ilza and Doctor Löw squeezed through, lay Janeczka down, and threatened Natka that if she didn't get a grip on herself, they would slap her. Finally, somehow, the car quietened down. Then we realized that we had stopped again. We could hear people running around very close to the car, and we stood huddling together.

"They're going to open the doors now, and they could shoot us!" I said to Rózia, who was next to me.

"For heaven's sake, do shut up." I was stunned at how sharply she had spoken to me. Then she took me by the hand. "Nerves bring out the worst in people."

I didn't answer, because I had learned long ago that fear and nerves often hide behind the mask of arrogance or anger.

What would happen now? It would be better to die while the train was moving. The movement was calming. But to stand still and wait like this was horrible.

The train was rolling again. We speeded up. I had to bring Mummy out of her lethargy somehow. "Does it hurt?"

"How should I know? Maybe. I'm not thinking about it. When it hurts, it means you're still alive. We're strong, we can take a little more."

"Mummy, maybe if I rub my head my hair will start to grow back."

"Don't do that. You've got dirty hands and it's rotten enough not to be able to sleep, without you messing up your scalp. It'll grow back. It'll be beautiful."

"And blonde," I added.

She didn't laugh, but I had succeeded.

"You're a dear child," she said. "You're trying to tear me away from my thoughts."

"Well, just a little, Mummy. There's nothing better to do."

"You're right."

4

Brünnlitz

There were grating sounds, screeching and jerking. This had to be our last stop. No one said so, but we were certain. We could hear people talking, mostly in Czech. No dogs barked, which was an enormous relief. Someone spoke in German, but calmly and without shouting. Then the door suddenly opened and the daylight blinded us. *"Raus!"* So they still employed that word. SS-men with rifles approached. We were numb and aching but we jumped out, helping each other. The women handed Janeczka down. Nothing was going on, and no one was beating us or pushing with rifle butts. We felt a mixture of amazement and horror: was it possible the regime could become so mild just before the end? Three hundred women lined up, with a few being carried out further down the train.

A car drove up. Two men got out: one of them rather tall and dressed in an SS uniform, the other massive, in a different uniform, with a slight smile on his face. A whisper ran along the row: the big, powerful man is Oskar Schindler.

Natka, who along with Rózia was holding up the feeble Janeczka, seemed to lose her senses and stammered, "On your knees, on your knees before him."

Janeczka mustered the strength to whisper, "Mummy, be quiet, he's not alone! Control yourself!"

We were counted, and it seemed that noone had died on the way. The SS-men stepped back, saying to each other, *"O, wie die Frauen stinken."*

I was registering everything instinctively. "Did you hear, Mummy? They called us 'women' instead of 'swine' the way they normally do."

"Yes, I heard. You understand well."

"Maybe it's a good sign."

"Time will tell, dear."

In the daylight, Mummy's ravaged face looked awful. The blood had clotted, half the skin was torn away, and one eye was swollen almost completely shut. As Schindler walked along the rank, he held his gaze on her for a moment. That burly man had a strange expression, a mixture of horror, pity and benevolence. It only lasted a moment; the SS-man was walking beside him with his head lifted proudly.

Our row moved forward. We marched through the small train station and onto the road, a real road with narrow verges. There were low houses, like villas and bungalows. I suddenly recalled Rabka, as if through a fog. That little town along the road was like Rabka. Nowhere did we see a soul. The place seemed to have died, although from time to time we noticed that a curtain moved in a window.

Suddenly, the road turned sharp left. The camp gate stood open and the sentries counted our stinking procession. We formed up in a small, oblong courtyard between two buildings. The structure on one side was like a long warehouse, grey, one storey, with several doors. Opposite was a larger, two-storey building with a walkway along the upper storey, divided by a wire screen. Iron stairs led up to the walkway at both ends. On the ground floor was a wide entrance, and we were being led there.

My heart was pounding, and not only mine, because we expected to see our men-folk as soon as we entered. They had been transported out before us, so they should be here. We entered an enormous factory workshop divided down the middle by a wire mesh fence. I noticed a lot of machines, some of them so huge they almost reached the ceiling. Then I noticed something strange. There, on the other side of the screen, was a moving sea of heads.

"Mummy!" I almost screamed, "The men are over there!"

"Yes, I can see." She was shaking feverishly.

218

A second later, there was an uproar. On the men's side, a powerful voice boomed, "Quiet!" He was trying to shout over the confusion. "Quiet! We will read out the names one at a time."

The noise subsided. Wives were called to their husbands and sons; there were shouts and the waving of hands across the wire barrier. I could not recognize anyone as I peered into the crowd because they all looked alike.

"Mummy, it's terrible. I can't see Daddy or Adam!"

"Wait patiently, wait. They must be there, if we could make it and you're alive..." She could not go on.

We waited.

"Stella! Where are you?" It was Daddy! I could not make a sound.

"Where's Stella?" Daddy called.

Mummy pushed me forward. I knew they were there, but I could not see through the flood of tears.

"Stella, call to him. I can't, with this damned face," Mummy whispered.

"We're here! Daddy, Adam!" I finally managed to scream.

Daddy was covering his face; he was crying, too. The greeting went on endlessly. Some cried for joy and others in sorrow.

Pots of soup were brought in, and several men stood over them serving. There was a crush of people; everybody wanted to help, to look, to touch their loved ones. Yet order was preserved. A wonderful smell rose from the tureens; the soup was hot and delicious.

We were led upstairs. There was a large hall without bunks or mattresses, but with its floor covered in straw. It was like a fairy tale; no one had screamed at us or hit us yet. I only wondered whether there would be enough room for all of us, but that seemed unimportant now.

In the doorway stood Oskar Schindler himself, massive, filling it with his silhouette. There was utter silence in the room, but even silence has different hues, and this was not the silence of fear.

He spoke. He had a voice that was powerful but very gentle. "I know that you have been through hell on your way here.

Your appearance says it all. Here also, for the time being, you will be forced to suffer many discomforts, but you are brave women. We did not have a great deal of hope that it would be possible to bring you here. That is in the past now. I am counting on your discipline and sense of order. I think that the worst has been overcome. The bunks should be here in a few days. Now you must put things in order yourselves. The doctors should report to the head physician, and you should elect block supervisors. Doctor Hilfstein and Pemper will show you where you can wash. The sick and those who need bandaging should go with the doctors."

He left. The silence lasted a long time.

Mietek Pemper and Mietek Penner came in. We exchanged hugs with Penner, who was laughing. "Tusia," he said, "what a softie that husband of yours is I had to keep reassuring him day and night that you were alive, when I was almost going crazy myself. But I've got a little flask of something that I'll pass on to Wanda later."

It turned out that only ten women at a time could fit into the washroom. We waited to wash in a orderly, peaceful way until late at night. Doctor Löw and Ilza took possession of the *krankenstube,* located right next to the factory floor. It was crowded there, with not more than ten beds. They were already dressed in white smocks, beaming despite their fatigue.

It was late. Ilza came running in. "Tusia, Janeczka and Stella, come with me to the *kranken."*

It was as clean as a real hospital. Doctor Hilfstein went to work immediately on Mummy's face.

"They really gave it to you," he puffed. I could not see what he was doing, but only heard his instruments clinking. "It's a wonder you didn't get an infection, dear. Now it's going to hurt a little, but I have to cut some of that mess out." He talked to himself all the while. "It should heal up without a trace. You're so beautiful. Oh, I remember you from the ball, you were there with the Grünbergs and I could only dream about a dance, you were in such demand. Yes, indeed. Now you're like new. What, you still can't smile? It'll pass. Save me a waltz at the next ball."

Ilza dressed my wound. Doctor Löw put Janeczka on a cot. Doctor Hilfstein ran around kissing us as if he were eighteen again. But he examined Janeczka for a long time with a serious look on his face. Ilza hugged me and said I was healing beautifully. Now I finally dared to look at Mummy. Although her face was smeared and sprinkled with something, it no longer looked a ghastly mask.

I really took a liking to Doctor Hilfstein, and perhaps that is why I went up to him suddenly, without even thinking first. "Doctor, I've got a big favour to ask."

Everybody looked at me, wondering what had come into my mind. Still in a cheerful mood, Doctor Hilfstein said he would do whatever I asked. I took a deep breath.

"Could you please, Doctor, allow my Daddy, Adam and Mr. Feigenbaum to come in here for a moment?"

He stood looking at me and burst out laughing. "Think for a minute, dear. Perhaps you'd like to invite somebody else, too? You've got nerve. But all right, just this once. My word is my bond. Just keep it hush-hush."

" Yes, of course."

Ilza and Doctor Löw brought supper: white bread with marmalade and hot tea, some sort of herbal tea instead of the real thing, but still wonderful.

Then they came tiptoeing in. Crying like a baby, Feigenbaum kissed his wife and daughter. "You'll get better," he stammered to Janeczka. "They said you were all dead, gassed. Schindler himself went to Auschwitz but they didn't want to let your group out." He was unaware of what had happened to Janeczka. "You've just caught cold, you'll get over it, it'll pass."

Daddy and Adam stood like two pillars of salt, looking at us. Tears ran down Adam's face.

"Don't cry," I shouted, and then started howling myself, as if all our wrongs had only now hit home.

And that big brother of mine said, "You know what? I made a spoon for you."

221

Daddy and Mummy hugged each other for a long time. "And here we are, together," Daddy said.

"So what's up, sister? Adam kept repeating.

"You know what?" I said stupidly, "We've finally changed roles. You've got the beautiful hair and I'm bald, so I can beat you up." I gazed at him admiringly. My brother was so tall, taller perhaps than Daddy now, and very handsome.

"What's that stink coming from you, sister?"

"Shit, I think."

"Stella, the way you talk," said Daddy in a shocked tone.

"You see, Dad," Adam cut in, "nothing's changed." There was so much joy on every face that even the reprimand sounded affectionate.

The initial wave of emotion was subsiding. Now, everybody had a story to tell. I was Adam's audience. He told how they were equipping the factory, which was to produce ammunition.

"Do you mean we're supposed to make weapons to kill our allies?" I was outraged.

"Don't be childish," he said in a superior way. "Schindler told us that none of those shells will ever kill anybody, but we have to work and he'll take care of the rest." Adam said this so proudly that you would have thought he and Schindler had planned it together.

Mummy was telling Daddy something and glancing at me every so often with a concerned expression. Doctor Hilfstein started signalling that the visit should end.

Before Daddy left, he hugged and kissed me and then touched on the tenderest point. "Did they shave your head today on top of everything else?"

"No, my hair must be offended at me or something. It doesn't want to grow back." I tried to laugh, but felt like crying.

Mummy made a sign to him, probably trying to communicate that he should drop the subject, but it didn't work. He kept stubbornly stroking my bald head and saying in an angelic voice, "You're beautiful, dear, even without hair."

Doctor Hilfstein was hovering around meaningfully. "So, enough of this love. The women are barely alive and need their sleep."

Daddy and Adam walked out backwards, just to keep us in sight longer.

It had been many, many years since I had fallen asleep with such a feeling of blessed peace, without fear, without screaming, without rats. Ilza had taken my striped uniform to be washed and said that she would keep me in the *krankenstube* until it was dry, which was legal in any case since my dressing would need changing. Doctor Hilfstein warned us that Leipold, the camp commandant, was dangerous and had to be watched. Schindler was doing everything he could to keep Leipold in line, but we should be careful.

In the morning, I woke up lethargically. Morning is a funny word to use, since it must have been after eleven. I tried to make sense of the extraordinary events of the last hours, touching myself and my bunk to make sure that I wasn't dreaming.

Then I remembered that Janeczka should be there. "Hey," I called, too lazy to raise myself from the bunk. "I'm ashamed of myself. Why didn't they throw me out? It's so late."

"Don't worry," she replied in her usual quiet, gentle voice. "Your uniform's still wet, and you could still get sick."

"Come on! I'm already healthy." I jumped up.

"We had such a laugh over you. They put a piece of bread right under your nostrils and you twitched your nose like a rabbit and smacked your lips like a piglet but you couldn't wake up. The doctors were laughing, and they announced that you were in critical condition. Doctor Hilfstein laughed the loudest."

To my joy, Janeczka seemed lively and kept laughing.

"What's so funny?"

"They wanted to play a terrible trick on you, but Ilza wouldn't let them."

"What?"

"You know, I can't say it." She was embarrassed.

"Come on, tell me."

"They were going to scream, 'Get up, you lazy whores!'" said the delicate Janeczka, blushing. "But Ilza told them to forget it."

"Has my Mummy gone to work?"

"Yes, the women are getting work assignments."

I ate breakfast, dry bread, but white and delicious, and cold herbal tea. I couldn't imagine that the freedom we dreamed of could be any better.

"You know, Stella, I'm jealous of you. I'd like to work too," said Janeczka gloomily. "I can't walk on my own. They said I have to stay in the infirmary for now."

"Don't they call it a *krankenstube* any more?"

"No, now it's the infirmary. I know there's something seriously wrong with me."

"Janeczka, you just need to rest and then you'll be able to walk. I have pains in my back too, sometimes."

"I know. From when Gargoyle beat you. But I can't do anything. It hurts really badly. I can't tell you how badly."

Her depression worried me.

"You know, if Mr. Schindler can do so much, then I'm sure he'll arrange for you to be taken to a real hospital where they'll make you better. You have to believe that."

"I'm trying. When you were in the epidemic ward of Birkenau, did you believe you'd make it?"

"Not very much, except that I could never imagine myself as a corpse being gnawed at by the rats, and then I thought that I had to live. You also have to believe that you're going to be healthy."

"It's a shame you won't be in the hospital. It's more fun when you're around."

"Ilza will let me visit."

Since I didn't have a uniform and the doctors weren't around, I climbed back under the blanket. I saw that the window was frosted over. It must have been below zero outside, but it was warm and quiet there.

"Is there a latrine here?" I asked Janeczka.

"There's a little lavatory against the wall."

That was where a small stove was giving out that wonderful warmth, and where my uniform was drying. Further on were several beds for male patients, but they were empty which meant that, fortunately, nobody was sick.

The doctors came and changed my dressing. They laughed about how the Czech air was doing wonders for me; I was healing well. Mummy also came to get her dressing changed. A long time would pass before her face healed.

"Starting tomorrow, dear, you've got a work assignment. I don't know how you'll make out. You'll be working on a lathe."

I cannot say that I was thrilled by this news. Would I manage? Mummy read my thoughts.

"Don't worry. You'll learn."

She reached out to stroke me, and I saw that her fingers were also bandaged.

"What's that?"

"Oh, nothing serious."

"Did it happen today?"

"No, it was when we had to find a way to get you out of that epidemiological ward. I forced poor Rózia to go looking for Bronia. We were crawling between the barracks at night to get to the ward, and there were these ditches, pretty steep, and we fell in. We couldn't get out, so I scratched footholds for Rózia to climb out and the ground was frozen..."

"And you hurt your fingers," I added.

"Well, there's no need for such a tragic expression. As you see, it was worth it." She smiled. "And poor Rózia still has the skin on her back torn. I tried to lift up the barbed wire while she crawled under but I didn't have the strength and it fell on Rózia's back and cut right through her uniform. She was afraid to cry out, and I pushed her through, poor thing."

"But Mummy, weren't you afraid that the wire was electrified?"

"No, I wasn't afraid of anything. Maybe I even wanted it to be electrified."

"Didn't you believe that you would get me out?"

"To tell you the truth, dear, I didn't believe it. Now I know that the only thing you can believe in is good people, and that's what those women turned out to be."

My mind went back to the nightmare I had recently lived through. I concluded, without sharing my thoughts, that

225

something must be wrong with me. Just the other day, I had been tormenting poor Mira over how I wanted to poison myself, and now little things made me happy and trifles made me angry. I didn't like myself. But was I the only one like this? After all, I had seen people who had lost their loved ones. Their behaviour was also normal or, if you prefer, abnormal. I was incapable of working out what was correct.

And yet, when I start agonizing over something, I agonize over it to the bitter end.

"Mummy, is it possible that, after all these years, I'm, well, a little abnormal?"

"What are you talking about?"

"I don't really know."

"Idiot," she commented.

"Ah, you see."

Janeczka's good-natured laughter interrupted us. "Stella has the most improbable ideas."

"Indeed," Mummy assented resignedly. "It sometimes seems to me that she's serious and really has become a little wiser." She waved her hand in surrender and changed the subject. "You know what? The men have carved wooden needles."

"Wooden needles?"

"Listen, blockhead, I'll explain. Wooden knitting needles to make sweaters with."

"I thought this was supposed to be an ammunition factory."

"It is, but let me finish for once! There used to be a spinning factory here, and the storeroom is full of yarn or thick thread. With winter coming, well make sweaters in our spare time. It'll help us survive. You've got a silly look on your face."

"Because I haven't got the slightest idea of how to make sweaters and I doubt if I'm going to like it."

"There you go," Mummy said indignantly. "She's already choosing what she'll like and what she won't like."

Fortunately, Doctor Löw and Ilza came in. They were carrying packages of medicine that Mr. Schindler's wife had collected for the hospital. I was surprised – so he had a wife! They told me she was a small, pleasant blonde.

"She must have been very ill. She holds her head to the left, as if she were slightly paralyzed," said Ilza. "She'll be coming here for massages."

"Do you know how?" Doctor Löw asked Ilza.

"Me? I'm a gynaecologist, but there's nothing to it. I've already got a plan. We'll teach Natka to do it, and that way she can work in the hospital and be with Janeczka."

"What will Doctor Hilfstein say?"

"We outnumber Doctor Hilfstein two to one. I've already talked to him and he agreed, of course."

So the problem of keeping Natka and Janeczka together was quickly solved. Natka was radiant.

Ilza went on: "I've also told Doctor Hilfstein that we need another woman to help with the cleaning, and a male orderly, too. Pick the weakest people."

"You've arranged a lot," we said with satisfaction.

"Yes, and I've also found out a lot. Commandant Leipold interferes in everything and without asking Mr. Schindler he has requested that *kapos* and *aufsejerki* be sent here."

"You found out too much. *Kapos* and *aufsejerki* are bad news."

"You're coming out with me, Stella," Mummy said.

Ilza objected. She said there would be no problem with my staying there where it was comfortable and warm and not overcrowded like upstairs.

"No, Ilza dear," said Mummy good-naturedly. "I know you want the best, but I had an unpleasant scene today. A woman told me that she thinks I'm under special protection. Her husband was left in Gross-Rosen while I have my whole family here and, in addition, my daughter is malingering in the hospital. You understand. Stella has to share the discomforts with everybody else."

Ilza was furious. "But I still have to look after the dressing on her leg. Let me go upstairs to tell that woman what I think."

"Please don't. Stella can come here to have her dressing changed."

It was dreadfully crowded up there. I learned that some of the men would be going out to work cleaning the streets and woods. Schindler was afraid that Leipold would come to the conclusion that there were too many people killing time in the factory, because in fact there weren't enough work assignments to go around. Mummy added that Leipold, a healthy young malingerer, ought to be happy he's not at the front. Hatred sometimes obscures common sense.

To me, the factory is black magic. All those machines stand in a line and I have no idea what the monsters are for. With one blow, they stamp a big steel plate into a pipe called *buksa*.

"You're going to grind the *buksa* on the lathe," our foreman patiently explained to me.

Mummy stood beside me to check whether I understood.

"And what happens to the *buksa* afterwards?" I asked.

"Afterwards, it's put in a crate and sent to another factory where they fill it with explosives."

I looked fearfully at the lathe, the devil's handiwork.

"Where will Mummy work?"

"Beside you, packing."

We got soup in the factory. Mietek Penner came by and gave us baked beets, which were wonderful. He also gave Mummy a cigarette; working outside the camp, he was always getting things.

I was surrounded by men. "Come on, little one. Time for your first lesson. The most important thing is to get a feeling for when it's finished so you don't burn the blades."

They showed me how to turn the machine on, which wasn't so bad. I burned the blades on the first *buksa*. After an hour I was exhausted and ready to give up.

"Couldn't I do anything else?"

"Out of the question. You're supposed to be a skilled worker. There will be inspections. You can't risk being sent back to Birkenau as unskilled."

Sent back from here? That possibility hit me like a lightning bolt. I felt numb all over, and started working. I was still standing by the machine trying not to burn the blades long after they had given out supper.

I learned that Dolek Horowitz with Ryszard and Doctor Gross with his son had indeed been left behind in Auschwitz. The fathers had stayed of their own accord rather than leave their children. Now I finally understood why Niusia Horowitz was crying all the time.

I had hoped that I had conquered the fear that had so often led to fits that looked almost like epilepsy. I had thought the night-mare was over forever. But the war was still on.

We went upstairs to the dormitory. That small space had to hold about three hundred women. When they lay down next to each other like sardines, there was no question of any room to walk about. It was a horrible night after the luxury of the hospital. At a signal, the whole row would turn over from one side to the other. There was bedlam when one woman got a stomach ache and couldn't make it through the crowd in time. The malicious ones, and there were a lot of them, screamed that she was a pig. The same thing happened again the next night. It turned out to be typhus.

Doctor Löw and Ilza quickly brought the situation under control. By agreement with Doctor Hilfstein and Doctor Aleksandrowicz, they decided not to tell anyone, except of course Schindler. He agreed that it should be kept a secret from Commandant Leipold. Schindler got the necessary medicines, the infected were somehow kept isolated in the hospital, and we were lucky enough to avoid an epidemic.

We were working two shifts, day and night. The women spent most of their free time making those horrible sweaters. It was a strange kind of thick, hard, springy wool, so stiff you could almost cut your fingers on it. In order not to be worse than the others, I learned how to knit a little. Mummy and I took turns making sweaters. They were terribly scratchy but they gave some protection against the cold, and the factory was chilly. The sweaters were life-savers for those who left the camp to work in the open air.

They finally brought mattresses and narrow bunks. Two people had to share, sleeping head-to-foot. It worked somehow if they liked each other, but there were also terrible fights.

Leipold was starting to make his influence felt. We got a *kapo* called Müller who was said to have a platinum plate in his head after being wounded on the Italian front. I looked him over discreetly trying to decide whether he would give us trouble. That piece of platinum must have affected his mind. From the first day he ran around the factory like a madman, carrying a whip, of course. He had obviously learned only one word in Italy and kept shouting *"Avanti!"* >From that time on nobody ever referred to him in any other way. I often wondered where the idiot got the strength and energy to run like that all day. Fortunately, the way he constantly shouted *"Avanti!"* made it easy to locate him. But there was more tension at work now.

The *aufsejerki* came a few days later. Schindler had tried to reassure us that they were harmless, just a couple of ordinary Dutch cows (they were indeed tall and heavy), but merely knowing that they were there, walking around the factory, was depressing.

Various commissions appeared in the factory, always accompanied by Schindler but also by Leipold. After such visits, we could hear drinking parties going on long into the night in Schindler's apartment. The strangest thing was that he was never seen drunk in the factory, although his voice was the loudest during the parties.

Sometimes the men coming back from outside work brought cooked potatoes that they had got from the Czechs. They had been afraid that the sentries would give them trouble, but the latter simply pretended not to see anything.

I was having a hard time at work because I kept burning the blades. During the day I was careful, but at night it was worse. I was afraid of Avanti and his shouting; I could feel instinctively that I'd end up getting it from him. So it was. He gave me harmless tap across the hands with his whip. It terrified me so that I stood there with my mouth open like a cretin. He stared at me, amazed at my reaction. The machine kept running until a blue haze rose above it, and then I switched it off.

"Auschwitz!" he roared, and mimed a chimney with smoke coming out of it. Then he shouted: "Sabotage!"

And I stood there nodding. When he had quieted down a little, I think I drew courage from my fear, because I stammered, as well as I could, *"Meister, prima zeigen, ich lernen."*

He understood, the idiot, and grinned. He took off his cap and rolled up his sleeves. Thus began my lessons with the help of Avanti. >From that day on, when I was on day shift, he stood by the lathe doing almost all my work for me. Nights, I sat behind him on the boxes and only got up from time to time to give cries of delight, which pleased him greatly. Once, he even brought me a piece of bread with sausage, and another time he said, *"Nicht Auschwitz."* I felt that I wouldn't get any more beatings from him.

One day, big shots visited the factory. A German stopped at my machine. I shivered from my bald head to my feet. I realized that without hair I looked even more childish than my real age of fourteen. They had all gathered round when I heard Avanti explaining that I was one of he best lathe operators. He pulled a few finished *buksa* out of the crate, showing how beautifully they were made. I will never know if he regarded them as his own work or mine. In any case, without knowing how I managed, I worked without error, silently telling the blades, "Just don't burn now, you idiots." They finally left.

Avanti must have been convinced of my skill because he came back a moment later and said, *"Prima arbeit, gut!"*

The other workers were happy about the way he spent hours at my machine. It gave them a little peace. He did hit people fairly often with his whip. He wouldn't flog them, but his single blows were forceful.

Only Mummy was unhappy with his patronage. For several days, she kept saying, "We have to transfer you, I don't know where, because who knows what sort of ideas could come into that idiot's patched-up head."

Wiluś Kranz finally took me back to the shipping department. Avanti went dangerously crazy, screaming that he had been deprived of his most skilled worker and would complain to Leipold. It was decided that it would not be advisable to get the commandant interested in a girl who now looked like an over-grown ten-year-old. I returned to my post at the lathe the next day. Avanti ran up happily, repeating *"gut, gut,"* and laying a piece of bread with liver sausage on my machine.

Regina Horowitz and Zunia Gross, in despair over their sons and husbands, got up the courage to go to Schindler with a request that he try to get them to Brünnlitz. He replied that he was trying, but had been threatened with the liquidation of the whole camp. He said the only good thing was that the war was drawing to a close. They were heartbroken, especially Regina. Small and petite to begin with, she was just a dried-out fragment of a human being now. Explanations by her daughter Niusia didn't help. All she cared about was Dolek, her beloved husband. It was plain that the end was approaching, but the Germans were still liquidating people.

Our rations grew scantier. Even Schindler was having trouble arranging provisions, despite the letters he kept sending about how essential we were to the salvation of the Reich. There simply wasn't any food. Mietek Penner kept changing jobs. Now, he went out with the group that cleaned the streets. This was a real sacrifice because it was well below zero. Yet he always managed to come back with something, usually grain from the nearby mill. The owner pretended not to notice when the prisoners filled their little bags. In fact, it was bran. After being ground between two bricks and mixed with some sort of husks and water it could be baked into little cakes. They were strange cakes, with the great advantage that they took a long time to chew and swallow. They tasted like sawdust.

Oskar Schindler's wife occasionally walked through the factory with the *aufsejerki* and her two Great Danes. When I saw the dogs for the first time, I froze. Then I realized that they were not the bloodthirsty monsters from Płaszów. They did not pay attention to anything, but walked calmly at Mrs. Schindler's heels. She was short and slender, with her head twisted to one side and a sad look on her face. When Ilza and Doctor Löw came to visit us, they reported that Mrs. Schindler was a very good person.

My leg and Mummy's face were almost healed although she still had scars that the doctors said would disappear with time. All the women had fine heads of hair by now, at least none of them was bald. But I could not find a single hair on my scalp. That hadn't seemed so important when I was unsure of surviving from one minute to the next, but now it was enough to drive me into a rage or despair. I tried to control myself, especially when I saw the frightened look on Mummy's face, but I couldn't always stay calm.

The New Year is coming, and the women have made Schindler an incredibly beautiful steel floral bouquet from the strips of metal left over from milling cartridge casings. I think that even the most devout Jews must pray to Schindler now, and not to God. He has been clever enough to hire two local Czech women as his house-keepers, rather than using prisoners. He does whatever he can to make it seem that we are all vital skilled workers.

The drinking parties he is always holding for reasons known only to himself have motivated him to get instruments for the Rosners. These are Regina Horowitz's brothers. Thanks to them, we can find out what is said during those binges.

During the last one, when Schindler was practically bathing his guests in alcohol, one of them cried out in his cups, "You know, Ossie, it's about time you scheduled the liquidation of your camp." Schindler's reply was "No, let those Jewish swine work for the good of the Reich. I'll squeeze them till the pips squeak." At that, one of the big shots stood up and declared with a reverent look on his face that a patriot like Schindler should be an example to them all. He promised to try to get some sort of nomination or medal for such an outstanding citizen. Then there were drunken embraces and backslapping. The Rosners said Schindler had tears in his eyes. The Germans thought he was so touched, but he was really just trying to keep from bursting out laughing.

The *aufsejerki* behaved rather decently. Mrs. Schindler often invited them for tea and although none of us believed that doing so could have been a pleasure for her, it allowed us free access to the latrine.

Both of the Schindlers did what they could to make our lives easier. Avanti had a bad day once and beat a prisoner. Schindler came into the factory then and, with a benevolent look, offered him some vodka. Avanti refused, pointing at his head. Alcohol must have been bad for him. Schindler roared, *"Das ist ein befehll"*

Avanti stood at attention and drank a whole glass of vodka. Then he went to his cubicle and dozed off for several hours.

Early on New Year's Day morning, before the *aufsejerki* and Avanti showed up, Schindler and his wife came to the factory. This had been arranged beforehand by Pemper. They were given that lovely steel bouquet, and then we softly sang *"Sto Lat"*.

Unable to control his emotions, Schindler thanked us. He said, "As long as I remain alive, so will you. The war is ending now and we have to try to survive. We cannot lose heart because of difficulties, especially with food. The road to survival, for you and for me, has not been easy. But you are alive. Keep trusting me, because there is no way to tell what sort of struggle for life lies ahead of us."

People wept and thanked him. His voice broke, and he left quickly with his unique bouquet. On the way out he said that we had the day off and could go to our quarters; he had arranged it with commandant Leipold.

We went upstairs. For years we had been unaccustomed to a life without harassment or work, and now we sat there in silence. Just as I had once been unable to imagine the war, I now found that I could not imagine freedom. The gate would open and we would walk out, with no one screaming at us or hanging over us with a whip, and we wouldn't have to march in ranks... No, I simply could not imagine it.

"Mummy! I'm going to look like an idiot in a dress and with a bald head."

She looked at me in puzzlement.

"What are you thinking about?"

"He said the war was ending, didn't he?"

"Oh, Stella dear, don't get carried away with your fantasies. It's not over yet. By then, you'll have beautiful hair." But I could not see any certainty in her eyes.

It might be a fault of mine that I swing so easily from joy into despair. Nothing came of my meditations on freedom, so I tried analyzing what Schindler had said. He had clearly stated that he did not know what dangers lay ahead of us, and yes, as I had heard many times, the front was fast approaching. They would want to get rid of us, to shoot us. Would Schindler be capable of helping us? After all, he was only a man who had been labouring stubbornly to save a handful of starved Jews, and the fact that he had managed so far was no guarantee that he wouldn't trip up some day.

Halinka "Baby" sat down beside me. She had already made her great plans and started telling me again with enthusiasm about how Zev was going to take her to America.

"Just you or your whole family?"

She looked a little embarrassed. "At first just me, because we'll have to make a start there. You know," she went on, "his father left his fortune in safekeeping with a friend near Bielsko, so first we have to go there."

I stopped listening to her tale, but couldn't stop staring enviously at her beautiful, shiny hair. Was it worth it to survive the war and be bald? I could not even become a nun because I didn't believe in anything, and they prayed all the time.

"Mummy, do the Jews have nuns?"

She was dumbstruck. Then she said, "Dear, I think you're still sick."

I had been crying a lot lately. As if at a signal, the tears streamed down my face.

"It's all right, dear," she hugged me. "I'm a terrible mother, because how could you know anything, poor dear?"

Rózia intervened. "What's she crying about now?"

"On, nothing serious," Mummy said in chagrin.

Rózia said, "Come on, Stella, let's go visit Janeczka."

"You could run into an *aufsejerka*" Mummy objected.

"Tusia, it'll be a good deed. Janeczka's really in a bad way and it'll cheer her up."

"Then go," Mummy said, without neglecting to add, "But be careful. Don't forget to say hello to her from everybody, Stella."

Rózia laughed and said, "Still teaching her good manners in camp, Tusia. Be patient, the time will come when you can really start her education. I wouldn't want to be in Stella's shoes then."

We sneaked into the hospital and there was great joy. Doctor Löw and Ilza both had to hug me and then they made me show them my leg. We crept up to Janeczka and kissed her, wordlessly. I was afraid I would cry. Janeczka looked very different, sallow and shrivelled. I made an effort and said, "Janeczka, you look a lot better."

"I'm glad you came, Stella." She ignored my remark on her appearance.

I chattered on trying to cheer her up and she seemed to enjoy hearing about my cooperation with Avanti. Mrs. Feigenbaum trembled with delight at seeing Janeczka laugh. In the end, I ran out of funny stories.

"Look at my head, Ilza," I said.

"It's lovely." She tried to sound jolly. "Don't scowl. You know what the most important thing is."

"Yes, Ilza," I recited, "a living head on living shoulders."

Doctor Hilfstein looked in, hugging me and joking about what a way this was to greet the New Year. Then he returned with steaming herbal tea. "My pleasure, my dear little one, I've always had a soft spot for you. This is supposed to be for the patients," he said, adding a spoonful of sugar.

What a feast.

That was how we greeted 1945. It was a pleasant day in comparison with the preceding years, when we had been treated to special massacres and harassment on holidays.

***

Work went on normally. The frost was heavy and even at the lathe I had to keep rubbing my hands together. Avanti no longer ran around madly; there was a little stove in his cubicle and the *aufsejerki* often sat there with him.

Schindler had to use all his diplomatic skills against Leipold. One day the commandant ordered roll-call to be held outside. Before the *aufsejerki* could get us outside, Schindler was in the factory. He objected strenuously, saying he had to have people capable of working and not frozen dummies. That was what the Fuhrer demanded of him. When he talked that way, Leipold stood at attention and looked admiringly at him. We knew well what Schindler was fighting for. "What an actor," people said.

We were bothered by increasingly frequent inspections. When they strolled through the factory, Schindler always talked the loudest, as if he wanted to reassure us: it's all right, I'm here. One day the men said they were sure they had seen Amon Goeth going into Oskar Schindler's apartment. We fell into a panic. What was Goeth doing here? Some people had it figured out: he had come to liquidate us. They talked all night. Some of the men were in favour of a mass escape, but others asked where 1,700 people could hide.

Mietek Penner came in the morning, aware of how frightened we were. He explained that immediately after our transport out of Płaszów, Goeth had been charged with appropriating Jewish valuables and dismissed from his post as commandant. There was probably going to be a trial. He had only come to see Mr. Schindler for a moment and had left immediately. The most important thing was that he had left. Mummy and I immediately felt joyful, because if Goeth was gone from Płaszów that meant that Aunt and Uncle Grünberg would survive the war. They would be alive for sure, and they might even be free now.

Having so much trouble feeding us, Schindler often went around the nearby towns with a truck. We were nervous every time he left, fearing that Leipold would decide to liquidate us while Schindler was away. He could just have us shot. He came into the factory once during Oskar Schindler's absence and beat a prisoner for no reason at all, and then led him outside for half an hour of *stillstand* in the bitter cold. The *aufsejerki* would only let us go to the toilet at set times, which never happened when Schindler was present.

We sent representatives to Schindler: Mietek Pemper, Mietek Penner, and Doctor Hilfstein, who reported truthfully that he had bandaged the beaten prisoner. From that time on, Leipold left us in peace. Whenever Schindler left the camp, his wife came to the factory and invited the *aufsejerki* to her apartment for tea.

The freezing spell continued through the end of January. One day there was nervous excitement in the factory from early morning. Wiluś Kranz, who was everywhere carrying things on his wheelbarrow or putting things in order, told us why. Oskar Schindler had been informed that a couple of railway wagons had been standing for several days at a siding in Zwittau. They were frozen over and the doors were sealed, but human voices could be heard from inside.

That evening, Schindler gave warm clothing, electric torches, axes and blankets to a couple of prisoners. He loaded them into the trucks, also taking one of the doctors along, and they drove there. It was unclear what was done with commandant Leipold. Penner claimed he had been sent off to drink with some friends and a woman, who had been instructed to keep him suitably occupied until morning. In any case, he was not seen in the camp that night.

Around sixty men were brought in the next morning in an indescribable state. They were complete wrecks, stinking of excrement and urine, frozen and barely alive. We learned that there had been more, but they were already dead. The corpses were frozen to the waste on the floor of the railway wagons and it had been impossible to remove them. Schindler ordered the little storeroom next to the hospital cleared out, and he placed the unfortunates there. He brought out the last reserves of corn meal that he had been keeping for a moment of real need.

Now a struggle began to save the lives of those poor men, who could not even tell us where they had come from or how long they had been travelling. Several more or less fit prisoners were taken from the factory to help nurse them. Within a week many had died, but the rest were saved. We were happy that at least a handful of men had been pulled out of the jaws of death. Of course, this made our food problems even worse. Leipold's wrath knew no limits. Even Schindler walked around looking upset.

At the same time, we got news that Kraków had been liberated. We had mixed feelings; we regretted not having stayed with Uncle Grünberg, and then again we worried that perhaps no one remained alive there. We finally asked Pemper to request that Schindler try to find out about the fate of the Płaszów liquidation party. Several days later, Mietek told us that Schindler had not been able to find out anything for sure, but he thought that Uncle Grünberg (Schindler knew him) and his family were alive, because they had supposedly been transferred out of Ptaszów at the last moment. The news raised our spirits a little. Perhaps they would last until the end of the war in some other camp.

Oskar Schindler has outfoxed Leipold again. He sent a letter to the authorities stating that he had succeeded in finding sixty highly skilled workers, and if he obtained permission to employ them, he could almost double his factory's vital production. Several days later he received permission to do as he pleased with the prisoners as long as they were productive. Ilza told us that several of those "productive workers" were recovering from the amputation of their gangrenous limbs.

Mietek says Schindler isn't himself. He paces around his office mumbling to himself that he has to do something about Leipold. Our imaginations run wild. What can he do with him? He could hardly shoot the commandant of the camp. Perhaps he could arrange an accident. No, because that would involve visits and enquiries that he cannot afford.

In February, Schindler convened a sort of meeting. He told us that we had to limit our food intake to a minimum, since his

239

supplies would hardly suffice to feed five hundred, and there were about 1,700 of us. He said that he was able to find less and less on his expeditions with the truck. Food supplies were running out. His connections with the local landowners were of no avail, because they were feeding the partisans.

A period of terrible hunger began. A new sickness appeared: scurvy. Many people lost all their teeth in the course of a few days. Their teeth simply fell out, as if they were not rooted in their jaws. These people with empty mouths looked ghastly. Now, aside from my manic rubbing of my scalp, I had to check my teeth every day.

The feeling of despair grew. People kept repeating, "He practically pulled us out of the gas chamber, and now we're going to starve to death." No one held it against Schindler. We held it against life.

The *aufsejerki,* and Avanti as well, constantly try to limit our contacts with the men. Yet they always manage to come over to our side under the pretext of carrying crates or steel in or out. We get a piece of bread every few days. Mummy and I set a little aside. Adam is losing weight quickly; he has sunken eyes in a sallow, emaciated face.

We have had our first cases of hunger swelling. I already know the symptoms. I look Daddy and Adam over carefully whenever we see them. Visits to the hospital are allowed only with the permission of Doctor Hilfstein or Doctor Bieberstein, and things are so bad that Ilza even scolded me impatiently when I went to visit Janeczka, so I withdrew quickly.

Daddy came at the beginning of morning shift, pushing a wheel-barrow full of scraps. He had a sly, radiant look on his face and signalled for me to stop my machine. I glanced around to make sure there were no "enemies" in sight.

"What is it, Daddy?"

He came up and hugged me.

"Happy birthday to the loveliest daughter in the world," he said with his voice trembling, "and I hope you grow up to be beautiful, that you're healthy and happy..." He couldn't go on.

Mummy came over.

"Oh, what a monster I am," she said. "I forgot that today is my own daughter's birthday." She took me in her arms. "My darling daughter, my child of camp misery."

I was moved, because I had also forgotten that I was fifteen today. But dear, good Daddy wouldn't forget anywhere, even here. "I've got something for you," he said tantalizingly.

I could not believe it. From his pocket Daddy took four perfect little apples, barely larger than walnuts. I held them. They were real, bright red, and had a lovely smell.

"But Daddy, where did you get them?"

"Do you think I would show up at my daughter's fifteenth birthday with empty hands?" he chuckled proudly.

"Daddy, it's been years since I've seen an apple. I had forgotten about apples. They smell so good!"

"Come on, eat them now," he urged. "Eat at least one."

"No, let me look at them." Then I grew sad and said, "Fifteen and still bald."

I knew that I would always be Daddy's sweetheart no matter what I looked like. My baldness could not diminish his joy. For the whole rest of the day I had a tremendous problem with those apples. I knew that I wouldn't eat them myself, but I also knew my parents would protest if I invited them to share.

In the evening I sniffed the apples and asked Mummy, "Janeczka's very sick, isn't she? Is it true she can't sit up?"

"Yes, dear, she's really unlucky. Doctor Löw says she has tuberculosis of the spine. She's in a bad way."

"I think Daddy would want it this way," I said, turning them over in my hands.

"Want what? Come on, let it out."

"I want to give Janeczka these apples." •

"You always were a strange one," Mummy said with a really puzzled look. "You can seem so nasty, and then turn around and give everything away just to make somebody happy. They're yours so, of course, give them to Janeczka. But it won't be easy for you in life with such a nature."

"Who knows? The war's still on."

"Yes, the war," she echoed. Then she opened up as she never had before. "I've been worried about you lately. I've been watching you. You've suddenly become so serious. You almost never laugh. You used to be impulsive. You never say anything any more. Look at Halinka, she's not much older than you and she's so cheerful."

"Mummy, I'm already fifteen."

"You're only fifteen."

"Are you so sure that I'll make sixteen?"

"Go along to Janeczka and stop tormenting me."

The last thing I wanted was to leave her in that mood. "I think I've seen more corpses than live people, and I still see them often."

That, of course, was the worst thing to say. She gave me a glum look, sighed, and told me to get going.

On my way into the hospital to give my treasure to Janeczka, I ran straight into Doctor Bieberstein, a terrible stickler. He barred my way. I asked him in a polite way – incredibly polite for me – to let me in for just a moment. "I have to see her."

He burst out angrily: "*Have* to! People *have* to die, and they *have* to go to the toilet!"

I got just as angry in return, and vulgar, too. "If they don't do it in their pants on the way!"

We must have been shouting because Doctor Löw and Ilza appeared. "What's going on, dear?" asked the latter.

"Dear!" Doctor Bieberstein mocked her. "What a spoiled child!"

"You worry about your own daughter!" I shouted. Then to the women, "How can you work with such a..."

Ilza clapped a hand over my mouth and pulled me inside.

Doctor Hilfstein was bent over with laughter. "You're fantastic. Somebody finally told Alexander off." He must have got on all their nerves. "For that, you get tea." Ilza and Doctor Löw signalled to him that he shouldn't praise my behaviour. I got the herbal tea without sugar, but it was still good.

The hospital was overcrowded. Janeczka tried to smile in greeting, but her face twisted in pain. When I set the apples down on her bed and said that they were for her, she almost fainted. She picked them up and smelled them as I had done that morning and then put them aside. "I can't accept these apples. Where did you get them?"

I had to tell her the truth about my birthday, but I lied and said I was afraid to bite them because my teeth were loose.

"I don't have much longer," she said.

"If you don't take them," I said, pretending not to hear, "I'll cry."

Doctor Hilfstein came to my rescue. "Take them, Janeczka. If she cries on her birthday, she'll cry all year. Can you imagine such a big girl crying?"

Ilza had caught the remark about my teeth and she ordered me into a corner. "Show me your mouth." I tried to joke that I wasn't a horse and whispered that I had only said that for Janeczka's sake, but it didn't help. "Open up!" She had a look. "Everything's all right for now." She took out some pills. "Swallow these. Come back every day. We have so few vitamins that we don't know who to give them to, so you'll get some."

"What about him?" I motioned towards Doctor Bieberstein, who had sat down nearby and was looking sulky.

"Tell that child that to her I'm 'Doctor,' not 'him'," he grumbled.

"You know," Ilza said, "We're all on edge. Patients keep coming in and we're short of medicine. It can't last much longer," she said equably.

But Doctor Bieberstein was clearly offended. He let loose with the worst thing he could have said: "What have you been doing to that girl? Did you shave her head here?"

That hit me like a bolt of lightning. "Old fool," I shouted, and ran out in tears. Along the way I remembered what Doctor Hilfstein had said about crying on my birthday, and wiped my tears. To make myself feel better, I silently repeated, "Fool."

We started a week on night shift. When one of the big, important machines broke down, Schindler was awakened. He came into the factory, looked at the machine and at our worried faces, laughed, and said *"Scheisse."* Then, translating, he said in a comical tone, "Shit," waved his hand, and walked out.

Avanti had been observing Schindler the whole time. He kept standing there, thinking. I watched in fear. If Avanti spent too much time trying to think with that half-brain of his, he might start beating people. Then, with a strange look on his face, he looked around as if he was seeing us for the first time.

"Hitler kaputt" he said and walked to his cubicle.

Things like that gave us hope. We felt the joy of survival, even though we were so hungry we could barely stand. If it hadn't been for common sense, we would have sung and shouted for joy.

***

Completely on his own authority, Schindler loaded several of our men into a truck every few days and went out foraging for food. It was familiar territory for him and he knew where all the restaurants and inns were. He also knew what the Germans had left behind. He took what he found, but it wasn't much. Once they brought back a large mouldy cheese, and although people said it had worms in it, we ate it. They found herrings, which didn't last long despite being portioned out sparingly, one per head per day. Another time they sweated horribly unloading some big barrels, only to find on opening them that they were full of mustard.

German dignitaries made regular pilgrimages to see Oskar Schindler. He always got them drunk, and we wondered where he had got such supplies of booze. He had obviously planned ahead. He once received an official shipment of a couple of sacks of potatoes. That was very important for us, and doubtless for him, too.

There were nights when Schindler and our men drove right up next to the factory. His wife always invited the *aufsejerki* for tea then, and he would order us to go to our quarters for half an hour. Something happened downstairs then. They tried not to make a noise. They were delivering something.

244

My curiosity became overpowering. Whatever was going on, it would affect us women, too. I asked everybody. Many men were now wearing leather boots, which was great progress. Mostly, these were the men who went out at night with Schindler.

Mietek Penner was one of them. I asked him as nicely as I could, "What's the surprise? What are you men bringing in at night?"

He just laughed. "Nothing for children. When we bring cakes, you'll be the first to know."

"Don't give me that," I said. "I already know."

As I had expected, this took the smile off his face. "What do you know?"

I took a wild guess. "You're bringing guns."

I knew immediately that I had hit it right. "Who told you such nonsense? Who told you? Keep your mouth shut."

Now, for a change, it was the guns that obsessed me. I looked around the factory trying to guess where they were hidden. And for what? Was there going to be an uprising? I couldn't make sense of if

I went back to Mietek. "What are the guns for?"

"In case anybody gets any ideas about liquidating the camp. Schindler's in touch with the local partisans, and they'll help us if need be. He's worried that Leipold is up to something. But remember, it's a secret!"

"Of course," I promised.

Mietek ran back to work, which by now was just a cover for the existence of the camp, since lately not one crate of those meticulously polished and packed shell cases had been sent out.

Sometimes when I lay in the bunk at night among the three hundred sleeping women, I thought I heard a faint, distant rumbling from below the ground. They said that the front lines were close. Or was it my imagination? I couldn't help wondering if they would reach us while we were still alive.

It wasn't very warm but winter was obviously ending. Daddy came in looking worried. He could never hide anything from us, but today we were struck by how he kept looking at the ground. He had something to say, but didn't know how to begin. It was terrible: Adam was starting to have hunger swelling. We were powerless and terrified. My wonderful brother Adam's feet were too swollen to fit in his clogs and his eyes had sunk almost out of sight in his yellowish face.

Mummy had madness in her eyes. She looked at Adam as if he were a spectre. She loved him so much. Then she said to herself, "Of course they'll help."

"Who, Mummy?"

"I'm going to Doctor Löw and Ilza to see if they've got anything to eat or any vitamins."

I imagined how she must have felt. She had never asked anyone for help. When she came back from the hospital she looked better. They had promised a little food at least twice a week. She also brought some vitamin pills. I decided that Adam could have the ones I was supposed to get.

"Mummy, let's give Adam half of whatever food we get. We can lie and say that the women get bigger portions."

"Don't be ridiculous. He won't believe it and, besides, you were just at death's door yourself. Do you think you won't swell up?"

"But Mummy, I don't need as much as Adam. I'm smaller and younger, and I might be stronger and have more resistance."

"You're acting as generously as you used to when you were a child," she said a little hesitantly.

"If he gets two extra portions from the hospital and two from us, he'll make it."

"My dear child," she said, hugging me.

She must have been exhausted, because she seldom permitted herself any tenderness. My poor, worn out mother. Many nights she sat knitting by the bunk so that I would have more room to sleep. I pretended not to notice.

So we gave Adam half of our food. We saw him more often now and he still looked terrible, but at least he wasn't getting any worse and it hadn't started to affect his teeth. The men transferred him to other work, or rather to no work at all, so that all he had to do was walk from one corner to another when somebody was watching.

Another small group of prisoners arrived at the camp. They were called *Budzyniacy* from the name of some town or shtetl. Many looked on them with hostility, since they represented additional mouths to be fed from our slender resources. Yet they also had the right to live.

The grown-ups often called me "kid," but I quarreled with them when they talked nonsense. I could still explode the way I used to in the Ghetto and in Płaszów. Then one day a woman called me a "bald, overfed brat." We had just finished our watery soup, and I gave it to her over the head with my bowl. There was a terrible uproar, but Wanda Penner and Rózia came to my defence as usual.

"We would have done the same thing a moment later, only harder," they said.

Our people, the prisoners, somehow found out that Oskar Schindler's birthday was approaching. They decided to offer Schindler a letter of safe conduct. I had no idea at all what that meant. I considered for a long time how I could find out without making an idiot of myself. Lately I was wary of asking questions that would be met with either head-scratching or laughter.

I finally concluded that Mummy would be my best source of information. Even if the questions were less than wise, she wouldn't jeer at me.

Evenings in the bunk were the best time to talk and ask questions. "Mummy, something's been bothering me."

"If it's bothering you, ask."

"What's a letter of safe conduct?"

"I was afraid you wanted to ask about something serious."

"Isn't that serious?"

"Well, of course it is." She explained to me with infinite patience what it was and why we had to give it to Schindler. It would guarantee his safety after liberation, stating that he wasn't a murderer and had saved us. I liked the idea. It was to be written in three languages, Hebrew, English and Russian, and all the prisoners would sign it.

I lay there sighing and squirming. "Is something else bothering you?"

"Two things. Do we have people who speak so many languages?"

"Of course. And the other thing?"

"Well, I don't know if I'll be able to sign my name. I might have completely forgotten how."

"There's nothing to worry about. I can sign for you."

"No!" I almost jumped out of the bunk. "I insist on signing it myself."

"Fine. I'll ask Pemper for a pencil and we'll practice."

"But you won't tell anybody?"

"Don't you trust me?"

There was nothing more to say.

Mummy kept her word. She found a scrap of paper. It was worse than operating the lathe. Every letter went in a different direction, but I was happy that I would be able to sign by myself.

It was later that I fell into despair. What if we really survived? Such a big girl, unable to write, not knowing anything. This line of thinking completely soured my outlook on life. I became arrogant and touchy. Mummy was evidently keeping an eye on my behaviour. One day she told me to go and visit Janeczka.

"I wasn't allowed to before."

"Even Doctor Bieberstein says you can come now. He was having a bad day when he flew at you."

I knew it was a trick but I went anyway.

Janeczka looked dreadful, and so did her mother, with deep worry lines around her mouth. I tried to talk with Janeczka and tell her about the letter, but everything made her tired.

All the doctors were there. Bieberstein gave me a friendly smile. We shook hands and made up. I kept feeling that they wanted something from me.

"Do you feel all right?" asked Ilza. "Are you weak?"

"No." I was irritated. "Tell me what's going on. Was Mummy here?"

"Yes, and she said you're acting strangely. We want to examine you," said Ilza sharply. "Undress. Do as I say."

She took out her stethoscope, listened, tapped. They all took turns listening, tapping, oohing and aahing. They went back to the left side of the clavicle, or whatever they called it, and finally let me get dressed.

"Sit down. Take this thermometer." Ilza had turned into a real doctor. "Her temperature has risen," she said curtly. "Have you got a cough? Do you get chills?"

"When it's cold."

They looked at each other and roared with laughter. "You know, Ilza, now I understand why you all like her so much," Doctor Bieberstein said.

I didn't understand anything. I really did have the chills when it was cold, and what was funny about that? I got tea. The herbal kind had run out and this wasn't as good. They also gave me a pill.

"So am I sick or not?"

They looked a little uneasy. "Yes and no," Doctor Löw said after some thought.

"I'm leaving. If you decide I'm sick, let me know." I kissed both of them. Ilza had a strange look on her face. The doctors glanced at each other. On my way out I knew I would be tormenting Mummy about why she had sent me to the hospital.

I didn't have time to do so immediately. Mietek came around with a big piece of paper as long as a towel for everybody to sign, and I was truly happy that I could write my own name there. Everything was arranged. We were supposed to be in the factory the next morning at five o'clock, before the *aufsejerki* came. A rostrum made out of crates had been prepared for the Schindlers.

When we were all assembled, Pemper and Penner invited them to the factory. In a shirt but no coat, Schindler stood beside his wife on the platform. The letter was read out, and I remembered the most important part, that all the prisoners ask that wherever they are, Oskar Schindler and his wife be given all help, be accorded the credit they deserve, and be received with honour.

Mrs. Schindler did not conceal her emotion, wiping her eyes, and he was close to crying as well but controlled himself. It all happened quickly. Quietly, without singing, we wished him *"Sto Lat"* three times. Schindler thanked us and said we had to stay alert because there was no telling what difficulties lay ahead.

In the evening it turned out that he had given our men a few bottles from his unending supply of alcohol. I also got a sip of something that burned and stank and was supposed to be fine cognac. Everybody raised the toast that we had gradually got used to: "Until freedom comes."

We were starting to believe in that freedom. I lay thinking what it would be like. I was afraid to ask anyone. Mira alone might have had enough patience for me. My heart was pounding. I had thought so little about her, and she might be alive. I asked impulsively, "Mummy, is Auschwitz free now?"

"Yes. what are you thinking about?"

"About that wonderful Mira, whether she survived."

"If destiny permits" – Mummy had picked up the tone of the women here, but at least she wasn't asking God for help – "we'll find her once we get out."

"I never even thanked her," I burst into tears.

"Why did I let you drink that alcohol?" she said angrily. "You're falling apart. I don't know what's wrong with you. Doctor Löw said it's nothing serious, but something's happening." She sounded sad. "First you hit a woman over the head with your bowl, and now you're crying again."

"I won't do it any more." I felt bad. "And why did they examine me like that in the hospital?"

"They said it's nothing serious, but they might be wrong. They said you should go back in two or three weeks."

"It doesn't matter." I waved my hand.

"It matters a great deal. And you know," she said, trying to change the subject, "I have the impression your scalp's getting darker."

Nothing helped.

"It doesn't matter," I repeated. Mummy fell silent.

The end of March was approaching. While we were having our dinner of watery soup, there was a great commotion in the factory. We learned that several badly beaten prisoners had been brought to the camp in the company of a *sturmmann* and a "V" *kapo*. We caught a glimpse of some men being led limping to the hospital.

We learned the rest that evening. Schindler and Leipold had had a serious quarrel. The commandant had demanded that the SS-men take the new arrivals off to be shot in a nearby wood. Schindler threatened that in such a case he would immediately report the SS-men as malingerers to be sent to the front. Not entirely sober, Leipold said he would agree to wait, but only because he would need the SS-men in the near future when he finally took care of the *"schweine Bande,"* meaning us.

>From that day on, Schindler looked preoccupied. He had to find work for the *kapo* who had brought the newest prisoners in. Two of them survived. They told us that the *kapo,* called Willi, had taken them out of a nearby camp and had killed more than ninety men with a steel club. The sentries had not taken part, except to put some terribly injured men out of their misery.

***

Avanti came to life now that he had Willi as a helper. He ran around with his whip, shouting like never before. Willi beat a man savagely on his first day. First he cracked his head open with one blow, and then made him do squats until he fainted, instead of letting him be taken straight to the infirmary. This happened while Schindler was away. Fear seized us again. Pemper went to Mrs. Schindler, but she said she wasn't allowed to interfere.

Schindler came back the next day and we felt better. Pemper worked next door to Schindler's office, and he eavesdropped. Schindler called Willi in and told him that this was an ammunition factory on which valiant German soldiers depended, and we had to be fit for work, not injured. If the previous day's incident was repeated, Willi would be arrested for sabotage and hampering the war effort.

Willi became Leipold's favourite, sleeping in his house and drinking with him. One day, Schindler discovered that Leipold sometimes took a detail of SS-men outside the camp. So he got one of them drunk and weaseled the truth out of him. Leipold was ordering them to dig ditches in the woods. Everything was clear now; they were preparing to finish us off.

Schindler stopped leaving the camp. He was constantly seen keeping friendly company with Leipold.

Mietek Penner or Mietek Pemper reassured us that Schindler would surely outfox the commandant. But no one knew how. Perhaps Oskar Schindler himself did not know. Legally, it was Leipold who had the power of life and death over us. Schindler passed word through Mietek Pemper that we should be prepared. He told him where the guns were hidden. The partisans had been notified and were observing the camp. If we were led out, we would have to fight and the partisans would help us. The front lines were near Brno.

That told me nothing. Where was Brno? Where was the front? I only knew that it would be a shame to die now. I imagined Adam unable to walk well, the people lying in the hospital, and Janeczka, who could not even sit up on her own.

Schindler decreed that we should stay absolutely calm, as if nothing was going on. But the men started to panic. They wanted to get the guns out and place them among the crates so that they could be used at a moment's notice. Others were against the idea, saying that nothing could save us if Willi or Avanti, who were everywhere, stumbled upon them. We had to wait. Everyone hoped that Schindler would think of something.

The food situation turned serious because of the fact that Schindler had not gone out for several days. He told a couple of men to leave at dusk and sneak under the fence to the nearby mill, whose owner had supplied us with grain or flour several times before and had now been alerted. The owner told them to return in two days. Two days later they dragged a couple of sacks of turnips and some strange flour back under our fence. It was something.

We received food, if you could call it that, twice a day. After a fast lasting several days we were given a sort of paste made of flour. It was good, hot and filling. The turnip soup was doled out with a pharmacist's precision, no bowlful containing more than five little cubes of vegetable. We still ate only half our rations. Adam's condition had not worsened, but, understandably, neither had it improved. People were starting to lose weight. We had to conserve our strength, but in such a way that our enemies did not notice.

We could definitely hear the dull rumble of the war. The sound gave us comfort and strength, although no one could say where it was, or how far. The men said that the Soviets were closer than the Americans. Whole columns of German armoured cars, trucks and tanks drove along the road outside the factory day and night.

Spring was apparent everywhere, even in the factory. The *aufsejerki* stopped watching us and preferred to sit with the SS-men, who had also ceased to pay any attention to us, in the sun outside. Only commandant Leipold and his inseparable companion Willi remained alert. Prompted by some inexplicable instinct, however, Schindler always turned up when they did. He would put his arms around both of them in a friendly way and disappear with them into his apartment, from which drunken shouts and singing soon issued. Avanti had gone back to sitting lethargically in his cubicle. Perhaps he was not such an idiot as he seemed.

Ilza summoned me to the hospital. I wondered why. Had Janeczka asked for me? I went there and sat down beside her. She opened her eyes with an effort.

"Just hold out a little longer, Janeczka," I said, "not long." But I knew it was almost impossible.

The Greek women from the epidemiological ward in Birkenau rose up clearly in my imagination: faces without expression, eyes without life.

Doctor Low again ordered me to undress. She and Ilza listened for a long time and exchanged incomprehensible words. They gave me a thermometer. It showed a slightly high temperature. I drank boiled water with a pinch of sugar; the herbal tea was long gone. They gave me a couple of vitamin pills. Neither of them was in a good mood, so I left quickly.

Mummy immediately asked, "And what did they say?"

"Nothing," I lied. "I'm healthy as a horse."

***

The days passed quickly. To our amazement, we noticed that the *aufsejerki* had gone. Oskar Schindler had supposedly explained to Leipold that they were no longer needed, giving him to understand that he had taken the decision to liquidate the camp. Leipold strutted around in enormous satisfaction. He asked Schindler each day when the liquidation would take place, and Schindler replied that it would be soon, as soon as "the filth" finished the last shipment. Leipold was so excited that he took Schindler into the woods to show off how carefully and precisely he had had the ditches dug that would hold the 1,700 corpses. Schindler praised him.

The German upper crust from the whole vicinity came by car in the evening. The binge went on until morning. The women on the night shift said that Schindler had come into the factory many times and sat in a corner laughing his head off. They suspected that he, too, had been drunk.

Several days later almost all of us were witnesses as the SS-men got into the truck and Schindler ceremoniously invited Leipold into his car. They all drove away. This was in the second half of April. Schindler returned many hours later with some new SS-men. They were older, jumpy, and carried their rifles under their arms like useless parcels. Schindler posted two of them at the gate and quartered the others in Leipold's house.

What was happening, what was this all about? An hour later, Schindler entered the factory wearing, to our puzzlement, his

Nazi party uniform. He sat on a crate and laughed. At first it was just laughter, but after a moment it seemed like the laughter of a madman. He stammered something about now the man had not yet been born who could outfox Oskar. He was not mad. But it would not have taken much more to drive us crazy.

Mietek Pemper and Penner told us the whole story, and we could have listened to it forever. Here's what had happened. Before holding that drunken binge, Schindler had prepared documents in which Leipold and his escort of SS-men requested, "as patriots who believe in the victory of the Third Reich and its great leader Adolf Hitler, to be transferred together to the front line." When Leipold was completely drunk, Schindler put the document in front of him and instructed him to sign, saying that it was the order to liquidate the camp. Without reading it and almost weeping for joy, Leipold signed. The document was immediately taken to headquarters by a confidant of Schindler's. Thus, Leipold is apparently fighting heroically on the front line near Ostrava. When Schindler told Pemper the whole story, he added, "and he will be buried with the highest honours."

Schindler ordered Willi to be locked up in the cellar under guard by our men. There were mixed opinions, with some in favour of doing justice immediately. The majority, however, were determined to wait until the liberating army arrived. Schindler advised Avanti to vanish, explaining that things could get dangerous in the camp.

The new SS-men walked around looking lost. Schindler told them not to let any German vehicles into the camp, because they could be partisans in disguise. They stood at attention before him as if he were Hitler himself. He ordered us to shut down all the machinery and act as if the camp were empty. We sat that way for many days. Sometimes Schindler dropped in. He was invariably smiling and full of hope that nothing bad could happen.

He went off looking for food. Even his wife's dogs were looking starved. Mrs. Schindler had given us the last of her food reserves. We had a little dried bread, but not even enough to go around among the sick. We weren't allowed to make soup from the hoarded turnips for fear the smoke from the kitchen would give us away. So we ate slices of the turnips raw. If the liberators didn't come in a few days, we would die of hunger.

Schindler requisitioned a little dry bread, but not enough for everyone.

The ground was rumbling and aeroplanes flew overhead occasionally. The SS-men hung around looking nervous, trying to start conversations with us. They explained that they had just been drafted, that they were too old, that they hadn't done any harm to anyone. It was quiet. For the first time in memory I heard the birds going crazy, singing in joy at the spring.

We learned that a group was preparing to escort Schindler and his wife to the Allies so that no harm would come to them. I was frightened at Schindler's leaving, frightened that something bad would happen once he left.

"I can't understand why he has to go," I pestered Mummy.

"He comes from around here and his neighbours might not want to listen to the good things he's done. They'll only remember that he joined the Nazi party, that would be enough to get him into trouble," she explained patiently.

"Is he leaving today? What's the date?"

"You know, I'm not sure. Either the sixth or seventh of May." Mummy had lost track.

Ilza came in the evening and talked to Mummy, Rózia and Wanda. Whenever I approached, they paused. Finally, I got angry. "Why do you stop talking when I'm near?"

Mummy took it as another sign. "You see, Ilza, how irritable she is? She can't control herself!"

"What are you hiding from me? Is Adam worse? Tell me, damn it!"

Halinka "Baby" came over with red eyes. Everybody started making some sort of signals. But all she could think about was her Zev who was going to take her to America.

"Stella," she said in a mournful voice, "It's such a shame about poor Janeczka."

"Yes, she's been in a poor condition for a long time. But they'll be able to take her to a hospital soon and operate."

"What for?"

"What for? So she can get better, you idiot."

"You're the idiot," she snapped. "Are they going to operate on a corpse?"

I looked around. Everybody had turned away.

"Ilza!" I grabbed for her hand.

"Yes, dear, she died last night."

"She died last night," I repeated. "Last night? She couldn't wait for freedom? Ilza, couldn't anything be done so she'd see even a minute of freedom?"

I could not get it into my head that people die by themselves all the time, every minute, without being shot or murdered. I stood there as though rooted to the spot. I could see her smelling the apples.

As she had done for so long, Ilza put her arms around me. "Go ahead and cry, Stella. We all feel so bad. You know, it might have been harder for her to die if she had seen freedom."

"I always said," I whimpered, "that there's no one there. If there was, He would never have let her die."

"You can't talk that way. Look around at all the people that have been saved."

"Have they all deserved it?" I didn't know what I was saying.

I started to retch. I was angry with everyone. As always, Wanda had a little alcohol. I drank a little. "The only thing that would make me feel better," I hiccupped, to Rózia or Ilza, I don't know, "would be to kill just one German, one God-damned little Hun kid."

"Stella!" Ilza cried out. "Get a grip on yourself! Children don't start wars, no matter whose children they are. I know how sorry you are for Janeczka but hatred won't help your sorrow."

The bitterness of all those years must have been flowing out of me. I could see before my eyes the murdering, the hanging, the killing of old people and children. I went back in my mind to the Ghetto, when the heads of infants were smashed against the wall. Was I supposed to forget all that? I felt sorry for

257

myself; for the rest of my life I would see men hanging from the gallows and corpses with rats nibbling at them.

"Where is Janeczka?" I had calmed down.

"Her father and brother are nailing together a coffin for her."

The next night, Schindler's luggage was loaded onto a truck and he was driven away towards the American lines under the protection of ten of our men. A wonderful man, and yet how often many of our people had cursed him, unable to believe that such a person could exist. If only they managed to get him safely into the right hands.

It must have been May 7. In the morning we saw that no one was guarding the gates. The SS-men had disappeared, leaving their rifles in a corner near the gate. With Schindler gone, they must have decided that their time had come. German vehicles full of soldiers kept rolling along the road; if they turned off into our camp, they would kill us like insects.

Our men returned at sunset. They recounted in confused terms how they would have never found their way back if Schindler had not drawn them a map. Finally, they gave us the most important news. They had turned Schindler over to a rabbi with the rank of colonel and given him the document. The rabbi had sworn that not a hair on Schindler's head would be harmed, nor his wife, nor even their dogs.

Without asking anyone, some idiot took a white-and-red Polish flag out of hiding and climbed up on the roof. As he was trying to tie it there, somebody in a passing truck full of soldiers let off several shots with a rifle. Fortunately, he was hit only in the buttocks. As they were taking the bullet out in the hospital, he screamed worse than I heard anyone scream in all those years of the war. He must have been in pain, but all we could do was laugh. We sat quiet as mice for the rest of the day, not even sticking our heads out.

A Soviet officer on a white horse stood before the camp gate in beautiful sunshine the next morning, as if he had ridden out of a fairy tale for good children. The gate was open, and others rode up behind him on horses. The road was still jammed with tanks and other vehicles, but now they were Soviet.

How many times during those horrible years I had tried to imagine freedom! Now I stood there feeling nothing. My thoughts flew past quickly. This is freedom, but no one is crawling along the ground, no one is going crazy. Mummy held me tightly by the hand, just as she had at Auschwitz. "Maybe something's wrong with us," I said despite myself.

"How?"

"I'm just wondering if this is what joy is supposed to feel like, joy at being alive."

"It'll come dear, it'll come," she repeated. "We're exhausted."

"Will we go out through the gate?"

"Of course."

"When, now? I might be afraid to go."

But Mummy was feeling very emotional, and she kept repeating, "It'll come, it'll come."

A camp stool was set up in the courtyard, the officer sat down, and our prisoner Willi, the "V" *kapo,* was brought out. Then he was taken away again. The lawyer, Schlang, sat beside the officer.

Daddy joined us with Adam, who still had his swelling. They both looked lost. "What are they doing?" I asked.

"Writing the charges against Willi and his sentence."

"Idiots," I said. "Why don't they just do to him like they did to us? Do they have to play around?"

"Stella," Daddy said gravely, "We can't act like ordinary bandits. We have to be different. You have to start feeling that there are certain rules of law."

"I don't have to do anything," I screamed hysterically. "I'll never have to do anything again."

"All right, dear, all right."

"I'm going for a walk," I said.

"I'd rather you stayed close," Mummy said.

"But I have to start moving around finally," I said, "Even if it's just in the camp."

"Well, don't wander off."

259

A few metres away, around the back of the factory, was a storage shed. The door was open, and I went in. Our labouriously manufactured shell casings were stacked to the ceiling in crates. I went in further and saw a barrel. I lifted the lid. Mustard. I dipped my finger in. Delicious! I sat on top of the open barrel and started eating, using my hands. It burned a little, but it was delectable. I heard voices outside.

"Here she is." I recognized Wanda's voice. "I told you I saw her go in here, Tusia."

I was still sitting there and was about to tell them how good it tasted, when Mummy and Wanda started shrieking, "I can't believe it. That child has no common sense at all. What are you trying to catch, typhus or dysentery? It's a miracle she's alive. Call Ilza."

"What's wrong?" I managed to get a word in. "Even when I was little I used to eat mustard and vinegar."

Ilza had arrived. "But that was on a full stomach," she explained. "This is no laughing matter."

"Ilza, I promise, I'll be all right."

We were already outside. "Look at you. You look like you're covered in..." she didn't finish.

I completed her thought: "In shit?"

They pretended not to hear, fortunately.

A field kitchen had arrived. "If she eats something she might be all right after all," Ilza sighed. I wiped my face on my sleeve. The mustard was in fact burning in my stomach like hell now, but I wouldn't say anything even if I burned up.

We lined up with out dishes. A lovely smell was coming out of the pots. A young soldier, not more than nineteen, was giving out the soup. Our people were used to obeying, and hungry as they were, they stood still in line for their first "liberated" soup.

"What's going on inside?" I asked as I waited.

"They're going to carry out the sentence on Willi."

"Who is?"

"The men that he brought here."

I got my portion. It was barley soup. Rózia had finished hers. "Not much of it," I said.

"It's just right. They're going to feed us often but in small amounts. There's fear of diarrhoea."

I took my bowl of soup and went inside. They were reading out the sentence. I looked around for the gallows. Willi was standing on a board between two crates. I looked up and saw a wire noose. Two men went up, put the noose around his neck, and then pulled the board out from under him. The noose apparently cut his throat, because blood spurted out. He must have still been alive, because he was kicking.

I was standing there not thinking about anything and eating my soup, and the mustard still burned a little inside me. They had told me to eat slowly, so I did. Willi's eyes turned up. Then I felt a tugging and spilled some of my soup. Mummy was standing beside me and her eyes looked just like Willi's. Her chin was trembling.

"Get out of here. Get out immediately!" She pushed me towards the door.

I was genuinely surprised.

"I'm going to leave this place with an abnormal daughter! You stand there eating soup with an idiotic expression on your face while they hang a man!"

I was flabbergasted at Mummy's reaction. "But Mummy, I stood at roll-call when they murdered and hanged loads of our people, and I had to watch."

"That's entirely different. Our people never murdered anyone. We stood for hours in the cold or the burning sun..."

"And now," I added with malicious relish, "I could stand and watch as they slowly pull the guts out of one of them."

As little inclined to tears as she was, Mummy covered her face and the tears rolled out from between her fingers like water from a tap.

Rózia came over. "What's wrong?"

I answered. "Nothing. Mummy went to pieces when she saw how they hanged Willi."

Rózia hugged her soothingly.

"She was standing there eating soup," Mummy said calmly. "I was just terrified. That's my daughter, the same daughter that cried over an insect somebody had stepped on."

"What are you talking about, an insect? Have you both lost your minds?" Now Rózia was furious.

"When she was little," Mummy explained.

"Tusia, you're a grown woman. Do I have to explain to you that Stella is going to have very bad associations now, because she has grown up in abnormal conditions? You're going to have a lot of patience. All of us have been harmed mentally, and what about a girl her age?"

They went on arguing. Finally, Rózia lost her patience and said, "Tusia, stop being hysterical. She's been through hell." And she walked away.

I hung around the courtyard. There were more Czechs now; they would come shyly into the camp, occasionally bringing us something. Some of the prisoners flocked around them, taking what they could get. I didn't go near, because I didn't want anything. I was dreaming of a pleasant, quiet room where I could shut myself in and not see or hear anyone for a long time. Where I could fall asleep without listening to the moaning and snoring of hundreds of women. That was what I wanted most.

I listened as an officer announced a two-week quarantine. I couldn't understand it; nobody had typhus. He also said that for our own safety we should not leave the camp alone; there were many armed Germans around from units that had broken up, and something bad could easily happen. It was funny, but I felt a kind of relief that I wouldn't have to go out of the gate that I had stared at continually, that had become an insurmountable barrier for me. How could we ever go out if not in groups of five, with an escort? I would not share this fear with anyone in the world.

A little embarrassed over the scene she had made, Mummy asked, "Are you coming to Janeczka's funeral, dear? Her parents said they'll bury her and then come back for her once they've settled somewhere."

"Ah, so they'll come back for a corpse?" I didn't want to be truculent, but I couldn't help it. "I'm not going."

"But you always liked her."

"I did, but I'm not going."

"Well, I am. It won't help Natka, but we're going."

"Don't wander off," I said as she left.

She looked back, worried.

I went around behind the factory where it was quietest. I saw them carrying Janeczka's coffin out. They carried it crooked because her brother Lutek was tall while Mr. Feigenbaum was on the short side. Her mother must have got a black scarf from a Czech woman and she had her whole face covered, but the scarf looked terrible with her striped uniform. There were a few of our people, and Soviet soldiers with rifles just in case.

One of those zealous rescuers of people's souls started singing a plaintive Jewish song. That made me furious, although if someone had asked me why, I wouldn't have known how to answer. I would have jumped out of the coffin to scream that I don't want any prayers.

I thought that all our women had gone to the funeral, but then I saw Wanda. She must have stayed behind to watch me, but why? A couple of locals came up. They were jolly and laughing. I could catch about half of what they said. They were staring at me. I sat down on a crate against the wall and didn't feel like talking. "You're so young, were you one too?"

"One what?"

"Well, what do you call it?" One of them hesitated, and then said gaily, "a prostitute!"

"What's that?" I asked.

They kept laughing. Wanda came over. "I see you've made friends," she said sarcastically.

"I can't understand them. They're asking if I was a prostitute. What's that?"

Wanda just about choked. When she could open her mouth, she screamed at them. "Get out of here before I murder you." They backed away, with stupid expressions on their faces. Wanda kept repeating. "On, God! Oh, God!"

"Stop saying that or the Germans will come back. Now tell me, if you know yourself, what a prostitute is."

"I'll explain," said Wanda, getting a grip on herself. "Remember how there was nobody on the streets when they brought us to this camp? The bastards had announced that we were a transport of women criminals and prostitutes."

"I know they were capable of such things, but what's...?"

"So I'll tell you." She had to stop and think about how to put it. "It's a terrible thing, and it means the same thing as when the block supervisor used to call us 'you whores'."

That did it. I understood and jumped to my feet. "I'll catch them and crack their heads open. How can they be such idiots? Didn't they have a war here?"

"Forget it. Can't you see that they're just ignorant, spoiled youngsters? What would they know about the war?"

I felt terrible. How could there be people anywhere in the world, except perhaps infants, who didn't know what had happened? "How is it possible, Wanda?"

"Now you're going to encounter a lot of things that won't make any sense to you. That's life."

"If that's life, to hell with it."

"Nevertheless, there will be things you know that others won't know. And vice versa." Wanda talked and talked while my mind raced. I could take being called such things in Birkenau, but not here, when we were free. I was ready to cry. She tried to make a joke of it, but I felt bitter.

A young soldier came up and Wanda explained something to him. When he tried to stroke my bald head, I hit his hand as hard as I could.

The women had come back. I couldn't, and didn't want to look at Mrs. Feigenbaum, who was so small and old and bent over.

"Come with me," said Doctor Löw in a tone that admitted no discussion. She talked that way sometimes even though she was so wonderful and good.

"Where?"

"Come on, I want to listen to your chest."

"I'm not going. It's warm and good here. Leave me alone!"

"You come, dear." Ilza had joined her. "We just want to listen and tap. It won't hurt. Imagine, of all our children only you and Niusia are left. You don't want to make problems for yourself and us."

264

"Go and examine Niusia."

"I already have. She's all right for now."

Mummy stood miserably off to the side. I felt bad again.

"I'm going, Mummy. I'll let them tap me."

We went into the hospital, were Janeczka wasn't lying any more. I undressed in the doctors' cubicle. "Well, you're lucky it's over. Your bones are poking out. You'd never make it through a selection," they tried to joke.

They took turns listening and tapping, and kept going back to that left side. Then the thermometer. They read it. They put it back in, saying it might not have been shaken down.

"So, have I got a fever or not?" I asked impatiently.

"You've got a slight temperature."

"What is it? Typhus, dysentery or mustard? I want to know! I have a right to know!"

"Of course. It seems to us, though we might be wrong, that you've got a slight murmur in the upper left lobe."

"Tuberculosis!"

"Don't jump off the deep end. It's a long way from a murmur to tuberculosis, but once you get home you'll have to have an X-ray."

"Home." I repeated. "How far is home?"

"Nearer than you think, and not long now."

I walked out of there full of new ideas. Home, to live in a normal home. Have we still got that beautiful apartment, which I seemed to see now through a fog? Maybe Mania was waiting. Yes, I'll be at home, and comfortable, and I'll have to forget. Forget. About Malina Rottermann, about Marek, about the Jewish dog they hunted down in Płaszów. But no, there in Kraków I would never forget. They would all be with me for the rest of my life. I would rather never go back there. But how could I say that? Daddy couldn't wait to see Kraków again, he could not imagine life without Kraków, and he had already promised that no teacher or professor would ever be able to tell me as much about the city as he could.

We had frequent meals but a couple of people came down with diarrhoea. To my surprise, I had no particular appetite.

For so many months, for years, it had seemed to me that when this moment came I would eat and eat, that my stomach would burst and I still wouldn't stop. Now, it was different. I had thought that when freedom came I would go mad with happiness, but it was different. My joy had fled. I could not even define that joy. Was it the joy of life? I did not know when, or with whom, it had been buried. I shouldn't be this way. I had my beloved parents and my wonderful brother, who was still a little swollen but was starting to look better.

I had become unbearable again. Adam brought a branch full of beautiful green leaves back from the funeral. He was happy when he gave it to me. What did I do? I got angry and said he had killed the branch. I could see he felt bad. I wanted to make it up somehow, to thank him, but I didn't know how, and I loved him so.

***

We jumped out of our bunks and ran down the iron stairs to the courtyard. There were gunshots and bells were ringing. The soldiers who had stayed to guard us were running wild, dancing, and firing their guns in the air.

"The war is over! Germany has surrendered!" Rosner was playing his accordion.

"*Hitler kaputt!*" Then something splendid and moving happened. With tears running down their faces, the prisoners were singing the Polish national anthem.

I was touched. Something responded inside me, and I looked around to see Daddy as they sang about Poland. There he was, standing at attention, terribly absorbed in it all. I went up to him. "Daddy!"

"Today I'm the happiest man in the world. Do you understand, dear? The happiest. I have my homeland, my Poland, and there's nothing more I need. I could spend the rest of my life in rags, but I'll always be happy."

I could have said that I couldn't share the joy, that I knew I would never be happy there in Kraków. I was different, or

I had become different. Something was always crying inside me, something sorrowful and bitter. I pretended to be as happy as he was.

People were dancing and singing. I wandered around the camp. Halinka and Zev were hugging each other and beaming. I was reminded of Bubik, who had also promised that he would take me to America when the war ended, that he would find me wherever I was. Was he alive? Was he in his America? Now Halinka was going to America with Zev. They stopped in front of me. "When will we say goodbye?" I asked. "When are you leaving?"

Halinka looked at Zev with big, calf eyes. "Have you got a cigarette?" I asked him.

He had one, gave it to me, and said with a smile, "Better go and smoke it in a corner somewhere."

"Why?"

"You know, without hair you look as though you're ten years old."

"That's my problem. I wanted to wear a scarf, but they yelled at me that it would be better to let the air get to it."

I saw Adam and wanted very much to talk with him. "Let's sit down," I said. "This is the quietest corner. How do you feel? You look better." I didn't know what it was that I wanted to say.

"What's eating you, sister?"

"So many things, you know, that I can't say what's worst."

"Your hair?"

"Not really. A little, maybe. Have you got used to freedom yet?"

He considered. "You know, not really. It's hard to define. Maybe when we get out of here... But right now it all seems sort of unreal. Do you understand? It seems false."

"Do you want to go to Kraków immediately, like Daddy? Because I don't." I had managed to say what was bothering me most.

"I don't understand," he looked at me curiously. "There is, or perhaps I should say 'was,' but anyway that's where our home will be again, those are our streets. Maybe we'll find our relatives. Well, at least the Grünbergs. You love them."

"Yes, but I'm afraid that my thoughts will keep going back all the time to what happened, and that I won't – I don't know how to put it – I won't be able to return to a normal state."

Adam was surprised. "Something will remain in all of us, sister, but you're in a normal state. You always had your problems," he laughed. "I remember how you said you didn't like one of your dolls and you broke it, and then you spent days sitting in the corner wondering if you had done the right thing."

Seeing that he could not understand what was really bothering me, I changed the subject. "Have you forgotten much of what you learned at school?"

"Some, but I'll make it up."

"You were at high school already. I have to start all over again."

"Don't worry, I know you. You'll manage." He was bored with our conversation.

"What's your greatest dream?" I asked hurriedly.

"When we get to Kraków, I want to take a big loaf of bread, cut it lengthwise, and smear it with butter. When I eat it, I'll believe I can start life all over again." He patted me on the head and left.

It occurred to me that he didn't want much.

Halinka dropped by in the morning, in tears. She ran straight to my bunk. It took me a long time to understand what was wrong,

"They've taken Zev away."

"Who would take Zev away. And why?"

"You're stupid," she sobbed. "His father took him away."

"And you're a complete idiot!" I screamed. "He's a big, grown-up boy. Did his father put him in a rucksack and carry him off? They just left together, that's all."

She maintained stubbornly that Zev would never have done that. Yet he had. I felt a little sorry for her, but I also knew what Halinka was like with boys and I was sure that before we left the camp she would find another one, again the 'one and only,' and whom she would be in love with forever. All it would take was for someone to tell her how attractive she was, that she was the most beautiful girl he had ever seen, and everything would be fine. I had envied her more than once. When I had cried after a mass execution, or when they took the children away or led people up the Hill, she would ask if something had happened to somebody in my family. Certain things went right over her head. I had been unable to understand this in Płaszów, and that was probably why I had stopped being so close to her. Now, perhaps, I knew why. Yet I had a terrible nature, and Mummy had been right when she said, "It won't be easy for you in life." As usual.

***

Boredom, simple boredom. I had not known before how many malicious women were here. Each of them had had her workplace and her little space to move around in; I had lived among three hundred and known a few of them. Now, with freedom, they've changed. They can quarrel until they're out of breath and beat each other over the head for the smallest reason, over a piece of clothing or a bit of food that one of them got from a Czech, over a place in the washroom, over anything. Once, I couldn't stand it and tried to break up a fight. They instantly turned on me: I was a little shit, but that wasn't bad enough. They accused me of being the doctors' pet and of having eaten the patients' food rations. That made me cry again. Mummy and Ilza couldn't get me to tell them what had happened. But I finally told them. Ilza went crazy. She insisted that I point out who had said that about me, after all my years as a prisoner. Now the roles changed. I was trying to persuade her that there was nothing really wrong, that it wasn't worth having a breakdown over every little thing, because there were so many little things. She sat silent for a long time.

"Do you know why I like you so, Stella? Or love you?" She hugged me. "I have nobody."

"Maybe somebody from your family is alive?"

"Maybe, but I was an only child. My parents never got over the fact that I married a Jew. Now he's been gone so long, and

269

he was everything to me. I didn't have many friends. That's why I worry about you so much."

"Because you don't have friends?"

"No. Because I see that you're a little like me. You take everything to heart and analyse it. Not everyone will like you, and you won't accept everybody."

"What does that mean, 'accept'?"

"That you're not always going to like what you see in other people, and then you'll be hurt. You're good, but you cover the good with aggression or silence. And do you know why? Because a lot of things hurt you."

I couldn't understand everything she was trying to explain to me, but I felt better. Every word she said helped me to sort out my own complicated feelings towards people and about things that I just did not understand.

Ilza went on: "You're a little bit different, and people don't like that."

"So what should I do?"

"Nothing, dear. Be yourself. We will all have to start life from zero, but you more than others."

"Why more?"

"We grown-ups had already been formed one way or another. You went through hell first, and now you have to learn how to live."

"But you'll be with us, Ilza! You don't have anybody, and I really love you."

"You know I'll help you as long as I stay in Kraków, dear. You'll always be a joy to me."

"And you're not going away?"

"For now, no. I also have to find a place for myself in this new life, and it'll be a problem."

"But you're a doctor."

"I doubt if that will fill the rest of my days."

"I'm glad you've explained so many things to me."

"It's just a first small step, and you've got miles ahead of you."

I felt a little better. I was less furious about the way those women started fights over trifles. She was right. People are different.

"I've got a request." I felt no inhibitions with Ilza. "Could you get me a mirror? I won't go into hysterics; I know I'm bald. I never liked my looks, but now I have no idea what I look like."

"Just remember," she said, "that to me you're lovely, but you can't expect everybody to have the same opinion."

Ilza kept her word. She brought me a mirror the next day, and it even had a little stand. I carried it around and looked for a private spot, which was not easy. I finally went behind the factory. I peeked with dread at the face reflected in the silvery surface. That couldn't be me! I looked again, more carefully. Despite all Ilza's warnings, I was appalled. Why hadn't I died? A tiny face, and those eyes, those enormous eyes, horrifying, set in very black sockets. Those thick black eyebrows, that shaved white head, round as a ball, and nothing more. A white skull and black eyebrows. I threw the mirror down. Immediately I regretted the act but, as usual, it was too late. I had asked Ilza to bring it, and she had. I tried to pick it up, but it was shattered. She would understand, if she ever asked at all.

Halinka come running up, looking vibrant and flushed, with her shining brown hair bouncing luxuriously.

"You know what?" she gasped. "The Rosners are going to play, and there's going to be a dance in the courtyard. And a handsome soldier keeps following me around and asking me to promise to dance only with him."

"So dance."

"Aren't you coming? You're weird."

"Are you going to return to Russia with him?"

"We'll see," she beamed and trotted off.

They really were dancing and having a party in the courtyard. As in a circus, the soldiers jumped and knocked their heels together, and kicked and leapt around. A soldier came up, took my hand, and pulled me toward the dancers. I broke free. Hardly discouraged, he ran to seek a more willing partner.

My family was there. I watched them enjoying themselves. "Where have you been?" Mummy asked with relief, happy to have us all together.

"Just walking around. Adam, do your feet hurt? Why aren't you dancing?"

"I'm waiting," he laughed, "to take my sister to her first ball."

"The first ball and the first waltz are reserved for me," Daddy objected.

Maybe I was wrong, but it seemed they were all pretending to be happy. Everyone was thinking of one thing: how freedom would work out for us.

***

Some people left the camp without permission. We waited for the transport. Our parents said that we were still too weak to walk off into the unknown. They pretended to be stronger, but were concerned about Adam and me.

A table was set up for the local mayor or whatever he was called. Our camp committee sat beside him, looking very dignified. The forms had been prepared. They wrote down our first and last names, date of birth, and destination.

We stood in line. Mummy asked: "Zygmunt, are you sure you want to got to Poland?"

"But, Tusia, love," he looked at her dumbfounded, "You've got your sisters and your mother there. We might find our relatives, my sister, Zygmunt, Ziuta." He did not have to explain that Kraków was the whole world to him.

"Fine. So we'll go to Kraków."

Daddy went on, to himself: "My father, grandfather and great-grandfather were Polish. I was born in Kraków..."

"Stop, please," she scolded him. As long as I could remember, Mummy had always had the last word about everything, with the one exception of Daddy's Polishness.

We finally got documents and stopped being numbers. At the very moment I took the paper into my hand, I ripped the tag with the number on it off my striped uniform. I do not know why, but that scrap of paper was a turning point. I felt nearly mad with joy that I had not experienced at all when the end of the war was announced. I could not hide my impatience, and tried to spell the words out to myself. Every letter added to my joy. I could not believe it. I grabbed Adam. "Read it out loud to me, clearly and distinctly."

"Haven't you read it?" He was surprised.

"I have, but now I want to hear it. Now I know that I'm really free. My first and last name are there."

"Sister, you're barmy sometimes. Whatever you want." And he translated it to me:

"The Local Council in Brnenec. The Council Office hereby confirms that the bearer of this certificate, Müller, Stella, born 5 February, 1930 in Kraków, was a political prisoner in the Brnenec branch of the Gross-Rosen concentration camp, and is entitled to transportation from Brnenec to Kraków, her place of residence. We request that all official bodies render any necessary help. Brnenec, 15 May, 1945."

I followed first Mummy and then Daddy around. I gave them no rest. When would we leave? Today? Immediately? I was happy.

"We can go. Let's try to find the right road, Daddy."

"Calm down, dear. They're supposed to arrange a train."

"Who needs a train?" I persisted. "I've got so much energy."

"Look how swollen Adam's legs still are." Mummy ended the conversation.

Epilogue

The great day arrived. We had been informed that the train A would not take more than a hundred people, so we were among the first to set out for the station. They gave us little bags with some sugar and half a loaf of bread in them. We walked with Ilza, Doctor Löw, Mietek Penner and his family, Rózia, and many others. Along the way, we laughed about how this was the last time in our lives we would walk in ranks. Never again. On this occasion the Czechs did not conceal themselves, but cordially led us to the station. Some of them offered us food for the trip. So we reached the station, where many months earlier we had arrived in a completely different state, as human rags filled with terror.

The sight of the cattle trucks, or rather coal trucks since they were open, extinguished my joy. I had been certain that we would travel in a normal train. Daddy read my thoughts: "It doesn't matter, dear. Every kilometre will bring us closer to Kraków."

We were already climbing on to the dirty platforms. Ilza said to Doctor Löw, "Aren't we idiots, Matilda. We never thought of blankets, and the nights could be cold." We were all in high spirits, however. It didn't matter; we had known worse cold.

The train moved out. We didn't look much better in those filthy railway cars than we had when they brought us here. But that wasn't important.

It was already completely dark when we rolled into Brno. There were crowds of people like us and a booth with the Red Cross insignia on it, where they offered us mugs of hot tea and sliced bread in a basket. Nobody could say how long we would have to wait for the next train. The Germans had apparently blown up a lot of tunnels and bridges.

We were warned that we would have to walk two sections of the route on foot to get to connecting trains. So we found ourselves wandering in growing crowds of emaciated prisoners. We trudged for many kilometres around demolished tunnels and bridges. When we stopped we got a little hot tea and one slice of bread per person; they had nothing more. The nights were really cold.

Our group stuck together. Some of the enthusiasm had left our faces, with the exception of my father's. He kept repeating, "We'll make it somehow." When people started talking about how nobody even knew what we were returning to, and whether there would be a place for us, he would say, "We'll make it somehow."

Mummy burst out angrily once, "How could I have been so stupid as to follow your sentiments? We should have gone to Sweden like so many others. They say that the organization of aid for prisoners there is excellent." "Former prisoners," she added.

"But Mummy," Daddy spoke up shyly.

"Zygmunt, if you say one more time that we'll make it somehow, I'm jumping off the train."

Rózia laughed: "Don't be in a hurry, Tusia. We'll soon have to walk again anyway, so why jump?"

I did not know how many days we had been wandering, because it could hardly be called a short trip. One night, in fact just as dawn was breaking, somebody shouted: "Everybody out! This is the border! You're in Poland!"

There indeed was a white-and-red flag flying. My heart skipped a beat, but Daddy behaved strangely. He got down on the ground, digging at it with his fingers and kissing it. I had never seen him in a such a rapture. Such love for his country – perhaps I wasn't old enough and hadn't had enough time to absorb and feel such love. I was more touched by Daddy's reaction than by the fact that we were in Poland.

Mummy started bringing him back to reality. "Enough, Zygmunt. You'll have lots of time for such emotions. Go to that building over there, and ask for something warm to drink. Stella and Adam are freezing." We were at a little border station and I don't remember for sure, but it might have been Zebrzydowice.

Daddy and another man walked over. They pounded on the door for a long time. A woman with frowzy hair came out. "Can't you let people sleep at night?"

They asked very politely for something warm to drink.

"Are you crazy?"

"We're on our way back from a camp, we've been travelling a long time, and we're thirsty."

"I don't care where you're coming from. I've got a right to sleep." Besides, she added, her stove was cold.

"We'll light it for you," they urged.

"Of course," she added. "I'm supposed to let some kind of gang into my house?" She slammed the door.

"There's your Poland for you," Mummy said. "Your Polish land. I told you we should have gone somewhere else."

"Forget it," Daddy said a little sadly. "One crazy woman with no heart isn't Poland." They snooped and asked around, and a railway man finally pointed to some wagons and told us we could start out as soon as they coupled a locomotive on. But when that would be, he couldn't say.

We were on the move again. There were more changes of train, there was more waiting. Now we saw little canteens, but they wanted money for food. We had to be happy with the sugar the Russians had give us, and from time to time a little water. But we were going home.

One night we heard, "All off for Kraków Płaszów." It sounded strange, but I was too tired to react strongly. I wondered how it would be when I walked into the Ghetto, without barbed wire now, when every home and every building would remind me of people and friends who I knew were dead, when I stood in front of the *kinderheim* where they had thrown children out the windows. Was there still a trace on the cobblestones of the enormous puddle of blood which had formed around that little girl bent over her doll? Mummy was right. We shouldn't have come back.

We lay until morning in a waiting room crowded with miserable, filthy people. Everyone lay on the floor, some with bundles under their heads and some without.

Mummy and the other women agreed to meet in two days. There were notices in the waiting-room about points for enquiries about missing persons. It was time to say goodbye, and I wept a little. I would have preferred that we went together. If Grandmother and my aunts were at home, we could stay with them.

Once again, the adults decided and once again I was a child whose opinions interested no one. We got on a number 3 tram. We were going to Azory, where Mummy's mother and sister, Aunt Hanka and Aunt Maryla, lived. It turned out that it was Pentecost. The people in the tram looked at us warily. We were dirty, terribly dirty after all those coal trucks and nights spent in corners. Everybody else was clean and beautifully dressed.

A conductor came up to Daddy. "Any more tickets, please."

Daddy was in a stupor. "I'm sorry, sir, but I haven't seen money for four years. We're on our way home from a camp," he stammered in embarrassment.

"I know all about people coming home from camps," the conductor said irritably. "No money for tickets, and as soon as they get off they buy a bottle of vodka."

I was speechless. Tears ran down Daddy's dirty, unshaved face. A man stood up. I noticed every detail of his elegant clothing. He was wearing a grey suit and a beautiful sky-blue shirt. He walked up the conductor. He was pale.

"You animal," he said, taking hold of the conductor's lapels. "How dare you!" He was shaking. "Look at these people. Haven't you learned anything from the war?" Then he regained a measure of self-control and said to us: "With your permission, I will pay."

Daddy looked terrible, heartbroken. Everything showed on his face and, just as he could never keep a secret when he was happy, he was also incapable of concealing his discouragement.

We rode along Starowiślna Street, where everything seemed half familiar to me, but only half. The voice of the man in the grey suit brought me out of my musings.

"We're near the Post Office. If you will allow me the pleasure, I propose that we go in a cab."

My parents hesitated a moment, but I jumped right out. I recognized it – the Planty! My mad rides on my scooter, my knees always covered in scabs! The Post Office. Around the top of it ran letters I had been unable to read then. Mania told me that they were an advertisement for Tungsram light bulbs. Whenever we walked there, I shouted "Sram!" which is a rude word in Polish. Mummy would reprimand me, and I would reply that I was only reading. I couldn't have been more than six then; it was before we moved to Szymanowski St.

Daddy's voice interrupted my reverie. "Come on, the gentlemen is very kind. We're going by cab."

It was crowded and the gentleman sat next to the driver, but facing us. He was not ashamed of us, dirty and ragged as we were. As if sensing our embarrassment, he smiled. "I was in the Uprising in Warsaw. I lost my family."

No one said anything. Decorated vehicles filled with merry, singing people passed us. "Let's drive through the Market Square," he told the driver.

I tried not to look at Daddy, whose eyes were still fogged with tears. The cab stopped at a sign reading "Restaurant." The gentlemen alighted. He returned a few moments later with a huge parcel, and again smiled shyly. "I haven't had my breakfast yet," he said. "We can eat together."

He unpacked lovely, brown rolls made into sausage sandwiches. He had bottles of orangeade in his pockets. I will never forget the taste of those sandwiches and orangeade. No other rolls will ever taste as good.

I registered every street we passed in my numbed memory. I squirmed around to make sure it was not a dream. The horse's hooves clopped monotonously and my eyelids started to droop; I had to open my eyes wide because it would have been a shame to doze.

I suddenly made everyone jump by shrieking, "The Park! Park Krakowski! Szymanowski Street! Here's where we live!"

The gentleman ordered us to stop. He was disoriented. "Should we turn here?"

"No, no," Mummy said. "I have no idea where we'll be living. First, I have to make sure that everything is all right with my mother."

We drove on towards Azory. I was no longer interested, because the area was unfamiliar. I closed my eyes, letting the hackney cab rock me and the sun warm me.

I heard the man asking, "How old is your daughter? She's just a child. How did she survive? Forgive my curiosity."

"She looks very young now," Mummy said. "She's been through a lot. When she was eleven, she was already in the camp. Now she's fifteen. But she's still a child."

I woke up. "But children like me fought in the Uprising, didn't they?"

"Were you only pretending to be asleep?"

"I wasn't pretending at all. I just had my eyes closed. And I'm not a child."

Mummy excused my behaviour. "She's got out of hand." I waited for the scolding to start, about how impolite I was and so on.

But the gentleman commented, "She has a right to be like that."

We were there. Mummy groaned, "Oh, no! This is where they lived."

I looked. Half of the little house was destroyed. The rest, including part of the chimney, was still standing. Mummy sat down on part of the wall. She didn't cry, but only looked around in terror. "Now what? What next? Now what?" she kept repeating.

A plump woman, all in frills with her blouse tied at her neck in a big bow, came out of the house next door. She stood there and looked at us. The gentleman in the grey suit asked, "What happened to the ladies who lived here?" He indicated the ruined house.

"Oh, they moved out. Yes, they were really lucky!"

Mummy leapt to her feet. "Where are they? Did they leave an address?"

"Yes, there's an address," the woman in frills chattered, "Have you got any news, perhaps, about any of their family? They're all said to have died. Those ladies are so religious. They made offerings and prayed to Our Lady for the souls of their relatives."

Mummy didn't say anything. I knew, I was sure, that nothing would keep me quiet. "They shouldn't have been in such a hurry," I said emotionally. "Here we are!"

The woman peered at us. "Oh, my goodness! Isn't this Mrs. Tusia Müller? I remember how elegant you used to look when you visited." She straightened her bow. "I would have asked you in." She looked at our rags and shifted her weight from one foot to the other.

"Please give us that address," Mummy said matter-of-factly.

Without pausing for breath, the plump woman continued, "Oh, what all of us women went through when that bomb hit the house! You can't imagine. We said Hail Mary's around the clock and that saved us."

"Mummy," I said in a muffled whisper, "I'm going to scream."

"And you must have been in a prisoner-of-war camp," she ploughed on.

"No!" I shouted. "In a Jewish camp!"

She opened her plump mouth. "Whoever would have thought," she considered for a moment, "that they had anything Jewish in them?"

I was ready to say something impolite when I felt the gentleman's hand on my shoulder. "Could we ask you for that address?" he said politely. "Everyone's very tired."

She ran in her frills to the house. None of us spoke a word. She returned, handing over a piece of paper and panting, "I would ask you in. It's 12 Kolberg Street."

"We can read." I could not deny myself the pleasure of one more word.

Mummy hesitated a second. "Do you know whether any of my sisters might have moved into our apartment?"

"No, certainly not. That was apparently a very large apartment, and they were sure..."

"Yes," Mummy interrupted, "That we were dead."

We were back in the hackney cab. The woman in frills was still huffing around us. "How fortunate you are that you didn't go through that terrible horror when that house was hit..."

Thankfully, the rest of her chattering was left behind.

"I don't want to go to Kolberg Street," I said after a while.

"So get out," Mummy grumbled. She was very irritated. "And then what?"

"Exactly. And then what," she repeated.

Daddy looked sad. Just as long as he didn't say "We'll make it somehow."

Probably just to have something to say, Mummy addressed the man in the grey suit who was sitting there silent and wrapped in thought. "We've caused you so much trouble. I hope we'll have the occasion to repay you some day."

"Please believe me when I say that I was dreading spending this holiday alone. This has been a pleasure, a very great pleasure."

We were there: a lovely house in a lovely, quiet street. I didn't want to go inside because the entrance hall seemed terribly dark. But everyone else had gone in, so I followed. Mummy was already ringing the doorbell.

We waited a moment, lined up behind her. The door opened. A little, white-haired, old woman stood there. "Can I help you?"

"Mother, it's us!"

There was a moment of silence. Then: "Hanka! Hanka dear! Maryla! My children have returned! My grandchildren! Hanka dear! They're alive!" Grandmother was crying. "They've returned!"

Daddy went back to invite the gentleman in.

"He's gone," he said. "We didn't even thank him,"

After the war Stella Müller lived with her parents and her brother in Kraków. Zygmunt Müller died there in 1982, Berta Müller in 1985, Adam in 1990.

Uncle Grünberg stayed in Płaszów until the camp was closed down and was then deported to Auschwitz; he was beaten to death in April 1945 by a Kapo.

Aunt Grünberg died in January 1945 while being transported from Auschwitz to Ravensbrück.

Ziuta Grünberg lives today in Ramat Gan, Israel.

The three brothers of Stella's mother – Uncle Adolf, Uncle Ignac and Uncle Juzek – did not survive.

The Rottersmann family were shot dead in Płaszów.

Bubik succeeded in fleeing during the journey from Hungary to Auschwitz. He went to live in the USA after the war.

Oskar Schindler lived in Argentina after the war and returned in 1957 to Germany. He died on 9 October 1974 in Hildesheim and was buried, according to his wishes, in the Catholic cemetery in Jerusalem.

Emilie Schindler lives in Argentina.

Amon Goeth was executed on 13 June 1946 in Kraków.

Chronology

Autumn 1925	The first part of *Mein Kampf* is published. Among the basic aims of his political programme, the future Führer includes the extermination of the Jews.
30.1.1933	Hitler becomes Chancellor of Germany.
April 1933	The first legislative measures are taken against German Jews.
9.11.1933	'Kristallnacht' – the first pogrom instigated by the German authorities against the Jews.
1.9.1939	Germany's invasion of Poland sparks the beginning of the Second World War.
3.9.1939	The first large-scale slaughter of Polish Jews takes place.
26.10.1939	Kraków becomes the seat of the German Governor General of Poland.
End of 1939	Oskar Schindler arrives in Kraków. The following year he becomes the manager of the Enamelware factory in the Zabłocie district of Kraków, which he ultimately acquires.
May 1940	The evacuation takes place of three-quarters of the Jewish population of Kraków.
20.5.1940	Construction of the concentration camp at Auschwitz.
2.10.1940	Creation of the Jewish ghetto in Warsaw.
20.3.1941	Creation of the Kraków ghetto.
22.6.1941	Germany invades the USSR. Large-scale massacres of Jews on Soviet territory begin.

3.9.1941	The first killings in the Auschwitz camp are carried out with the use of gas.
20.1.1942	The Wannsee Conference establishes the main course of action decided upon by the Nazi administration, aimed at the total destruction of European Jews.
1.6.1942	The Kraków ghetto is sealed off and the first transport to the extermination camp at Bełżec takes place.
8.6.1942	The second transport leaves the Kraków ghetto.
Summer 1942	Construction of the Płaszów camp begins.
23.6.1942	First selections are made for the gas chambers at Auschwitz.
Autumn 1942	First movements from the Kraków ghetto to Płaszów takes place.
27/28.10.1942	Third transport of Jews from the Kraków ghetto to Bełżec and Auschwitz. The ghetto is divided into sections A and B.
11.2.1943	Amon Goeth is transferred to Kraków.
13/14.3.1942	Liquidation of the Kraków ghetto and transfer of its Jews from section A to Płaszów. Those from section B are sent to Auschwitz and exterminated.
March-April 1943	Himmler and Hitler draft the "Informe Korherr'. This confirms, on the basis of statistical data from the SS, that by the end of 1942 the Nazis have been responsible for the deaths of four million European Jews.
Summer 1943	Final Transport from the Kraków ghetto to Płaszów.

7.5.1944	'Health review' at Płaszów. One week later the transfer to Auschwitz takes place of some 1500 children, elderly and infirm people – considered useless for labour purposes – with the object of exterminating them.
Summer 1944	High point of the occupation of Płaszów as its population reaches 25,000.
13.9.1944	Amon Goeth is arrested for trafficking in currency. He is replaced at Kraków by Arnold Buscher.
15.10.1944	Transfer of the men from Płaszów to the camp at Gross-Rosen.
22.10.1944	Transfer of the women from Płaszów to Auschwitz.
22.10.1944	The men from Gross-Rosen arrive at Brünlitz.
End of November 1944	The women from Auschwitz arrive at Brünlitz.
14.1.1945	The final transports from Płaszów to Auschwitz. Around eight thousand people remaining in Płaszów are killed.
26.1.1945	Auschwitz is liberated by Soviet troops.
7/9.5.1945	Capitulation of Germany.
8.5.1945	Brünlitz is liberated by Soviet troops.

Glossary

Antreten – To line up, take one's place, report.

Apelplatz – Central clearing in camp where roll-call was held.

Aufsejerka – German policewoman.

Aussenkommando – Detail sent to work outside the camp.

Bauleiter – Building supervisor.

Blokszper – Search of barrack.

Chalat – Overgarment worn by Orthodox Jews.

Hauptscharführer – Platoon or squad leader. (Nazi)

Hauptsturmführer – SS company commander

Kapo – Work supervisor (usually a trustee recruited from within the camp population).

Kartoffelkeller – Cellar where potatoes are stored.

Kinderheim – Children's home.

Konzentrationslager – Concentration camp.

Krankenstube – Sick bay.

Lagerszper – Search of camp.

Laufer – Runner, messenger.

Muzulmanka – Emaciated woman in camp (lit. a Moslem woman)

Oberka – Head of the female police unit.

Obersturmführer – SS company commander.

Ordnungsdienst (OD) – Jewish police service in the ghetto.

Polenlager – Polish camp.

Rassenschaden – Harm, injury, damage caused by proximity of other racial groups.

Schreibstube – Book-keeping/ records department.

Sto lat – Title of Polish song in which the singers wish the addressee a hundred years of life.

Strafkommando – Punishment detail.

Sturmmann – Member of Nazi unit, company.

Szrajber – Writer, book-keeper.

Waschraum – Bath-house.

Zahlapel – Roll-call at which prisoners are counted.

Zugangen – Arrivals, newcomers.

Zwangsarbeitslager – Forced labour camp.

Stella Müller, 1936

Berta Müller, Stella's mother, before the war

*August 1939 (two weeks before the outbreak of the war) left to right:
the Müller family's cook, Stella, Mania – her nanny*

Stella Müller in Krakowski Park (Kraków), 1938

The Kraków Ghetto, in the first days after arrival there;
Stella Müller, family and relatives, 1941

Zygmunt Grünberg (far right) in the uniform of a Polish army officer before the war

Kraków: Zygmunt Grünberg and family on the balcony of their home, 1938

Kraków: the Ghetto after it had been reduced (Archives)

Kraków: the main gate of the „original" Ghetto (Archives)

Initial construction work by Jewish prisoners at the Płaszów concentration camp

Auschwitz-Birkenau: the railroad entrance

Auschwitz: survivors after liberation (Archives)

Auschwitz: interior of the women's barracks (Archives)

Auschwitz-Birkenau: child prisoners at the moment of liberation (Archives)

*Oskar Schindler, with a group of workers, at the „Emalienfabrik"
(enamel factory) in Kraków* (Archives)

Dr Mengele, head physician,
who conducted criminal experiments
on prisoners at Auschwitz-Birkenau
(Archives)

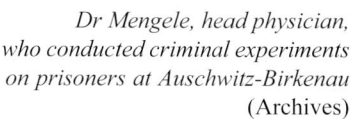

Amon Goeth at his trial (Archives)

Engineer (Bauleiter) Huth from Płaszów (Archives)

Stella's parents and brother after liberation, 1946

Stella's brother Adam, 1955

Stella Müller, 1950, still partially bald five years after liberation

Stella Müller, 1955 or 1956

Stella Müller-Madej in 1995, in the courtyard of Józefińska Street no. 29, her second „apartment" in the Kraków Ghetto © Ryszard Komecki

Jerusalem: Stella Müller-Madej and her husband as Steven Spielberg's guests at the conclusion of filming „Schindler's List". King David Hotel

*Stella Müller-Madej at the entrance to the Auschwitz concentration camp,
winter 1995* © Kristina Eriksson